The Dangers of Nuclear War

A Pugwash Symposium
Edited by Franklyn Griffiths and John C. Polanyi
Foreword by Pierre Elliott Trudeau

University of Toronto Press /Toronto Buffalo London

The Dangers of
NUCLEAR
WAR

© University of Toronto Press 1979
Toronto Buffalo London
Printed in Canada

Library of Congress Cataloging in Publication Data

Main entry under title:
The Dangers of nuclear war.
Based on papers originally presented at the 30th
Pugwash Symposium on the topic "The Dangers of Nuclear
War by the Year 2,000" held in Toronto 4-7 May 1978.
1. Atomic weapons and disarmament—Congresses.
2. Atomic warfare—Congresses. I. Griffiths,
Franklyn. II. Polanyi, J. C., 1929-
JX1974.7.D35   327'.174   79-18825
ISBN 0-8020-2356-8
ISBN 0-8020-6389-6 pbk.

This book has been published with the help of
a grant from the Social Science Federation of Canada.
using funds provided by the Social Sciences and
Humanities Research Council of Canada.

Contents

Contributors / vii

Foreword
PIERRE ELLIOTT TRUDEAU / ix

Preface / xiii

Statement by the Participants   3

1 Consequences of Nuclear War   7
J. CARSON MARK

THE AVOIDANCE OF NUCLEAR WAR
UP TO THE PRESENT

2 The Avoidance of Nuclear War since 1945   25
W. McGEORGE BUNDY

3 An Assessment of Nuclear Crises   34
JOHN STEINBRUNER

4 Existing Systems of Command and Control   50
VICE-ADMIRAL G.E. MILLER (Ret.)

5 The Achievements of Arms Control   67
GEORGE IGNATIEFF

FUTURE DEVELOPMENTS AS THEY
AFFECT THE THREAT OF NUCLEAR WAR

6 A World of Many Nuclear Powers   85
WALTER SCHÜTZE

7 Weapons Developments and the Threat of Nuclear War   93
RICHARD L. GARWIN

NUCLEAR WAR

8 Nuclear Terrorism and Nuclear War   109
WILLIAM EPSTEIN

9 Local Wars and Their Escalation   125
SHALHEVETH FREIER

10 Nuclear War between the Super-powers   135
GEORGE W. RATHJENS

RETROSPECT AND PROSPECT

11 Forum: Remarks Made at a Special Session
with the Prime Minister of Canada   149
GEORGI A. ARBATOV
P.R. CHARI
RICHARD L. GARWIN
GEORGE IGNATIEFF
LORD ZUCKERMAN

12 A Forecast   169
FRANKLYN GRIFFITHS

13 The Dangers of Nuclear War   182
JOHN C. POLANYI

Glossary   195

Contributors

J. CARSON MARK, a physicist, was formerly head of the division of the Los Alamos Scientific Laboratory concerned with the theoretical design of nuclear weapons. At present, he is a consultant on nuclear problems – both weapon and non-weapon – to several US government agencies.

W. McGEORGE BUNDY, President of the Ford Foundation, was formerly Special Assistant to the President of the United States for National Security (1961-66).

JOHN STEINBRUNER is Director of Foreign Policy Studies, The Brookings Institution.

VICE ADMIRAL GERALD E. MILLER was formerly Commander of the US 2nd Fleet and the US 6th Fleet. He has also been Deputy Director of Joint Strategic Target Planning Staff.

GEORGE IGNATIEFF has been Canadian Ambassador to NATO, Canadian Ambassador to the United Nations, Canadian Ambassador to the Conference of the Committee on Disarmament and to the Office of the United Nations at Geneva.

WALTER SCHÜTZE is a foreign affairs analyst at the Centre d'Etudes de Politique Etrangères, Paris.

RICHARD L. GARWIN is an IBM Fellow, Thomas J. Watson Research Center, Yorktown Heights, New York, and Adjunct Professor of Physics at Columbia University. He is a former member of the President's Scientific

Advisory Committee, USA, and is Senior Consultant on military questions, and on civil uses of nuclear energy, to the US Department of Defense and the US Department of Energy.

WILLIAM EPSTEIN, Fellow of the United Nations Institute for Training and Research, was formerly Director of the Disarmament Division of the UN Secretariat and Special Consultant to the Secretary General of the United Nations and to the Canadian Government. He was a member of the Canadian delegation to the UN Special Session on Disarmament, May-June 1978, and to the 33rd session of the General Assembly, September-December 1978.

SHALHEVETH FREIER is a physicist at the Weizmann Institute of Science, Israel. He was head of the Israel Atomic Energy Commission (1971-76) and Chairman of the Presidential Panel for Science Policy in Israel (1971-78).

GEORGE RATHJENS, Professor of Political Science, Massachusetts Institute of Technology, was formerly Chief Scientist and then Deputy Director of the Advanced Research Projects Agency (ARPA), US Department of Defense, and a Special Assistant to the Director of the US Arms Control and Disarmament Agency (ACDA).

GEORGI A. ARBATOV is a Candidate Member, Central Committee of the Communist Party of the Soviet Union, and Academician and Director, Institute of the USA and Canada, Academy of Sciences of the USSR.

P.R. CHARI is Director of the Institute for Defense Studies and Analyses, New Delhi.

LORD ZUCKERMAN, formerly Chief Scientific Adviser to the Ministry of Defence and to the Government of the United Kingdom, is Professor Emeritus at the Universities of Birmingham and East Anglia, and President of the Zoological Society of London.

FRANKLYN GRIFFITHS is Professor of Political Science and Director of the Centre for Russian and East European Studies, University of Toronto.

JOHN C. POLANYI is University Professor and Professor of Chemistry, University of Toronto.

Foreword

PIERRE ELLIOTT TRUDEAU

It is easy to forget the dangers of nuclear war. Most of us prefer not to think about disagreeable prospects or, if we do, to believe that all will turn out for the best. In matters of war and peace, we also tend to assume that private citizens can do little about them, or that the threat of nuclear war is in the hands exclusively of the nuclear powers. The great value of this book is that it reminds us both of the terrible dangers that threaten humanity as long as nuclear weapons continue to be produced, and of our obligations as citizens and governments to face the consequences of this situation.

Most of the participants in the Pugwash symposium on the dangers of nuclear war, of which this book is the result, believe that these dangers are increasing. Their reasons are credible. As the numbers and types of such weapons increase, the temptation and the occasion to take them for granted (what is called lowering the nuclear threshold) tend to be reinforced; and the incentive for other governments that fear for their security to hold open the nuclear 'option' is greater. Paradoxically, as a number of contributors suggest, the existence of nuclear weapons is also a powerful deterrent against the outbreak of 'world' wars as we have known them in this century. In the words of Dr Polanyi: 'The legitimate objective was seen, by most, to be the exploitation of nuclear weapons to avoid nuclear wars.'

In response to these concerns, the Canadian government has followed a double strategy. It has participated actively in efforts to slow down and eventually reverse the nuclear arms race, through such means as research into seismic verification techniques, contributions to negotiations on partial arms control measures, and appeals for a ban on the flight testing of new strategic delivery vehicles and on the production of fissionable material for weapons purposes; and it has sought to restrict the use by other countries of Canadian nuclear technology and materials to peaceful purposes, through the application of full-scope safeguards. We have not called into question the principle of nuclear deterrence itself, nor in consequence have we endorsed appeals to the nuclear powers never to use nuclear weapons; for we have accepted that in the world as it is the system of nuclear deterrence is essential to our security. We have also believed that Canada must contribute her fair share to Western defence arrangements as long as threats to Western security exist. Canadians decided thirty years ago that neither unilateral defence policies nor unilateral disarmament policies were appropriate in a nuclear world.

Most thoughtful citizens agree, by and large, that national security is both a matter of military deterrence and of arms control. The balance to be struck between them will vary from time to time, but the concept of balance is important. Ever higher levels of deterrence may impose intolerable strains on control procedures; but if arms control measures give rise to lack of confidence in deterrence the political consequences can be equally dangerous. As the essays in this volume indicate, the threat of the inadvertent use of nuclear weapons may have become serious enough to weigh the balance in favour of significant measures of nuclear disarmament, provided that each side maintains confidence in the good faith of the other. In any event, great power implies great responsibility. To lay stress on the dangers of nuclear war is to call to account both those who carry this responsibility and those whose actions may endanger its exercise, and to insist that this accounting satisfy the conditions for planetary citizenship.

Preface

We all have our own – seldom articulated – assessment of the likelihood of nuclear war in the coming decades.

Could we make that assessment more explicit and attempt to document it?

The result of such an undertaking would surely be uncertain, but we might succeed to a useful extent in sharpening our perception. This perception is of fundamental importance in determining the shape of the future. What the nations of the world are willing to venture in imaginative thought and action in the hope of providing a new framework for peace depends ultimately on their assessment of the dangers inherent in continuing to sustain the risks attendant on current policies.

An undertaking of the scope envisaged for this Symposium suffered from the disability of excessive breadth. Any single heading would have been a suitable subject for a four-day symposium – and many had been. What was lacking, however, was a contemporary attempt to take the measure of these various topics at one time. This totality is of such profound importance to us all that the venture appeared well worthwhile.

The Symposium had its origins in informal discussions held at Thinker's Lodge, Pugwash, Nova Scotia, in the summers of 1976 and 1977, at the invitation of Cyrus and Anne Eaton. A further planning meeting was held at Trinity College, University of Toronto, in October 1976, with the financial assistance of the Laidlaw Foundation (Toronto). Since the organization of this Symposium was in the hands of the Canadian Pugwash Group, which operates under the twin sponsorship of the international Pugwash organization (with its headquarters in London) and the Royal Society of Canada (Ottawa), the format for the meeting was based on established Pugwash practice. In addition to its annual international meetings which address a wide subject area, Pugwash has for years past sponsored international symposia on more narrowly defined topics. Typically twenty to thirty invited participants meet for a period of some days to discuss up to a dozen papers which have been circulated in advance of the meeting; these papers have been carefully selected, both in regard to author and subject matter, so as to constitute a systematic exploration of the chosen subject area.

The 30th Pugwash Symposium, on the topic, 'The Dangers of Nuclear War by the Year 2000: An Attempt at Assessment', was held in Toronto from 4 to 7 May 1978. It was attended by 26 invited participants from eleven countries (a list of the participants and their countries is given at the end of their Statement on pages 4 and 5). Ten papers were solicited for prior circulation to the participants; these comprise chapters 1-10 of the present volume. In inviting these papers the hope was expressed that 'we can address these topics with sufficient clarity and authority that a broader public can benefit'; it was intended from the first that this Symposium would lead to a published volume.

The papers having been circulated in advance, they were taken as read at the meeting. The four days were devoted to lively debate, which guided the authors in their subsequent revision of the manuscripts, and the editors in their preparation of their retrospective surveys (chapters 12 and 13). The editors are particularly indebted to the participants who furnished written comments during and following the meeting as well as to the two rapporteurs, Mr James Dow and Mr Alisdair MacLaren. Chapter 11 of this volume had its genesis in a session, near the close of the Symposium, attended by Pierre Elliott Trudeau, then Prime Minister of Canada. Observers at this and other sessions included Dr John Brenciaglia, Mrs Anne Eaton, Mr Klaus Goldschlag, Mr Duncan Gordon, Mr Walter Gordon, and Mr Ivan Head. The Symposium took place at Trinity College, University of Toronto, at the kind invitation of the Provost, Mr George Ignatieff. The Symposium was made possible by a grant from the Walter and Duncan Gordon Foundation of Toronto; it would be hard to exaggerate the indebtedness of the organizers of this Symposium to the generosity and understanding of Duncan and Walter Gordon.

There was no lack of lively, often impassioned, discussion at this meeting. A wide range of viewpoints was represented and found expression. None the less a shared sense of concern transcended differences, enabling the participants to find common ground in a Statement which, though prepared at the close of this discussion, is reproduced as a preamble to the present volume.

This meeting, and the spirit in which it took place, testifies to the qualities on which our hope for the future must rest; the ability to imagine (feebly), to comprehend (dimly) and to learn (at historic moments, rapidly).

The greatest peril for the future, lies in a fatalistic tendency for leaders and led to deny these very qualities; to suppose that new realities cannot be understood and new patterns of international conduct accepted. Our peril has never been greater than at a time when global expectations soar, resources dwindle, and weapons spread. If we survive, it will be because we have harnessed these same forces of technological change and of improved education to the task of bringing ourselves and our fellows to an appreciation of a changed world. The present Symposium marked a small step along this path.

Toronto, March 1979   FRANKLYN GRIFFITHS
                                         JOHN C. POLANYI

THE DANGERS OF NUCLEAR WAR

Statement by the participants

We have spent the past four days in discussion of a wide range of topics which bear, on one way or another, upon the dangers of a nuclear war occurring in the coming decades. Our meetings have taken place in closed sessions so as to promote as frank as possible an exchange of views. Papers prepared by participants were circulated in advance so that the entire period of our meeting could be devoted to debate.

Somehow we have survived for 33 years since the first demonstration of the appalling effects of nuclear weapons in Hiroshima and Nagasaki, with no further use of these weapons in warfare. To what do we owe our good fortune? This question was tackled under such headings as the analysis of past crises, the systems for command and control of nuclear weapons, and the attempts made to control the quantity and nature of armaments (arms control).

Our over-all conclusion from this portion of our discussion – having regard to the events of the past decades – was that, while the avoidance of nuclear war up to the present time was a testimonial to good management, it was a still greater testimonial to good luck.

The nuclear weapons that were used at the end of the war in Japan, awesome as they were, represented a destructive power and level of sophistication characteristic of a prehistoric nuclear age. The advent of the H-bomb and the ICBM does not, however, constitute a final stage of weapons development. In the next phase of our discussion we considered future changes in the weapons picture as they affect the threat of nuclear war. The topics for discussion were the proliferation of nuclear weapons and the hazards of a world of many nuclear powers, the implications of further technological developments in nuclear weaponry, and the possibility that terrorist activity could take on a much more threatening character as a consequence of the greater availability of nuclear weapons material and technology.

In the third and in some ways the central portion of our discussion we confronted the question of scenarios for the outbreak of nuclear war. These were considered under two headings: local wars and their escalation, and war between two major powers. Here we were speaking for the most part of war by inadvertence or miscalculation – for example, the threat of use of nuclear weapons that, at a time of high tension, might move by degrees to a point of no return.

Considering our imperfect understanding of the past, it is no surprise to discover that attempts to project even so far as two decades into the future are fraught with uncertainty. As much as anything, our discussions have had to do with the extent and nature of that uncertainty. Risks can only be assessed in context; a risk that would be tolerable in one area of human activity is intolerable in another. A war that unleashed the nuclear weaponry that exists in the world today would be a disaster beyond anything the world has known, and surely beyond our imagining.

The risks that face us are thus a matter of the gravest concern. We must find ways of moderating and then sharply reducing the political and technological competition of the last three decades. Many current trends, among nations of very different size and strength, run in dangerous directions, and the instruments and institutions for increasing international safety are still alarmingly weak. We have not mastered the paradox that the avoidance of nuclear war requires both stable general deterrence and deep restraint in reliance on nuclear weaponry of any sort.

What is needed, if there is to be no nuclear war in this century, and after, is a new readiness for imaginative political action both for drastic arms limitation and increased international understanding. Only so can we serve the imperative human requirement that nuclear war shall never happen.

Georgi A. Arbatov
USSR

Carl Kaysen
USA

Frank Barnaby
Sweden

Martin M. Kaplan
England

W. McGeorge Bundy
USA

M. Mahfouz
Egypt

5 The Dangers of Nuclear War

General E.L.M. Burns
Canada

J. Carson Mark
USA

P.R. Chari
India

Admiral G.E. Miller
USA

William Epstein
Canada

Baruch Raz
Israel

S. Freier
Israel

Uwe Nehrlich
West Germany

Richard L. Garwin
USA

John C. Polanyi
Canada

John Gellner
Canada

George W. Rathjens
USA

Franklyn Griffiths
Canada

Walter Schütze
France

J. Handler
Switzerland

John Steinbruner
USA

Brigadier K. Hunt
England

Lord Trend
England

George Ignatieff
Canada

Lord Zuckerman
England

1

Consequences of Nuclear War

J. CARSON MARK

Many thousands of pages have been written about the effects of nuclear weapons and the possible consequences of nuclear war. In a short discussion it is necessary to focus on a very limited selection of items. For this, we shall consider only a war in which the firepower is predominantly nuclear – not as in the Second World War where the use of nuclear weapons, though decisive in the short range, was incidental to the outcome. As to consequences, we shall examine mainly those effects of direct importance to populations rather than to military forces. We shall also consider mainly those effects that are distinctive to nuclear weapons.

Within an area of heavy destruction from a single nuclear explosion there are unlikely to be any unaffected islands which may be used as points of refuge or bases for aid. Moreover, a number of large explosions may yield not a series of isolated wounds which may be tended and bound with resources drawn from the fabric of surrounding organization but might well destroy the social fabric itself.

MODES OF USE

A nuclear war between opponents such as the USSR and the USA who have a large and diversified stockpile of weapons with appropriate delivery systems would include some – and could include all – of the following elements.

Battlefield use
Picture a fluid zone of perhaps 100km width along a front, with tanks trying to advance from one side and defensive units in small mobile formations trying to prevent this. The scenario often presented consists of

open, rolling country with a few clumps of trees spotted about, an occasional farm house, with a hamlet and church spire pictured serenely on a hilltop off to one side in the background. The scene is marred by widely dispersed units of defensive armour and numerous tanks sneaking up behind the trees. Spotters on either side call up nuclear rounds on short-ranged carriers directed at the more troublesome enemy targets.

In this and adjacent sectors of the front quite large numbers of nuclear fission weapons with yields of 1 to 20 kilotons (a KT is the equivalent of one thousand tons of TNT) might be used. All, or almost all, would be detonated as airbursts. Against exposed persons or buildings the lethal radius of blast and thermal effects would, depending on the yield considered, extend to a range from a few hundred yards to a mile. But the range at which tanks would be put out of action would be considerably smaller. Any built-up area which might be involved in such a battle-zone, whether used by the defenders as a strong point, or by the attackers as a screen, would probably be completely flattened.

In the war-games vernacular, blast damage of this sort is called 'collateral' (meaning incidental), since the objective is to stop tanks and since the incapacitation of the tank crew by heavy radiation exposure may be the most reliable means for that purpose (the hull of the tank provides rather little protection from radiation). This, of course, is where the so-called 'neutron bomb' comes into its own. In the absence of knowledge of weapon design no precise comparison can be made between the normal fission weapon and its neutron bomb (fusion) counterpart. It seems reasonable, however, to assume that a given level of weapons effectiveness by means of radiation could be met either with an armament of fission devices having yields of several kilotons or with a similar number of neutron bombs (fusion devices) having explosive yields a few times smaller.

Following an engagement of this sort the residual effects in the battle-zone would include both the collateral blast damage and any lingering radiation on the surface. Had normal fission weapons been employed, very heavy concomitant blast damage would be certain in any built-up area within the battle-zone, since the radius of heavy blast damage is comparable to the lethal radius for radiation. Had the same number of neutron bombs of a similar radiation effectiveness been used at the same heights of burst, maximum overpressures and areas subjected to given overpressures would have been smaller and collateral blast damage could have been markedly reduced because of the smaller blast yields. On the other hand, had a different tactic been employed, such as using lower heights of burst for the lower-yield weapons (neutron bombs) so as to increase the area of effective radiation coverage, the mitigation of blast damage, though still possibly significant, would not be so great. Thus, considerable collateral blast damage would still be likely, and heavy blast damage would still be possible despite the use of neutron weapons. Under each burst point there would be a patch on the surface, about 200m in radius, in which neutron-induced activation of surface materials would result in a residual radiation level of significant intensity. Using either fission devices or neutron bombs to provide the same level of radiation effectiveness, the intensity and nature of the residual radiation in these patches would not be importantly different, though obviously employment of higher radiation levels or larger areas of coverage would be reflected directly in the level and extent of the residual radiation.

In all cases the intensity of the residual radiation would depend strongly on the composition of the surface materials. For example, it would be much lower in the case of a very wet soil than in the case of dry soil of otherwise similar composition, since in the wet soil a large fraction of the neutrons would be absorbed in ordinary hydrogen to produce deuterium which is not radioactive. Indeed, no significant residual radiation surface activity would result from a burst over a fresh water pond or swamp a foot or so deep. However, for fairly dry soil of average composition the level would be extremely high immediately following the detonation (on the order of 10^4r/hr at the point below the burst, and half that much at a radius of 100m.).

The dominant source at very early times would be ^{28}Al (half-life, τ =2.3min.), so that in less than half an hour this source would have essentially disappeared. At a time of 1 hour the sources from ^{24}Na and ^{56}Mn would dominate, each contributing on the order of 10^2r/hr; but by 10 hours the source from ^{56}Mn (τ = 2.6hr) would have dropped out of sight, and from then until about 10 days the source from ^{24}Na (τ = 15hr) would dominate. Evidently a patch with the particular radiation history described could be reclaimed within a few weeks after the event and put to at least some kinds of use. Evidently, also, the actual radiation history could vary widely from one location to another depending, as it would, on such factors as the moisture content and chemical composition of the soil.

So far, it has been assumed that the height of burst was high enough that the fireball did not reach the ground. If that should happen, in addition to the effects described there would be some area under the detonation point on which there would be a deposition of fission products. The radiation from such a source would fall off less rapidly than that from the neutron-activated soil, and the time before any extended activity could reasonably be resumed in the area might have to be measured in years rather than weeks.

Apart from collateral damage, and the possibility that some of the weapons had misfired in such a way as to provide a surface burst rather than an air burst, the above description will indicate the prospects which would confront the survivors among the inhabitants of the battle-zone. Such survivors could include those who had managed to get clear of the area early in the proceedings, or who had reached well-prepared shelters – if any were available – or who had been fortunate enough that the nearest target point had been a mile or so away.

Of course, in addition to the small weapons used along the front where the opposing troops were in fairly close contact there would probably have been larger weapons directed at targets behind the front, as prudent commanders called for fire on what they might consider to be command points, staging areas, supply bases and supporting airfields; and the line between these activities and the use of quite large weapons at quite large ranges – which might seem to represent a rather different mode of use – would be hard to define.

It has been assumed that the weapons used in the battle-zone were of low yield, as would be required in the self-interest of the person using them who would wish to bomb locations fairly close to the position of his own troops. It has been further assumed that all bombs exploded in the air at a height sufficient to avoid intense local fallout (essentially the same requirement as having the fireball keep clear of the surface). This last assumption is at least likely to apply since it would be an absolute requirement for the forces on the downwind side of the front, and for those on the upwind side if they should hope to advance, and for the forces defending their own territory unless they adopted the ludicrous position that it was necessary to destroy the place in order to save it.

On this last assumption the fission debris would be carried up into the atmosphere without the large quantities of condensable surface material required to induce a rapid and concentrated fall-out, and would return to the surface on an essentially world-wide basis. A possible exception to this would be the occurrence of 'rain-out'. The debris cloud from a low-yield explosion may travel at an altitude lower than a rain-forming stratum in the atmosphere. During the first several hours, before the cloud would be widely dispersed and diluted, a moderate or heavy rain falling through the cloud could scavenge the debris and result in the concentrated deposition of radioactive material in local areas at distances up to as far as a few tens of kilometers from the burst and at levels which could be damaging, unless evasive or protective measures were taken. The probability of an event of this kind in such an extreme form as to have directly lethal effects is quite small; but the probability of having a radiation level at some location which would deliver an infinite-time whole-body dose of the order of 100rem is significant. With a large number of detonations events of this kind would be likely.

A further point concerning the consequences of battlefield use of nuclear weapons should be mentioned. In non-nuclear war the surviving troops, whatever physical injuries and disabilities they may have suffered, could not transmit these physical effects to later generations, though they may often have transmitted psychological scars. In nuclear war, those (whether troops or civilians) who have been exposed to serious levels of radiation, but nevertheless survived, may have been injured genetically; and the effects of this, including possible disabilities, could be transmitted.

Large airburst over industrial civilian targets
This mode of using nuclear weapons has frequently been discussed, and little need be added here. Prompt radiation would be of little significance since the lethal range of the blast and the thermal effects would be much larger. The effects of residual radiation introduced into the biosphere, which would be proportional to the yield, would be of a long-term, long-range nature rather than local. The direct effects on the population directly exposed would be tremendous if they were caught by surprise, very much less severe if they were emplaced in well-prepared shelters. Except for the possibility that some shelter exits might be blocked by rubble or engulfed in large fires which might result from explosion, the sheltered population could leave immediately following the event. The distinctive feature – different from the situation applying in connection with most Second World War bombings – would be the immediate and total blanketing of a very large area, several miles in radius, within which no undamaged facilities would remain. The inhabitants of the desolated area would have to be evacuated, presumably to locations outside the city, and only if the area should be rebuilt could the displaced persons return – which many would never do.

Large surface burst in (or near) industrial civilian targets
The direct blast and thermal effects of this would be quite similar to that referred to above, with the exception of a crater region in which no one would survive, and with a further major exception that the region in

which inhabitants would have to take shelter to avoid fatal injury from fall-out radiation would be much larger than that affected directly by the explosion. This region would extend for tens of miles downwind from the scene of the detonation, and the surviving inhabitants could not safely leave their shelters for many days. Nothing could be done – at least for a week or two – to assist persons who, though surviving, may have been trapped in shelters by rubble or fire. In all cases, both within and beyond the blast-damaged zone, in order to keep people indoors where they would have to remain for safety, shelters would have to be able to provide adequate heat, light, air, water, food and sanitary facilities as well as being able to cope with births and deaths. The number of persons who would have to be evacuated when that became possible could be many times larger than that in the previous case; and even those whose homes, though still intact, had been subjected, say, to a radiation exposure of $\sim$1000r in 4 days would be unable safely to return to their homes for about a year.

Heavy attack with surface bursts on military targets
There are about fifty strategic targets in the continental US: SAC bases, shipyards, and ICBM bases, for example. Even in a so-called 'limited' attack, in which targets were limited to purely military installations, any or all of these could qualify as targets for megaton-like weapons. It has often been supposed that an attack on an air base would be made by airburst because of the larger area of moderate blast pressure; but there is nothing to guarantee this, and since there might be no planes parked on any particular base at any particular time an alternative tactic could call for the use of surface bursts which would put the field out of use for a longer time and cause more disruption in the area.

A Minuteman silo is a very hard target, requiring a blast pressure of about 300psi to be destroyed. Because the radius of such a high pressure from a megaton weapon is comparable to the error radius in delivery by ICBM it is supposed that it would require two megaton weapons directed at each silo to obtain an acceptably high probability of destroying the silo. A quite low height of burst is required; and because a surface burst would be very nearly as effective, as well as being somewhat easier to implement, it could well be the preferred mode of attack. With from 150 to 200 silos on a single Minuteman base, a determined attack on the base could entail several hundred megaton surface bursts within a short period of time in an area $\sim$60 miles wide and $\sim$100 miles long.

Effective attacks against the strategic targets other than the six Minuteman bases might require only one or a few megaton weapons per base. Except for those strategic targets embedded in metropolitan areas – as naval bases and shipyards tend to be – the direct effects (blast, incendiary, or prompt radiation) of an attack on one of these strategic targets would not necessarily involve any civilian areas. However, in all cases where surface bursts were employed, the residual fall-out radiation would affect areas far outside the base.

From one megaton surface burst a cigar-shaped strip about 75 miles long and 12 miles wide downwind from the burst point would receive enough fall-out to give a radiation exposure in excess of 1000r to an unprotected person in the four days following the explosion. In a smaller (inner) contour about 40 miles long and 10 miles wide the 4-day exposure would be 3000r; while on a larger contour ($\sim$30 miles by 200 miles) the 4-day exposure would be down to 100r. The effects from several bursts only a few miles apart would be cumulative and result in higher intensities as well as larger areas exposed to a given intensity. From an attack of the sort pictured in connection with a Minuteman base the 4-day 1000r contour would be about 200 miles wide and 650 miles long. Depending on the wind pattern the intense fall-out regions from attacks on the Minuteman bases in Wyoming and Missouri could run together and overlap, and possibly have the effect of including Kansas City, St Louis, and Cincinnati within the same 1000r contour. At the 4-day 1000r contour the incremental exposure between 4 days and one month would be $\sim$75r; and between 4 days and one year $\sim$135r. At the 4-day 3000r contour these increments will be about three times larger.

It is supposed that a radiation exposure larger than about 600r received in a time as short as a few days would have lethal effects within a short time (days). It is expected that all persons receiving 400-450r within a few days would require medical care, and that about 50 per cent of them would die. The National Council of Radiation Protection (NCRP) has concluded that an exposure of about 200-250r in a time less than a week marks the dividing line between doses that will and will not cause sickness requiring medical care. This fits reasonably well with the experience of those on Rongelap Atoll, 105 miles from the weapons test of 1 March 1954, who received 175r in the two days before they were evacuated. None was incapacitated, though all displayed serious anomalies in blood counts over a period of about fifteen years, and there was a very high incidence of thyroid disorders requiring attention starting about ten years after their exposure. Since a larger total exposure can be tolerated if it is delivered over a longer period of time, the NCRP has concluded that no medical care would be expected to be necessary for persons receiving a total of 300r in a period of four months provided that no more than 200r of this total were received in any one month, nor more than 150r in any one week.

To keep below these thresholds a person at the boundary of a 1000r, 4-day contour would have to maintain an intensity-averaged shielding factor greater than 6 during the first week. The shielding factor for the first or second floor of a brick dwelling is only about 2 to 4, though the shielding factor in a basement without windows or exposed walls may be about 20, and it could be much larger in a shelter designed for the purpose. The NCRP criteria are only sufficient to avoid having a person actually fall ill. A group of persons just meeting these would be expected to experience about twice the normal incidence of fatal cancer cases in the 20 to 25 years following such exposure, and to see about twice the normal incidence of genetically transmitted disease in their offspring.

With these considerations in mind it is clear that not only would the whole population within (and even beyond) a 4-day 1000r contour have to find and maintain themselves in adequate shelters throughout the first week or so just to avoid becoming immediate casualties, but the area would then have to be evacuated. Unless weathering or decontamination measures could be effective in removing the fall-out particles it would be at least several months – and more probably longer than a year – before it would seem reasonable or attractive to have the displaced persons return to these areas and resume normal operations. If peacetime standards were applied, by which an area might be evacuated if the exposure were expected to exceed 10r in the course of a year, the period of evacuation would certainly not be as short as a year. For reference, the inhabitants of Rongelap Atoll were only permitted to return after three years following the explosion of March 1954. Though the part of the atoll on which persons were located at the time of this shot had only a 4-day exposure of 220r, other parts of the atoll had exposures greater than 1000r.

Although we have focused attention on the 1000r contour, it must be kept in mind that the population in a much larger area with lower exposure levels would also have to take protective measures, possibly involving evacuation. For example, in connection with the limited attack under discussion (an attack on Minuteman bases), Baltimore and Washington DC could be subject to exposures greater than 350r in 96 hours – that is, twice the level experienced by the inhabitants of Rongelap. Obviously, with different wind patterns the path of heavy fall-out might avoid these cities though it would probably still extend to about that range. Considering the size of the areas which might be involved it can be seen that many millions of people might have to be evacuated. Most of these would have to travel many tens of miles to reach places where further protective measures would not be required. The direction and location of safe areas could only be determined after the event.

Various estimates have been made of the number of fatalities resulting from such a 'limited' attack. These have ranged from less than a million to about 22 million – which suggests that, though there is no really good basis for estimating the number, the number would evidently be very large. After considerable study, the US Department of Defense concluded that a number of about 7 million fatalities would be 'most representative.' The number of non-fatal radiation injuries would almost certainly be larger.

In addition to the immediate effects on the human inhabitants of the areas affected there would be serious effects on agricultural activity, food production, livestock, and even plant life. An exposure of 5000r would be lethal for all fruit trees and most deciduous trees, while 1000r would be lethal for all coniferous trees. An exposure of approximately 3000r would be expected to reduce the yield of growing wheat or corn by 50 per cent (as well as making it unlikely that it could be harvested, or would be worth harvesting). An exposure or approximately 500r would be fatal for cattle in feed lots; and in addition such animals could not survive unless people should come out to supply them with food and water within a very few days. An exposure of approximately 180r would be fatal for cattle on pasture or range since, in addition to the γ-radiation, such animals would be exposed internally to β-radiation from the contaminated forage they would ingest. Out to about the 100r contour the milk from cattle on pasture would probably be unfit for immediate human consumption because of contamination with radio-active iodine, though it might still be usable for food if converted to dry milk or cheese and stored until the iodine activity ($\tau = \sim 8$ days) had died away.

As with human fatalities, there is no way of making a good estimate of the quantitative loss to US food supply from such a 'limited' attack on military targets, except that it would be very large. The area affected to the extent that agricultural work would have to be suspended or seriously interrupted would be larger than that from which evacuation might seem necessary. Though the particular areas affected would depend on the wind pattern at the time, an attack with surface bursts against all the US Minuteman bases could have the effect that agriculture production would be lost for at least the year of the attack in more than half of the important food-producing area between the Canadian border on the north to the southern borders of Kansas and Missouri, and from the Wyoming-Nebraska border to the eastern borders of Ohio and West Virginia. Put differently, the area affected to this extent would exceed the combined areas of France, West Germany, and Britain. All the land in such an area (or more) would be so contaminated with ^{90}Sr, in particular, that by peacetime standards it would be judged to be unsuitable for the growing of new crops for a year or so following the fall-out because of the uptake of ^{90}Sr into the plants. Under duress, such standards might be relaxed; but a massive program of monitoring soils and crops would be necessary through some extended period following the attack to evaluate the contamination level of possible food crops and determine their proper disposition.

DIRECT EFFECTS OF MAJOR NUCLEAR WAR

The battlefield use of nuclear weapons would be devastating for the immediate area involved. However, the number of people affected, the potential number of fatalities, and the extent of the physical damage from a *strategic* use of nuclear weapons would be enormously greater. We shall therefore consider further only situations in which metropolitan areas are either engaged as targets or receive heavy fall-out from weapons delivered at military installations.

A frequent question is that of the extent to which civil defence shelters and related measures could defend against the most serious consequences of a nuclear attack on a city. With respect to protection against blast the situation is quite different from that experienced during heavy bomber attacks in the Second World War, since those bombardments required several hours to accomplish, and a large fraction of the population could gain shelter after the raid had begun. In the nuclear case only those already in the blast shelters before the attack would benefit from them. The likelihood that a large fraction of the population would already be in shelters at the moment they would be needed would depend not only on the adequacy and convenience of the facilities available but also on the number of false alarms that had already been raised.

With respect to protection from fall-out in more distant areas free of blast damage there would be a warning time of something like 20 minutes, or more, between the detonation and the time fall-out particles from the cloud began to accumulate on the land at points beyond the blast-damaged zone. In principle, the immediate need for protection from radiation could also be met by the use of deep basements or the middle portions of large multi-storied buildings; but unless a supply of stored water were at hand, in the likely event that the city water system had been put out of commission by blast, people might be forced to leave before it was safe to do so.

Some matters would not be reduced to manageable proportions by the mere availability of shelters. Among these is the extended length of time for which people would have to remain in such quarters, and the fact that on leaving they would have to proceed rapidly and directly to a distance sufficient to get clear of the contaminated area and to reach some emergency station hastily set up at a location which could only be chosen after the fall-out pattern had been established. Thus, though civil defence facilities could possibly bring about a large reduction in the number of immediate fatalities, they could not alone ensure the continued well-being of the survivors.

A metropolitan area subjected to heavy fall-out, whether or not it suffered any blast damage, would first be immobilized and then, as possible, evacuated. One immediate consequence would be that the particular goods and services provided by the city – such as hospital facilities or supply warehouses depended on by the surrounding region, or supplies of tools, parts, pharmaceuticals, and the like on which the whole country might rely – would be cut off. More dramatically, of course, the million or so inhabitants of the area would be displaced in a short span of time into some refuge area having supplies and facilities of all kinds totally inadequate to meet the sudden demand. The logistic problems of meeting even the basic necessities would be enormous. Much would depend on just which stockpiles of supplies and which transportation routes, etc., had been destroyed or made inaccessible by fall-out, and which could still be used. Much would also depend on the availability of skilled people. As much would depend on the weather.

A great deal would depend on whether or not this was a well-isolated case to which a large surrounding area could rally in support. In the event of a major nuclear war this last condition would be quite unlikely since, even in the case of an attack directed only at targets such as the Minuteman bases, all the surviving inhabitants, both urban and rural, in a swathe several hundred miles wide and many hundred miles long – and, more probably, several such swathes – would nearly simultaneously have need of similar assistance. Some might consider that plans to cope with contingencies of this sort (whatever such plans could consist of) should be a part of civil defence; but the use of 'defence' in this context is misleading in the extreme: 'disaster mitigation' would be a more realistic term.

Apart from the immediate effects and disruptions already indicated, the question has been raised of whether a nuclear war would poison the biosphere to such an extent as to imperil prospects for the continuation of human life. As the result of a study conducted in 1975 by a Committee of the US National Academy of Sciences it was concluded that, after a war involving the detonation of ten thousand megatons of nuclear explosives, the fall-out at locations remote from the major target areas – at distances, that is, of the order of 1000km or more, beyond which fall-out is no longer local but is reasonably uniformly distributed on a world-wide basis – would provide an incremental radiation exposure approximately equal to that provided by natural background over a 30- to 40-year period. This would apply to the hemisphere (presumably northern) in which the detonations occurred; in the other hemisphere such effects would be about one third as large. The gross total of megatons considered was felt to be of about the right order to allow for as much as the major powers might be in a position to deliver.

In addition to fall-out radiation, other phenomena were identified which would lead to troublesome and undesirable effects – enhanced ultraviolet radiation persisting for at least a few years, for example, and possibly changes in climate and average surface temperatures which might substantially shorten growing seasons for particular crops and could restrict the areas in which they could be grown. Though the extent of such effects could not be estimated with any precision, it was not expected that the changes induced would be large enough to be catastrophic. In the most elementary physical sense, then, it was concluded that, with some increased difficulties and disabilities, the human species could continue to inhabit a major part of the northern hemisphere. This mere continuation, of course, does not tell one all one could wish to know about the quality of life, since the species already inhabited the northern hemisphere during the Dark Ages.

INDIRECT EFFECTS OF MAJOR NUCLEAR WAR

In many discussions it seems to be assumed that the effects of nuclear war are calculable and that the consequences could be managed and accommodated within the existing context. It is as if one should ask: after so and so many bombs, each destroying such and such facilities, how long would it take to repair the damage and return things to the *status quo ante*? This might be a relevant question with respect to an attack involving one, or a few, weapons; but following a general, or even a 'limited', nuclear attack many much more primitive and urgent questions would dominate.

Very large numbers of displaced survivors having almost nothing in the way of material goods, but much in the way of worries about actual or possible radiation injuries and concern over the basis of long-term as well as short-term subsistence, would have to be provided for. Their response would be greatly dependent on the rapidity and adequacy with which their most elementary needs could be met. Unless, within a very few days, evident progress were being made towards meeting these needs, bands of survivors, larger in numbers than the local residents, could be imagined setting out to forage for themselves. Attempts to counter or suppress such tendencies might or might not succeed; but in either event there would be a corrosive residue.

One may consider the problem of trying to locate and maintain an adequate food supply for a city full of displaced persons as an example. Evidently this would be a matter of great difficulty under the best circumstances; but it is to be expected that there would be at least some complicating circumstances. For instance, there would probably be several large groups in the same general region in the same predicament; normally important storage facilities could well have been destroyed or put temporarily out of reach by fall-out, along with a considerable amount of the equipment usually available for transport; a large part of the area from which new supplies were customarily drawn might have had to be abandoned; to say nothing of what a spell of extreme weather could add to this. Under an unfavourable, though not particularly unlikely, combination of such circumstances the business of delivering an adequate food supply for the displaced survivors could turn out to be impossible.

Food is only one of a number of items which might constitute urgent necessities, since such things as vaccines, plasma, heating oil, water treatment supplies, and others would also be required. Probably those individuals dependent on the most highly specialized assistance – such as dialysis machines and regular administration of particular hormones – would have been 'weeded out' of the surviving population at an early stage. Though the conditions favouring an outbreak of water-borne disease, or of some contagion such as flu, would be considerably greater than normal, trouble of that sort might not really be necessary to plunge a group of frustrated and worried survivors into a desperate and militant frame of mind.

Even after those displaced could return to their homes, they would not immediately be able to resume previous patterns of activity. Apart from the possible lingering effects of radiation injury and the possible consequences of civilian blast damage, serious dislocations would persist. Many of those returning to the agricultural sector would have to start very far back, obtaining new seed and rebuilding herds and otherwise requiring time, measured in seasons, before they could re-establish normal operations. Many in the non-agricultural sector – as those engaged in distribution, production of equipment, and processing – would be directly affected by this; and all would share the effects of a reduction in the food supply. Whether acceptable solutions to this and other similar problems could be found within the context of our present system of private ownership and free enterprise is at best unclear; so that these, too, might be casualties of a nuclear war.

The effects of disruption of food production in the US to the extent which could occur would by no means necessarily be limited to those felt within the country. In spite of the very high (average) standard of consumption maintained at present, the US is still a major exporter of grains, for example. This would be interrupted, and supplies from the US might no longer be available to help mitigate the consequences of a crop failure in one of those many regions of the world where food production is at best marginal with respect to subsistence levels. For other areas, such as coffee-growing regions whose specialized economic base may depend heavily on trade with the US, serious dislocations in the US could result in acute economic problems and shortages of various kinds.

The particular matter of food supply has been used here merely as an example. Other classes of products such as manufactured goods, machinery and chemicals, though not as basic as food, are nevertheless essential to the way we live now. The production of these may not be as sensitive to fall-out as food products, but would be more sensitive to blast damage; and they could have their production and supply cut back just as effectively by the direct consequences of a nuclear war. One has only to imagine the effects of a concerted attack on US oil refineries and major power plants, along, possibly, with a few transformer stations – which are much softer targets than Minuteman silos, and most of which would require at least several years to replace – to see that a successful attack of that sort, even without the concomitant dangers from fall-out, could force people out of their present modes of existence in large metropolitan centres and in other sections of the country which are not self-sustaining. The life of much of the developed world – including, but not limited to, the US – is now so heavily specialized, and so absolutely dependent on the continued performance of other groups and plants and processes far from the local community or section of the country, that it has become vitally sensitive to major disruption of any of these. More or less in parallel with this development, nuclear war has become capable of imposing such major disruptions.

The Avoidance of Nuclear War
Up to the Present

2

The Avoidance of Nuclear War since 1945

W. McGEORGE BUNDY

In the first years of the nuclear age it was widely believed that mankind faced an early choice between nuclear disarmament and catastrophe – 'between the quick and the dead'. Not many would have predicted that 33 years after Nagasaki there would be no international control over tens of thousands of thermonuclear warheads or over delivery systems of unpredicted speed and sophistication – but not a single use of nuclear weapons. It is quite right that the organizers of this meeting have asked us to address ourselves to the implications of this astonishing chapter in history. Broadly speaking, the work that has preoccupied students of the nuclear age has been work on the present and future. It makes sense to look back a little too. Have we been wise, or merely lucky?

A good first question for us is why there are so few states with a nuclear weapons capability today. In the late 1950s, after the surprisingly rapid achievements of the Soviet Union, it was widely believed that there would be a quick and drastic increase in the numbers of nuclear weapons states. Gloomy forecasts were made by such knowledgeable observers as Hans Morgenthau and Charles Snow. Indeed in the name of stable deterrence Henry Kissinger once went so far as to conclude that on balance the diffusion of nuclear weapons technology would be to our net strategic advantage. But in fact, I think by very good fortune, things have gone much more slowly than we feared twenty years ago. Why?

By my personal estimate there are seven states with nuclear weapons today – China, France, Great Britain, India, Israel, the Soviet Union, and the United States. All but India and Israel are self-proclaimed and universally acknowledged as such – though their capabilities are widely different. India has had one explosion, and Israel none, but I believe no neighbour of either one can assume for a moment that there could be a threat to the survival of either without heavy risk of a speedy nuclear response, and that seems to be the best test. Yet I intend no combative definition, and if one or more of these seven states prefers to describe itself differently, I do not object. (In particular one must welcome the clarification of Indian policy announced by Prime Minister Moraji Desai in 1978. His renunciation of further nuclear explosions clearly places India among the countries working for the restraint of nuclear weapons, even though there is no way in which India can forget what she has learned how to do.)

Why these seven and not more? Let us begin with some of the things the seven countries have in common – there is much more than the images of their national personae might suggest as one quickly lists their names.

Technologically, each of the seven, by traditions already lively thirty years ago, has had access, *through its own nationals*, to physics, chemistry, and engineering of high quality. (It is unwise to forget, for example, what the Indian nuclear effort owes to Homi Bhabha – scientist, artist, passionate patriot, and student of Rutherford at Cambridge.) Politically each of them has an intense tradition of deep conviction that its own national life is near the centre of man's aspirations; there are modest nations to be found, but not among these seven. And historically, each of the seven governments, at the time when it was deciding to 'go nuclear', had compelling reasons to believe one or both of two things: either that this decision was essential to its safety, or that a decision not to have the 'best' weapons would be the abandonment of a national tradition. What the United States did because of Hitler, the Soviet Union did because of the United States – though both would probably have come out at the same point somewhat later in any event. The drives behind the British and French efforts are less intense and more traditional. They represent the almost inescapable reflexes of political and bureaucratic energies channelled by centuries of existence as Great Powers. The Chinese imperative needs no new analysis. What is remarkable about the case of Israel is less that the capability exists than that it still remains publicly ambiguous. The danger in which Israel lives makes it hardly conceivable, in retrospect, that her leaders could have neglected nuclear weapons development. Only the Indian case was marked by any significant delay beyond that imposed by the pace of technology, and that temporary policy of delay was probably the product of the personal authority and restraint of Prime Minister Nehru. To the military and technical bureaucracies of India the natural drive to achieve a fitting capability may well have been as strong in its own way as the parallel earlier pressure in Britain and France.

To see that a political imperative was a necessary part of each national decision we need only note briefly the positions of others who have refrained from attempting to have weapons, in spite of ample technical, economic, and political capacity. Germany and Japan, two of the great nations of the thirties and forties, have been constrained by their parts in the Second World War. Moreover, the decisive constraints, except in the case of East Germany, have been internal – stemming from the general unwillingness of effective political opinion to support such a decision. Another group of nations – exemplified by Sweden, Canada, Switzerland, and Australia – have constrained themselves for varied reasons all of which, in the end, sum up to 'safer not'. I think myself that Mrs Alva Myrdal is right when she concludes that in logic the argument that prevailed in Sweden could have been as strong in London or Paris as in Stockholm – but there is a world of difference between the historical memories of Sweden, neutral and at peace since 1814, and those of the British or French. In some quite serious sense these middle countries were less proud.

Now let us note one further, and I think essentially lucky, characteristic common to the nuclear seven: that at the time of its effective acquisition of a nuclear capability each of the seven was, as it is today, essentially a satisfied state, in that no urgent requirement of expansion has been the inescapable determinant of its behaviour. I am not suggesting at all that these seven states have no interests or ambitions beyond their borders. Most of them have seemed aggressive to one or more other states, and all but India have used some force against someone else since they first had nuclear capabilities. But I believe that none of them has been governed, in its time of nuclear readiness, by any drive to expand as implacable as those drives that only a few years earlier dominated Japan and Germany, or even those that have governed the imperial or continental expansions of the British, the French, the Prussians, the Americans and the Russians at various times in the past. These seven, in relative terms, have all been satisfied powers, vastly more concerned with self-defence than with expansion.

This is lucky. It would require only a modest rearrangement of the history of technology and politics to put the first arrival of nuclear weapons in Germany, and not the United States, for a first use by Hitler and not Harry Truman. I cannot believe that such a rearrangement would be meaningless. Nor is it comforting to think of the temptations that might have faced some of the present seven nuclear states if their capability had been at hand at some earlier moment of revolutionary or military struggle. In the largest and most general sense none of the seven has had explosive ambitions while it has been nuclear, and not one has been pressed to the edge of a disaster so large and imminent that every weapon must be used. Nor has any one of the seven been torn by internal conflict so violent as to overturn the solid command and control of these weapons by national political authorities – and here too one can easily think of times and places where the outcome could have been different. The nature and condition of the seven nuclear powers is the first and most important reason for our relative good fortune.

The United States did use the weapon twice, to end a major war it did not start. The decision will be debated for ever, and I will not waste your time by repeating the arguments that prevailed at the time, though I find them persuasive. What I will say is that I think this decision, right or wrong in its own time, has had deeply important and constructive effects over the last thirty-three years. We know, and have known from the beginning, what even a primitive nuclear explosion can do to a city. I cannot improve on the sober conclusion of Bernard Brodie:

'The cold war was to develop soon enough, in a mood of soberness deepened by knowledge that war, that is, what we have come to know as "general war," had entered a wholly new and hitherto unbelievable dimension of horror. In any new war between the superpowers, the terrible devastation of the two world wars would be at once immeasurably surpassed. Certainly the clarity of this realization was heightened and made more acute by the knowledge of what had happened at the two Japanese cities that had been struck, accounts of which were soon widely published with no want of detail. After more than a quarter of a century they are still the only nuclear weapons to have been used in war, and their use has not made one iota more likely any future use. One would suspect that quite the contrary is the case. Though the people of the two cities paid bitterly for it, their sacrifice unquestionably contributed to the significance and the effectiveness of the "balance of terror," which thus far has shown itself to be an exceedingly stable balance.' *War and Politics* (Macmillan, 1973), 56.

It is impossible to overstate the general political and psychological importance of the instant and durable perception that these weapons were different in kind from anything before them in history. At various times and for various reasons both military men and civilian analysts have argued that these – or at least some of them – are weapons like any

others, but that has never been the view of either ordinary citizens or
heads of government. What was terrible enough in 1945 became more
terrible still when the thermonuclear age opened in the early 1950s. Still
more orders of magnitude of unimaginable destructiveness have been
added in succeeding decades as the number of warheads has steadily
increased. There has been no substitute, in all that time, for the horrors of
Hiroshima and Nagasaki as reminders of what would be fantastically
multiplied in any general nuclear war.

Just here we have the second important reason for the fact that those
who have these weapons in hand or in reach have never used them – or
even, I think, come very close. Nearly everything that has happened to
nuclear weapons since 1945 has intensified the general public and political perception that they are terrible. Thus the political dividing line between any other use of arms and the use of nuclear weapons has widened
and thickened from year to year, and the political cost of using them has
gone up. Probably the moment of greatest danger came in October 1962,
in the Cuban missile crisis, although I do not myself believe that the
danger even then was as high as some words of some of those engaged
might suggest. As far as we know there was no moment in this crisis in
which anyone on either side was planning any early use of any nuclear
weapons at all. I think the real risks of that crisis were risks of a more
conventional – though still enormously harmful – conflict. But whether I
am right or wrong on that point, I think we can be sure that the experience was one that neither the USSR nor the US has wished to repeat. That
too is fortunate, though perhaps not merely lucky; great states can learn
from shared danger.

Certainly it is not merely the increasing and world-wide revulsion
against nuclear weapons that has made their possessors refrain from
using them, it is also the fact that this absolute weapon has so far turned
out not to be usable, at least as between nuclear powers, without a wholly
unacceptable risk of a direct and terrible reply. Whether or not nuclear
weapons might be 'the absolute weapon' against an enemy without them,
they have not seemed absolute as between nuclear weapons states, even
when the imbalance between them has been very wide. Indeed, if we
begin at the beginning, there was never any high chance that the United
States would use its nuclear monopoly against Stalin's Russia, if only
because one probable price of such use would have been a Soviet occupa-
tion of Western Europe. And as the weapon slowly spread, there was
never a moment when it would have been attractive to any one holder of
nuclear weapons to attempt a pre-emptive attack on a rival. As Raymond

Aron has said, to make such an attack 'would be to throw oneself in the water for fear of getting wet', and the leaders of nuclear weapons states have known it.

For all its extraordinary power, the nuclear weapon so far has not provided its possessors with the capacity to make a safe first strike. The technology of delivery systems, so far, has validated the striking image of the scorpions in a bottle – able to kill one another only at the price of death. This again, I think, must be called a matter of good fortune, because there is no intrinsic requirement – nothing in the very nature of things – which assures that there will always be a high risk of self-destruction in any effort to use this weapon against another well-armed nuclear state.

In this respect the most important case is also the most instructive: the largely bilateral nuclear rivalry of the United States and the Soviet Union. In one way or another nearly every effort of either country in the field of strategic weapons systems has been designed to give assurance first of all against the danger that the other might be tempted to strike to win. There have been other objectives along the way; in particular both powers have had to contend with the fierce desire of military men to define both their own weapons systems and those of others in terms of what they could actually do in warfare. But whatever the 'war-fighting' doctrines of generals and marshals on both sides, the first and dominant objective of the two governments has been to deny to the other any temptation to try a first strike. And technologies have made that purpose achievable – different technologies in different decades.

To understand that this objective might not have been achievable we need only recognize that the most obvious ways of dissuading attack turned out to be ineffective – and perhaps worse. Neither defence against aircraft nor defence against missiles nor defence against submarines has proven sufficiently effective to neutralize those weapons systems. Moreover, some of these forms of defence might have been dangerous if they had been more successful, in that a capacity to defend can create an incentive for one's own attack. It is only by the device of 'survivable forces' that deterrence has been assured, and there has been almost continuous change in what has been needed, on both sides, to maintain such forces.

We here confront an unpleasant reality – and one often overlooked by critics of the two giants. Believing, I think correctly, that in the course of their contest both have at times been grossly overarmed, many critics have supposed that it would be wise for one or both simply to stop the

technological race. But when there is both danger and hope in the un-
known, it is hard to take, and harder still to enforce, an oath of ignorance.
The record of the past shows that repeatedly a new capability has been
discovered, and a new and timely deployment effected, in ways that have
clearly contributed to the stability of the strategic balances. The nuclear
weapons submarine may be the most notable example here, but the
development of technical intelligence has also been highly constructive.
Obviously not every advance has been helpful in this respect: the world
would be a safer place, I believe, if MIRVs had been unmakeable. Still it
seems a painful fact that both great states, at least until they are able to be
much more open with each other, with feel it imperative to press on with
what they know and do, if only to keep a sharp eye out for anything that
might cripple their own deterrent strength. In technology, if not necessarily in megatonnage, we seem condemned to continuing rivalry.

You will note that in counting our blessings I have not referred to such
widely discussed efforts as the struggle for non-proliferation or the SALT
negotiations. I intend no disrespect to either one, and have been an ardent
supporter of both. But I would argue that both have been less important
than, and derivative from, the larger forces I have been describing. The
movement against proliferation has been pressed, in nuclear and non-
nuclear states alike, by those who have seen most clearly that the nuclear
weapon itself is a durable menace to us all, so that the fewer the leaders
who could ever decide to use it, the better for everyone. And the SALT
process has been most important not for its achieved limitations on weapons, which have been few, but rather for its reinforcement of recognition
on both sides that the common danger of thermonuclear war requires at
least a modest amount of verifiable information helpful to both sides.
SALT has been important also as a demonstration by the two great powers,
to each other and to the world, that the final judgment on these matters is
rightly and necessarily political. If both sides have had to concede much –
too much I think – to military bureaucracies, still there is no way to read
the decision of SALT I and the emerging outline of SALT II as anything but a
significant and two-sided recognition that the most important, indeed the
decisive, role of nuclear weapons on both sides is to ensure that none of
them will be used. The 1972 Treaty that bans anti-ballistic missiles is
ineluctably dependent on the mutual acceptance of mutual deterrence.
Both non-proliferation and SALT, with all their imperfections, are policies
that help to widen the gap across which any decisions to possess or use
these things must jump.

Yet there is also value to uncertainty, and I cannot omit the remarkable fact that the long peace of Europe in these thirty-four years may well owe much to the fact that no one really knows what would happen if war should start there, even in a small way, between East and West. I am far from saying that nuclear weapons have been a net benefit to Europe; they are still too dangerous for that. But I do believe that since it is a fact that they do exist, it is a good thing for the freedom of Western Europe that there has been no way for the Soviet Union to impose its strength beyond its bloc without a wholly unacceptable risk that nuclear replies would come. The confusion over strategy in NATO has been almost continuous, but in this respect constructive. NATO's incoherent mixture of deployments, conventional and nuclear, tactical and strategic, while it has served no serious war-fighting scenario, has none the less served the common peace. There is here a tantalizing paradox which applies also, in a different way, to the general strategic balance: war-fighting at the level of thermonuclear exchange has become unreal as an object of policy, but a real capacity for it, and the possibility that it could happen, are real elements, vital elements even, in the calculus that keeps the peace.

We have found some partial explanations for our relative good fortune. The number of nuclear powers stayed relatively small, because the capacity to make the weapons and the political will to have them did not often coincide. The powers that did achieve the weapons were never insistent on great new victories or desperate in the face of disaster. The weapons themselves, by their very frightfulness, built a steadily stronger barrier of feeling against their use. And no nuclear power has ever been in a position where it could hope to use its weapons against another nuclear power without deeply self-destructive results.

But we have had to observe that there was a lot of luck in all this. Just as an example, nuclear weapons could have been easier to make than they were for each of these seven technologically modern states – and they probably *are* easier to make today; thus the technical barriers to thoughtless and imprudent proliferation may not be as high as they once were. Similarly technology could have favoured the first strike more than it did; it may yet do so in the future. Nor can we be sure that all who have such weapons now or in the future will have the combination of internal stability and lack of an explosive need to expand which have so far characterized the nuclear seven. The list of those who could choose to 'go nuclear' in the next decade contains some states whose long-run stability seems fragile. And perhaps most important of all, we cannot be sure, from one year to the next, that there will be no moment at which some present or future state with nuclear weapons will feel that it has no other choice than to break the taboo.

I began by asking whether we had been wise or lucky to get through these thirty-three years so well. I end by suggesting that we have been more lucky than wise, although some of our luck is that the men in final control of these weapons have been wise, or at least prudent, in the face of danger.

It is not my task to predict the future, but I allow myself two further comments. First, I suspect there is no state among those that have chosen nuclear weapons in which some men have not learned to wish they could live without them, and I think there is no state among those that have deliberately chosen not to have them in which the majority today would wish the choice had been different. In this important sense the record of the last thirty years is not in itself an incentive to proliferation; these are not weapons whose possession has been so obviously advantageous that every one must rush to have them. The nuclear weapon is neither the transistor radio nor the automobile nor even the jet plane of contagious technology. Nations able to make future choices of their own may indeed be glad if they are not pressed to take this fateful step either by some inertial sense of greatness or by the dangers they see around them. Unfortunately there is great force in the view that those considering this option in the future may simply think that it is different for them.

Second and finally, if any present or future nuclear weapons state should become dominated by some imperative of aggressive expansion, then the rest of us may need kinds of wisdom and will that have not been needed so far.

3

An Assessment of Nuclear Crises

JOHN STEINBRUNER

There is every reason, in reviewing the past three decades of the nuclear age, to rejoice in the fact that during this period the world has been spared the direct use of nuclear weapons in warfare. With the prospect of disaster hanging over industrialized societies, some basic restraints seem to have imposed themselves on the behaviour of nuclear powers. Analysis of the strategic situation cannot merely celebrate this central fact, however, but must face as well the more exacting question as to how securely restraint has been achieved. If the often discussed nuclear threshold has even been closely approached, then there are important lessons to be learned.

Precisely because the use of nuclear weapons has been avoided since 1945, experience from the intervening period is an uncertain guide in assessing the stability of peace. History does not directly reveal its possible extensions or the alternative directions that events might have taken, had decision-makers acted differently than they did. One can assert with some confidence that since the attacks on Japan nuclear weapons have been in the near background of all serious international conflicts and there are many reports of varying credibility regarding actual discussions of their use, at least by the United States government whose deliberations are more extensively recorded than those of the other nuclear powers.

Scholarly sources suggest, for example, that the Eisenhower administration invoked a threat to use nuclear weapons in order to bring the negotiations ending the Korean war to a conclusion, and that delivery systems capable of carrying nuclear weapons were ostentatiously moved to Okinawa to bolster this threat.[1] The Eisenhower administration also officially contemplated the use of nuclear weapons in the defence of

Quemoy and Matsu.[2] Those events, however, at least as far as they are publicly known, do not seem to constitute a serious enough approach to nuclear war to carry very powerful lessons on the subject.

It does appear that the Kennedy administration in the course of the Berlin crisis in 1961 seriously confronted the possibility that a defence of Berlin might require nuclear weapons and insight from that crisis is more likely to be pertinent. Documentary details remain protected by security regulations, however, and from what is publicly known, military preparations undertaken by the American government in response to the Berlin situation involved only conventional military forces. There is no indication that the actual preparation of forces for nuclear attack was begun before the crisis broke. For the Berlin situation as well as for most of the major crises of the period, in the absence of detailed documentation from the decision processes of the governments involved, there is no basis to suggest imminence of nuclear war.

There are, however, two crises of the period which offer some leverage on the questions posed, not because they are immune from historical uncertainties but rather because in some sense nuclear weapons were more prominently involved than they were in other episodes.[3] During the crisis over Cuba in 1962 and the Middle East war in 1973 some of the preparations required to use nuclear forces were actually undertaken. In the Cuban crisis the United States strategic forces were placed on alert and some of the physical procedures required to bring nuclear weapons to combat status were actually completed. In that case both the political leaders and the military commanders appeared to believe that nuclear war might conceivably develop. During the Middle East war in 1973 United States political leaders, under what they took to be strong diplomatic provocation from the Soviet Union, ordered an alert of US strategic forces largely as a signal of resolve. On that occasion the US military command structure did not seem to consider the actual use of nuclear weapons to be a serious and imminent possibility. A comparison between these two situations offers some insight into the conditions which affect the likelihood of nuclear war.

CUBA: 1962

As with all such matters the crisis over Cuba in 1962 was the product of complicated historical circumstances, but the immediate issue which raised the possibility of war was simple and well defined.[4] Without announcing its intentions and in contradiction to diplomatic assurances which the United States government believed it had received, the Soviet Union in the late summer of 1962 began a clandestine emplacement in Cuba of medium- and intermediate-range missiles designed for nuclear attack. The United States discovered the missile sites in an unfinished state of construction and determined that the missiles, some bombers capable of carrying nuclear weapons, and other pertinent equipment, were being transported to Cuba on ships. The United States secretly prepared a naval blockade of Cuba and then established a confrontation by a dramatic public announcement that it would prevent further shipments and would take such other military action as might be necessary to secure the removal of offensive weapons from the island. After six days of extreme public tension the crisis was resolved by a diplomatic formula relating a pledge by the United States not to invade the island to the removal of the Soviet missiles and bombers to which the United States objected. During these days government officials and ordinary citizens throughout the world shared the perception that nuclear war had become a serious and immediate possibility.* That circumstance has never been repeated and the Cuban crisis stands in nearly universal judgment as the closest approach to a two-sided nuclear war that has yet been experienced. Even those who doubt that general war was in fact imminent do not appear to question that it was more so then than at any other time.

There were several circumstances particular to the Cuban crisis which served to diminish the chances of nuclear war. An assessment of how near the threshold was approached depends largely on judgments as to how powerfully these aspects of the situation affected the governments involved. In the first instance, the United States enjoyed in the Caribbean area an extraordinary advantage in conventional military power and from that derived at least in principle a wide range of coercive actions that could have been undertaken without resort to nuclear weapons. Indeed there was probably no place in the world outside its own borders where the United States enjoyed a greater potential superiority over the Soviet Union.

Second, whether by coincidence or as an underlying stimulus to the Soviet actions, the United States possessed at the time of the crisis a sub-

---

* Because of the elaborate controls imposed on nuclear weapons under normal peace-time circumstances, a meaningful threat of the use of such weapons requires a political situation in which that threat is perceived to be real. Without the crisis situation, the legitimacy of instructions to prepare weapons for use is likely to be questioned, at least in the United States. Hence, these widely held public perceptions are probably a critical indication of the approach of actual war.

stantial advantage in the number of operational delivery vehicles capable of carrying nuclear weapons over intercontinental ranges under combat conditions. This fact precluded any appeal by the Soviet Union to a global level of warfare as a means of reversing the effects of the conventional force balance in the Caribbean. Once the incomplete sites were discovered and disclosed, Soviet strategic forces were heavily burdened to maintain basic deterrence and had no residual capability to block American military actions directed at the Cuban sites.

Third, the United States strategic forces, despite their numerical superiority, were still under development, and their actual capabilities inherently constrained any serious temptation for pre-emptive war against the Soviet Union. The early missile systems had a number of technical imperfections and the more developed bomber force was still constrained by the imperfectly developed organization of strategic attack capability. A decisive, disarming strike against all Soviet strategic forces could not be undertaken with the confidence a rational decision-maker would require, and thus the United States also had a strong incentive to restrict its actions to the Caribbean area and to the conventional level of warfare.

Given all three circumstances, a resort to nuclear weapons by either of the governments involved should have remained a remote possibility.

In retrospect it is not obvious, however, that the actions of either government were completely dominated by such cool rational logic. Apart from natural doubts that governments ever act in perfect accord with such principles, there are a number of documented features of the crisis which directly suggest that events approached actual nuclear war more closely than would be expected from the basic strategic circumstances. This is all the more striking in that it did not occur from a failure to recognize such a danger or from carelessness in attempting to prevent it.

In the United States during the Cuban crisis there was an extraordinary effort to co-ordinate the actions of the government and to subject those actions to exhaustive deliberation. As is well known, a special decision-making body, an *ad hoc* Executive Committee of the National Security Council, was established which clearly centralized authority under the President and which integrated policy across all the major divisions of the government participating in the crisis. The President and all the top national security officials set aside all other business for the critical weeks in October. Because they were aware of inherent dangers of nuclear war they accepted the task of controlling the crisis as an overriding responsibility. They adopted a policy of measured response at the lowest level of coercion and they pursued matters in such detail that they involved themselves in such questions as whether the American destroyers participating in the naval blockade had Russian-speaking officers on board and whether the officers in communication with ships approaching the blockade line were carrying loaded revolvers. Despite all this, the American military response to the crisis developed farther in the direction of global strategic operations than the President or the Executive Committee either intended or imagined in advance.

The strongest instance of this effect concerned anti-submarine operations in the North Atlantic. As noted, the Executive Committee in exercising control over the crisis went to enormous trouble to implement the coercive pressure of the naval blockade gradually, and to begin the process with the least provocative measures. The intention was to allow the Soviet government time to arrange a graceful withdrawal from a deployment operation that was well underway. Recognizing that accommodating decisions on the Soviet side could not be made and implemented instantly, the President and his advisers considered it important to withhold stronger military measures until it became apparent that the weaker ones had failed to secure compliance with their demands.

Until well into the crisis, however, it escaped their attention that the US Navy would pursue Soviet submarines in the North Atlantic as a normal operational measure in support of the large US naval deployment establishing the blockade. In fact, the naval commanders, with ample operational authority to do so (unless it was specifically denied), chose to pursue this mission very aggressively from the outset. Since Soviet submarines carrying cruise missiles with nuclear warheads were inevitably one of the targets of American anti-submarine warfare (ASW) operations, and since these submarines were one of the prime force elements the Soviet government would have to rely upon should they have to undertake retaliation for strategic attack, the actions of the US Navy constituted extremely strong strategic coercion and violated the spirit of the Executive Committee policy.* It is not unreasonable to suppose that American ASW

---

* With only a handful of operational strategic missiles and a long-range bomber force that had not been developed into a ready strategic weapon, the cruise missile submarines probably constituted the prime Soviet deterrent at the time. Once they had been found and brought under close surveillance by American destroyers, they were in effect removed from effective use since firing the missiles required that the submarine surface and the launching apparatus be prepared. Observing American destroyers would have no difficulty in stopping any attempt to launch the missiles. The fact that the Executive Committee was unaware of this feature of the Navy's activities is documented by the dramatic confrontation which occurred between Admiral Anderson, the Chief of Naval Operations, and Secretary of Defense Robert McNamara on 24 October, when the latter first learned of what was occurring.[5]

activity in the North Atlantic was in fact the strongest message perceived in Moscow in the course of the crisis, and if that is true, then the efforts to bring American policy under central direction must be said to have failed.

There are other, somewhat more subtle instances of the same effect. The Executive Committee, for example, undertook special efforts to co-ordinate the alerting of American military forces with the President's speech announcing the American position. This was done so as not to give the Soviet government an opportunity to make a pre-emptive diplomatic move. Despite this effort the coming of the crisis was perceived and anticipated in military command channels and a great deal of activity having to do with preparing military forces for combat was accomplished well before the official order to go on alert.[6] Since the American newspapers were able to perceive this activity in advance of the President's speech, it is a reasonable presumption that the Soviet Union was able to do so as well.

The precise intentions of the President and the Executive Committee with regard to the role to be played by American strategic forces are not entirely clear from published accounts, but it is apparent that they ordered these forces into an advanced state of alert – with bombers dispersed and nuclear bombs distributed – as well as the tactical forces which would have conducted conventional operations in Cuba.[7] They did not appear to intend, however, the incursion into Soviet airspace of a reconnaissance aircraft on Saturday, 27 October, the most tense day of the confrontation. That incident also gives some clue that preparations for strategic attack may have been somewhat more advanced than American policy officially mandated.*

Though there is reason to be concerned about the implications of these incidents, they cannot be explained away simply as unusual mistakes or aberrant behavior on the part of a few individuals. They reflect rather the sort of thing that must be expected to happen when high crisis strikes the very complicated, inevitably decentralized, very large organizations that constitute modern strategic forces.

Once military command channels perceive that actual combat may be in prospect, there are a large number of organizational preparations which must be made. It is not possible for the President or any other single individual to control or even be informed of all aspects of this activity. In

---

* Though this incident has been officially explained as an accident and an ironic coincidence, it is difficult not to notice that increased reconnaissance activity, somewhat like increased ASW surveillance, is a routine measure that would be taken in the initial stages of preparation for strategic operations. The incursion may well have been an accident, but it is not likely that it was a mere coincidence.

order for the complex organizational system to work at all a great deal of authority to make preparations necessarily resides at low levels of the command structure. This very basic fact unfortunately provides ample means for the events of a crisis to exceed the control of central political authorities and the decisions they make.

The actions of the Soviet government in the Cuban crisis are much less documented and inherently more uncertain, but there are reasons to suppose that they too were not dominated, even on important points, by a cool logical assessment of strategic conditions. The emplacement of missiles in Cuba in the first instance is a strong suggestion that nuclear weapons were being harnessed to political objectives ranging well beyond basic deterrence. Though some attempt to redress an unfavourable strategic balance is logical enough, Soviet motives for the particular risk taken cannot be easily derived from basic strategic circumstances. Their behaviour in the crisis, moreover, shows some hint of turbulence within their internal decision processes. The significantly divergent letters from Khrushchev received on 26 October and 27 October with no intervening American response indicate, for example, that important diplomatic actions were responding to conflicting influences, even conflicting political jurisdiction.

In the end, it cannot be objectively established just how close the Cuban situation actually came to the outbreak of nuclear war, but it is also not possible to dismiss lightly the testimony of participants to the effect that it was all too uncomfortably close. Robert Kennedy and Theodore Sorenson – the two men personally closest to the President – appear to have believed so, and they ascribe this judgment to other members of the Executive Committee as well.[8] President Kennedy himself was seized with an analogy to the outbreak of the First World War, and in the midst of the crisis he quoted the odds on the occurrence of nuclear war at 'somewhere between one out of three and even'.[9] Chairman Khrushchev directly expressed a sense of the imminence of war in communications with Kennedy during the crisis.[10] Even if the objective validity of these perceptions is discounted and if a close approach to nuclear war is doubted, there is sober warning in the fact that those who believed it was near were not thereby deterred from military actions. The initial argument of the American Secretary of Defense – that the missiles placed in Cuba would merely hasten by a few years the inevitable development of strategic parity, and that therefore the importance of the event should be minimized[11] – was quickly set aside as politically unacceptable despite the sense of danger. On both sides, it appears, a signifiant increase in the seriously perceived risk of nuclear war was being accepted in pursuit of immediate political purposes.

THE MIDDLE EAST: 1973

If ever there were circumstances which would appear to carry the potential for precipitating a serious strategic confrontation, they were present in the autumn of 1973.[12] On 5 October, Egypt and Syria, with apparent foreknowledge and obvious military support of the Soviet Union, began a surprise attack on Israel, a close ally with a very strong claim on American political emotions. The campaign was the most effective military action yet taken by the Arab governments against Israel, and it produced the largest tank battles since the Second World War.

These events occurred, moreover, at a time of pivotal change in the economic circumstances of all Western industrial societies. As a result of a number of long-term trends in energy supply and demand conditions, Arab oil producers were able to exercise much greater leverage over the world petroleum market than they had ever enjoyed before.[13] They discovered this fact in the course of the crisis, and in service of the Arab cause they began a sequence of actions (most notably oil production cutbacks and sharp price increases) powerful enough to have strong immediate effects on American, West European, and Japanese consumers and to bring about lasting changes in world economic conditions.

This was happening as the American Vice-President was resigning under indictment, and as the dismissal of both the Watergate Special Prosecutor and the Attorney General made it apparent that the political viability of the Nixon administration was in serious question. It is a natural presumption that the chances of nuclear war depend to some extent on large matters being at stake, and seldom have so many large matters been at stake as in October of 1973.

In addition to these volatile political circumstances, the Middle East crisis also occurred with the strategic forces of both the United States and the Soviet Union in a far more advanced state of development than they had been eleven years earlier and with the balance between them far more evenly drawn. In 1962, as noted, the actual deployment of modern strategic weapons was in a relatively early phase and the sophisticated hardware involved had not been fully integrated into military organizations to produce operational capabilities flexible enough to respond effectively to the special circumstances of a limited crisis. By 1973 that process was much more advanced, and the difference was particularly dramatic for the Soviet Union. They had completed the deployment of their third-generation land-based systems, and had proceeded far enough with the SLBM (submarine launched ballistic missile) deployment to have a serious capability. The crisis also occurred in an area which was within range of many Soviet medium- and intermediate-range systems.

Beyond that, the balance of tactical forces in the Eastern Mediterranean in 1973 was not decisively advantageous to one side as it had been in the Caribbean in 1962.[14] Both the US and the Soviet Union were capable of extensive tactical operations with conventional weapons and both, if they so chose, could have supported tactical nuclear operations in the area.

Though the closer approximation to tactical and strategic parity was an important source of restraint on the two major governments, it also presented an incentive to undertake the first attack if one side happened to judge that fighting could not be avoided. It was an important fact, therefore, that the limits on actual military capability which affected the Cuba situation were less confining in 1973, and that fact certainly worked to make the military situation potentially more dangerous.

Finally, as a third significant element of the situation, the direct Soviet-American confrontation and the alerting of strategic forces by the United States also came about under immediate circumstances which seemed dramatic enough to act as a precipitating event for a serious crisis. After emergency negotiations between Secretary of State Kissinger and Soviet Communist Party Chairman Brezhnev in Moscow, a jointly sponsored UN resolution was issued on Monday, 22 October 1973, asking for a cease-fire between Egyptian and Israeli forces, with the latter in position on the West bank of the Suez Canal. A series of violations of the cease-fire then ensued which resulted in Israeli forces virtually completing the encirclement of the Egyptian Third Army just prior to a second UN cease-fire deadline at 1.00 am, 24 October. This left Israel with the means of cutting off supplies to the Egyptian forces, and thereby bringing about their destruction. Had that occurred, Egypt itself would have been left effectively defenceless.

In order to prevent such a possibility Egyptian President Sadat asked for a joint US-USSR peace-keeping force. After pre-emptory rejection of this proposal by the United States, the Soviet Union, by means of a secret note from Chairman Brezhnev to President Nixon, raised the possibility of a unilateral Soviet intervention. The implicit threat was supported by the US intelligence analysts who had observed that seven Soviet divisions (50 000 combat troops) had been placed on alert in the Soviet Union, and who inferred from the pattern of air traffic that airlift capability was being assembled for those divisions. It did not require much imagination for either side to see grave consequence for its interests in the immediate flow of events, and it is plausible that each might have contemplated drastic action to prevent a sharp, unfavourable, and irrevocable turn in the course of history.

Despite all these conditions, however, which could reasonably be expected to bring about a more serious confrontation, there is every indication that in its strategic dimensions the Middle East crisis played itself out in a far milder fashion than did the Cuban missile crisis. Upon receiving the 24 October communication from Brezhnev, a sub-group of the National Security Council, apparently with President Nixon's rather passive concurrence, did order a world-wide alert of American military forces. This involved an increase in the state of readiness of some strategic weapons units and some movements of forces, including apparently a transfer of fifty to sixty B-52 strategic bombers from Guam to the United States. It appears, however, that this was done almost entirely as a signal to bolster diplomatic resistance to Soviet intervention rather than as a measure undertaken in anticipation of possible use of those forces.

The critical fact is that the American military command structure did not appear to consider that the actual use of strategic forces had become a serious possibility. Elaborate decentralized preparations – the preliminary tuning of forces for combat – were not triggered.* The response to the alert order was minimal and *pro forma*. On the day the American alert went into effect, 25 October, UN resolution 340 was adopted, with concurrence and support from the Soviet delegate, calling for a Middle East peace-keeping force explicitly excluding Security Council members (notably the US and the USSR). This removed the threat of unilateral intervention. On 26 October the general alert of US forces was rescinded and the aspect of the crisis directly involving nuclear weapons thereby ended.

In his press conference on 25 October which centred on the alert of American forces, Secretary Kissinger made some reference to the possibility of nuclear war emerging from the confrontation. After the crisis

---

* An interesting vignette about the alert has been described by an observer in an informal background communication to the author. According to this report the SAC commander was playing golf at a critical point in the affair when the military machinery underneath him began the staff work associated with the preparation of options. Though military aides came out to inform him, he continued playing golf in what could reasonably be seen as a significant act of statesmanship. If the strategic command channels know that despite an increase in official readiness status the SAC commander is still on the golf course, that is a powerful signal to remain calm. Though the story cannot be set forth as historical fact, the importance of this sort of informal signal is difficult to exaggerate. Given the discretion inevitably in the hands of local commanders a great deal depends upon their mood and perceptions of the situation.

President Nixon stated that it had been the most difficult situation since the Cuban crisis in 1962.[15] These references were very much milder than what their counterparts had said in 1962, however, and there was no unanimity of perceived danger. Defense Secretary Schlesinger said on 26 October for example, 'I think we were very far from a confrontation.'[16] Whatever its potential, the Middle East crisis just does not seem to have brought nuclear war into immediate prospect.

It is always possible to explain events after they have occurred, and there are many plausible reasons that can be adduced as to why the more ominous circumstances of the Middle East crisis produced a much less severe confrontation, given that there was some manoeuvring of strategic forces. It is possible to attribute this to more powerful stabilizing effects of fully matured mutual retaliatory capability, or, perhaps, to the more formalized, more widespread recognition of this condition and the concomitant passing of the cold war atmosphere.

It is possible as well to ascribe the difference to particulars of the immediate circumstances. The Soviet operation which the United States government was resisting in 1973 was only potential; it was not under way. The US Sixth Fleet quickly manoeuvred into position to threaten the air routes a Soviet invasion force would most probably use and there was little beyond that that could be immediately done by way of preparation for combat.[17] US forces in the area did not have the excess capacity to conduct far-flung operations, such as the search for Soviet submarines in the North Atlantic that occurred in 1962. The entire NATO apparatus which might have produced a great deal of associated military activity was held in check by the political effects of the Arab actions regarding oil supply, if for no other reason. US strategic forces had developed to a much higher state of readiness than those of the Soviet Union, and the realization of this removed the incentive to prepare further unless the Soviets increased the readiness of their strategic forces. They did not. The strategic interaction developed in a context in which high-level negotiations on the immediate issue of the cease-fire had already occurred and a mutually accommodating position in which neither Israel nor Egypt would be accorded a decisive victory had been worked out and had been publicly set forth. There was no equivalent to President Kennedy's opening speech in the Cuban crisis which articulated the political principles justifying a major confrontation. Indeed, President Nixon's ability to give such a speech, to marshall US forces in service of foreign policy objectives, was undermined by inherent suspicion that he might be motivated in such an enterprise by his domestic difficulties.

All these many aspects of the Middle East crisis could plausibly have contributed to the result and, as with any single event, it requires inevitably uncertain, disputable judgment to infer which actually did, and in what proportion. There are a few obvious facts, however, that any analysis must take into account. The Middle East crisis in the midst of inherently dangerous circumstances produced a very limited confrontation, distinctly one-sided in character as it related to strategic forces, and short in duration. For the strategic forces on both sides (as opposed to the Mediterranean fleets), the extensive preparations in which military organizations engage when they seriously expect they may have to fight were not triggered. The United States alert was limited to what it was intended to be – a formal change in status meant to support diplomatic action.

THE LESSONS OF EXPERIENCE

Uncomfortable as the fact may be the most important lesson that can be derived from experience with nuclear weapons in crisis concerns what is not and cannot be known. Pertinent experience is extremely limited. There is only one instance – the Middle East in 1973 – which occurred with nuclear arsenals in an advanced state of development. One may develop theories, beliefs, hopes, and firm convictions, and one may appeal to events of the past thirty years for support, but one cannot objectively determine by inference from the historical record just what it is that has preserved peace in the face of enormous destructive capabilities. Nor can one establish where the most serious threats of war are to be found. Thirty years is far too short a time to produce clear answers. Humility and intellectual caution are the first requisites of wisdom on the subject, whatever fashion may preach about decisiveness and bold judgment.

Beyond that rather chastening lesson, it is reasonable to infer from the limited experience offered that the answer to questions about the security of peace is a complicated one. If deterrence by threat of nuclear retaliation were really as impressive as sometimes imagined, if the enormity of potential destruction were really able to dominate the decision processes of modern governments, the Cuban crisis should not have occurred. Both the original Soviet action to place offensive missiles on the island and the dramatic, confrontational style of the American response, which preempted diplomatic moves not immediately based on coercion, appear more risky in the estimate of the political leaders of the time than the issues at stake seemed to warrant. Simple logic strains to explain the course of events. If, however, serious threats to stability stem from some of the more obvious sources, the Middle East affair should have been more serious than it was, and should certainly have been the more serious of the two. A comparison of the two crises plants the suspicion that the stability of peace and the risk of war are determined by interactions among a rather large number of circumstances and that the problem requires a deeper analysis than is yet available of the way modern governments generate and respond to strategic challenge.

In the category of ideas, as opposed to firm conclusions, there is more to be said. Experience with the Cuban and Middle East crises emphasizes first the distinction between explicit policy calculations and diffuse organizational reactions, and second the relative importance of the latter in determining the course of a crisis. The complexity of military operations is such that many critical features of a government's response to a crisis are not and cannot be completely determined by the decision-makers who set policy. In the American government during the Cuban crisis, extensive preparations of military forces for possible use were triggered distinctly before high-level policy channels were engaged in the crisis. These preparations proceeded through the crisis, independent in important ways of explicit policy formulation. This fact seems in retrospect to have a great deal to do with the seriousness of the Cuban crisis. Similarly the very restricted, localized response of the American military apparatus to the Middle East crisis seems to have held the seriousness of that situation well below its potential. These observations recommend more thought on the subject of what triggers the diffuse organizational reactions of modern military forces.

The same reflections also suggest more consideration of the way in which national policy and military operations interact. If the standard image of military forces carrying out the formulated intentions of policy officials is too simple to account for what occured, it does not follow that there was no relationship. In both cases it appears that the manner in which the crisis was dealt with in the highest forums of national policy did play quite a significant role, even apart from the specific decisions made and the implementing instructions issued. The actions of national policy officials set a general political construction on the course of events; and, though the effect was probably not consciously realized or directly intended, in both instances the diffuse organizational reactions of military forces seem to have followed these very general political signals. In the Cuban affair a presumption of confrontation and an ominous hint of surprise attack was implicit in the basic character of the actions being taken;

military deployments were secretly prepared and diplomatic contacts were used to cover these operations – even deliberately to deceive the opposing government. The political uses of force inherent in the initial Soviet missile deployment and in the American naval blockade were undertaken in advance of direct negotiations on the specific issues involved. In the Middle East affair, though these elements were not entirely absent, there was a much stronger presumption of accommodation from the outset. The habit of direct negotiation was more developed as the expected mode of US-Soviet interaction and that background factor was reinforced by special negotiations immediately preceding the crisis made highly visible by Secretary Kissinger's unusual trip to Moscow.

Whether or not these specific features of the two crises were actually the operative factors, there is a basic thesis which emerges: general political signals which set the expectations of attentive military organizations do appear to be a very important element determining the course of a crisis towards nuclear war.

NOTES

1 George Quester, *Nuclear Diplomacy* (New York, Dunellen, 1970), 96. Quester cites as documentation John Robinson Beal, *John Foster Dulles: A Biography* (New York, Harper and Brothers, 1957), 181-2.

2 Quester, *Nuclear Diplomacy*, 125. As documentation on Quemoy and Matsu, Quester cites Chalmers Roberts, 'The Day We Didn't Go to War', *The Reporter*, 14 September 1954, 31-3.

3 As with most historical judgments this one is subject to some dispute. In the Suez crisis in 1956, for example, Nikita Khrushchev did appear to threaten Britain and France with strategic attack and United States forces world-wide were put on alert. The Strategic Air Command, however, was to a noticeable extent exempted from this alert, apparently because the Commanding General Curtis Le May did not want to risk revealing the tactical operations he would actually use in the event of war. (Quester, *Nuclear Diplomacy*, 124; Charles Murphy, 'Washington and the World', *Fortune*, January 1957, 78-83). Both this deliberate withholding of strategic forces and the fact that the forces themselves were less developed than they were during the later episodes seems to put the nuclear dimension of the Suez crisis into a more limited category. Similarly, the movement of American strategic bombers to Britain during the Berlin blockade in 1948 occurred at a time when these forces were maintained in a much lower

state of readiness than they were a decade later; hence the action taken did not represent nearly as direct an approach to actual strategic operations as was the case when bombers were dispersed and a constant airborne alert undertaken during the Cuban crisis.

4 Historical accounts of the events of the crisis are to be found in E. Abel, *The Missile Crisis* (New York, Lippincott, 1966); G. Allison, *Essence of Decision* (Boston, Little, Brown, 1971); Robert F. Kennedy, *Thirteen Days* (New York, W. W. Norton, 1971); A. M. Schlesinger, Jr, *A Thousand Days* (Boston, Houghton Mifflin, 1965), chaps. 30-31; T. Sorenson, *Kennedy* (New York, Harper & Row, 1965), chap. 24.

5 Abel, *The Missile Crisis*, 154; Allison, *Essence of Decision*, 138

6 It requires somewhat greater precision than offered in the published accounts of the crisis mentioned, however, to establish the relationship between military preparations and alert orders issued by policy officials. The assertion here is based on background interviews with a few partici-pants who had the opportunity to observe this aspect of the crisis. Robert Kennedy, *Thirteen Days*, 25, asserts that the order to US forces world-wide to go on alert was given as the President was flying back to Washington from Chicago – i.e., mid-day, Saturday, 20 October 1962. Schlesinger, *A Thousand Days*, 809, observes that the *New York Times* had noted the troop movements by that weekend and that apprently on Saturday, 20 October President Kennedy called the *Times* to prevent publication of the story. There appear to have been some US preparations, however, even in advance of the U-2 flights which photographed the missile bases under construction.

7 Kennedy, *Thirteen Days*, 30

8 Ibid., 71, 75-6, and 83; Sorenson, *Kennedy*, 680 and 714.

9 Ibid., 705

10 Kennedy, *Thirteen Days*, 65-8

11 Abel, *The Missile Crisis*, 51

12 Details of the Middle East crisis are provided in a number of newspaper accounts: e.g., David Binder, 'An Implied Soviet Threat Spurred U.S. Forces' Alert', *New York Times*, 21 November 1973; Murray Marder, 'Kissinger Closing off Discussion of Confrontation', *Washington Post*, 22 November 1973; Marilyn Berger, 'Brezhnev Note: "I Will Say It Straight"', *Washington Post*, 28 November 1973; Marvin Kalb and Bernard Kalb, 'Twenty Days in October', *New York Times Magazine*, 23 June 1974.

13 Raymond Vernon et al., 'The Oil Crisis: In Perspective', *Daedalus*, fall 1975, 15-37

14   The Middle East war happened to occur as the United States was just
     relieving one of the two carriers normally stationed with the Sixth Fleet in
     the Mediterranean. Hence, the third carrier task force could be quickly
     recalled and US forces were stronger than usual. Soviet naval deployments
     were somewhat lower than normal levels by contrast largely because a mod-
     ern carrier, the *Nikolov*, left the Mediterranean through the Turkish
     straights on the day the war started. Because of regulation of transit through
     the straits, the Soviet cruiser could not return as readily as the American
     carrier. None the less, the Soviets were able to double their complement of
     combat ships (from 17 to 36) in the Mediterranean by the end of October. See
     Admiral Elmo R. Zumwalt, Jr, *On Watch: A Memoir* (New York, Quadrangle
     Books, 1976), 447ff.; Robert G. Weinland, 'Superpower Naval Diplomacy in
     the October 1973 Arab-Israeli War', Professional Paper #221, Center for
     Naval Analysis, Arlington, VA, June 1978.
15   Marder, 'Kissinger Closing off Discussion'
16   Ibid.
17   Weinland, chap. 6.

4

Existing Systems of Command and Control

VICE-ADMIRAL G.E. MILLER (Ret.)

In attempting to assess the dangers of nuclear war, one must give some attention to the command and control of the various elements of armed force that would be involved. The record of the past for all nations possessing nuclear weapons has been excellent in this regard. Numerous fictional episodes have, however, created the impression that there are now so many nuclear weapons, so many terrorists, and so many irrational leaders in existence, that a nuclear war may start through a breakdown in command or control – either in the hardware, procedures, or the security and reliability of the systems themselves. Responsible journals contain articles depicting an irrational president with his finger on the nuclear button, giving the impression that one man can start a nuclear war.[1] Articles appear declaring that the commanding officer of a nuclear submarine carrying a load of Poseidon missiles is the third most powerful man in the world because, should he choose, he can fire the missiles under his command and initiate a nuclear holocaust. The United States Congress has become aroused and in 1976, a total of 92 members of the House of Representatives submitted, in all, twelve resolutions calling for legislation which would restrict the President of the United States from the first use of any kind of nuclear weapon in any situation without Congressional approval.[2] The concern for the command and control of nuclear forces, particularly civil control, continues to mount.

The real danger may be that so many constraints are imposed as to jeopardize the reliability of command and control systems. But the record of the past is good. There have been no nuclear wars or incidents close to initiating nuclear wars that can be attributed to breakdowns or deficiencies in command and control systems.

How about the future? Will existing systems and those planned for the future be able to match the abilities of those in the past in successfully controlling the nuclear elements involved?

One of the great difficulties encountered in analysing command and control systems is the security classification that is placed on information about such systems. Naturally, the knowledge of how a possible opponent has organized the control of his forces is one of the most essential items of intelligence information one can possess. Consequently, specially sensitive classification labels are assigned to most information dealing with command and control systems. Nevertheless, enough has been published in the open press to permit some degree of analysis.

This paper will attempt to deal with three elements of the command and control process: first, the hardware, including communications, that will be involved; second, the procedures for the release and use of nuclear weapons; and third, the security and reliability of the whole process. Most information will relate to the United States, although some limited information is available about NATO allies, the Soviet Union, and China.

HARDWARE

The hardware involved in command and control runs the gamut of the communication spectrum, from ultra high frequency (UHF) to extremely low frequency (ELF). It includes the customary circuits (secure and open), antennae farms, automatic switching systems, computer banks, and relays. There are satellites for reconnaissance, for early warning, and for communications, which directly or indirectly link forces controlling nuclear weapons. There are also anti-satellites now in being or in the planning stages, to threaten or destroy command and control satellites.

There are programs for extremely low frequency communications with submarines, such as the US Navy Seafarer program. Superpowers continue to invest in airborne command posts, with hook-ups to land and sea-based terminals. There are emergency procedures and equipment for directing operations from the airborne posts, with much discussion about the ability to retarget missiles and other nuclear forces from these same airborne command centres. There are warning systems to detect the launch of certain types of nuclear weapons systems. There are concepts for the development of systems which will automatically launch certain nuclear weapons systems upon receipt of warning (the launch-on-warning concept).[3] It is highly doubtful that these last systems will ever become part of the United States hardware, but they could be implemented by others, should they become extremely apprehensive as to the probability of a surprise nuclear attack. There are trailing wire antennaes, airborne antennaes, and hardened antennae sites. There is redundancy or duplication in most systems with back-ups for back-ups – all part of the program to provide an 'assured' launch of any or all of a nuclear force, under any conditions, pre-emptive or retaliatory.

There are computer-constructed key codes, coding devices and interlocks, and there are permissive action links (PALs). Since there is so much attention being paid to these devices, with some scientists suggesting that PALs be incorporated in all weapons, nuclear and conventional, it might be well to repeat what has been published in the *Congressional Record* on these devices:

'The Permissive Action Link (PAL) Program consists of a code system and a family of devices integral or attached to nuclear weapons which have been developed to reduce the probability of an unauthorized detonation. The devices are designed to preclude the use of a nuclear weapon without first inserting the correct numerical code. The code system is a highly secure system which permits the using unit to obtain the proper numerical code only after PAL unlock has been authorized.'[4]

Satellites

It seems apparent that future command and control systems will rely more heavily on satellite systems, since the United States and the Soviet Union are both devoting a considerable amount of their space effort to that mission. The Soviets have been particularly energetic in this area, with space probes designed for electronic ferret, early warning, ocean surveillance, radar calibration, and communications store and dump missions.[5] Based on the experience of January 1978, when a Soviet reconnaissance satellite failed in orbit, the malfunctioning of these satellites, even those carrying nuclear power cells, does not seem to be cause for concern that they, in themselves, will precipitate a nuclear weapons exchange. As editorialized by the *New York Times*: 'The superpowers cooperated to an unusual extent in assessing the likely hazards as Cosmos 954 circled down toward the atmosphere. That precedent offers hope that they can cooperate further to find safeguards against another possibly more serious accident.'[6]

The Soviet use of satellite communications for direct control of and contact with naval forces has been impressive and is expanding with each global exercise they conduct. While the United States seems to have a capability to produce satellite systems of higher quality, the evidence indicates that the Soviets are putting such systems into operational status, while the United States keeps them on the drawing boards. Also there is increased attention to anti-satellite systems, with the Soviets now being credited with having an operational capability. The United States does not have such an operational capability, at this time, according to the Secretary of Defense.[7]

Hardware reliability

Some mention should be made of the reliability of this hardware. Given the redundancy in individual systems and the various back-up systems that are incorporated, there seems to be little cause for concern regarding the ability to communicate reliably with forces that are land-based. Ballistic missiles, bomber forces, and the so-called tactical nuclear forces are generally considered to be well provided with reliable hardware. This applies to the Soviet Union as well as the United States.

One area of expressed concern is that of submarine-launched missile systems. Communication with deeply submerged submarines is still a perplexing and unresolved problem for the technical community of any nation, at least according to the open literature. Much is made of the question of the ability of the United States to communicate reliably with its Polaris, Poseidon, and Trident forces. This has been one of the reasons for the initiation of the Seafarer program, designed to enhance the reliability of command and control for submerged submarines. The Seafarer system involves a buried communications grid capable of transmitting an extremely low frequency radio wave carrying command messages to submarines deep beneath the surface of the ocean, thereby enabling them to receive communications without having to approach the surface with an antenna.[8] The signal is more resistant to jamming than other more conventional radio emissions.[9] With the increasing emphasis on submarine-based systems as an essential element of nuclear forces, particularly in the United States, it is reasonable to expect that some form of Seafarer will eventually be approved for installation somewhere in the United States, although it is a political issue at the present time. In late January 1978, President Carter endorsed Seafarer by stating:

'Yes, I think we need a submarine communications system of that kind. When a submarine is submerged, it is imperative, in case our nation's security is directly threatened to have communications with them.

'The only means of fairly rapid communication is with the very low frequency, ultralow frequency transmission systems, and there are certain geographical or geological structures in our continent that permit the transmission of signals underneath the land and water.'[10]

Whether the Soviets have a similar system in being or in planning is an interesting question on which there seems to be little or no available open literature. What are the systems the Soviets use to communicate with their Yankee, Delta, and other ballistic missile submarines?

A second area of concern is satellite reliability for the command and control function, which is becoming the focus of some attention. *Aerospace Daily* reports on an article appearing in *Strategic Review*, in which it is contended that 'one of the ways of interfering with satellites – in addition to direct attack – is sending them false commands'. The author, Lieutenant Colonel R. E. Hansen (USAF Ret.), is further quoted as saying:

'A hostile nation with the capability to send spoofing or suicide-inducing commands to highly important satellites at the outbreak of hostilities or in time to conceal war preparations would have a distinct advantage. With these spurious commands, properly coded and appropriately timed, it is conceivable that the enemy could alter a satellite's position; cause it to leave its position in geosynchronous orbit; deny it power by disorienting sun-pointing antennas; fire thrusters causing orbital decay; trigger and receive stored radio transmissions ...; falsely cause nuclear power sources to self-destruct; render electronic counter-measures equipment inoperative; or render inactive defensive maneuver gear or defensive weapons.'[11]

At a press conference, when confronted with reports the Soviets had or soon would have the capability to disrupt United States sending of military orders by satellites, President Carter responded that his information was that the report was not accurate.[12] Subsequently it was reported that President Carter, 'according to FY 79 budget documents, is proposing that the Pentagon "conduct research and development to improve satellite surveillance, reduce satellite vulnerability and develop an anti-satellite capability" – all, apparently, under the omnibus space defense effort.'[13]

Defense Secretary Brown's remarks on the subject indicate increased attention to ensure reliability. Again from *Aerospace Daily*:

'Comparing the Soviet operational anti-satellite program with the U.S. effort which is still in the research and development stage, Brown said in his annual posture statement, "While eventually the U.S. ASAT capability may be technologically superior, a definite U.S.-Soviet asymmetry exists in this area."

'President Carter has concluded, Brown continued, that the United States "cannot permanently accept such an asymmetry and has directed a vigorous U.S. effort in this area."

'Brown noted the President's appeal for both sides to join in an effective and adequately verifiable ban on anti-satellite systems.

'"However," he continued, "the Soviets with their present capability are leaving us with little choice. Because of our growing dependence on space systems we can hardly permit them to have a dominant position in the ASAT realm."'[14]

So it is apparent that as one side develops an edge, the other will take whatever action is necessary to develop a counter for protection of the command and control process.

Summarizing what has been said on the subject of hardware, we may note that there seems to be plenty available, with much redundancy incorporated and back-up systems deployed to ensure reliability. Even supposing the most severe exchange of nuclear blows between super-powers, it seems that enough redundancy exists to ensure reasonable communications for command and control of nuclear forces. The most significant areas of concern are those relating to the reliability of communications with deep submerged submarines and with satellites. These probably will be resolved in the coming period with the advent of some form of Seafarer system and new developments in satellite programs.

PROCEDURES

Of primary importance to the procedures used in the command and control process are the strike plans designed for the use of nuclear weapons. These can run the gamut from a single integrated operational plan designed to launch the entire strategic force in a pre-emptive strike, to a single, small-yield weapon used as a warning shot in an isolated area. The plans developed for the use of nuclear weapons depend on the philosophy or policy adopted by the country concerned. The nature of the policy has considerable bearing upon the complexity of the command and control system. A simple first-strike plan based on a policy of massive pre-emption would require a relatively simple command and control system. A more sophisticated policy such as one calling for the so-called 'flexible response' concept with limited attacks – that is to say, limited nuclear warfare – would require a much more elaborate set of procedures and hence a more elaborate command and control system.

Not much is published on the nuclear warfare plans of any country, particularly the Soviet Union. The United States discusses its single integrated operation plan (SIOP) in open terms, but never in detail. It is apparent, however, that many options do exist in the plans[15] and that the command and control procedures associated with them are complex, numerous, and loaded with checks and balances.

Release of weapons

Perhaps the single most significant area of concern about procedures for the command and control of nuclear forces is the authority for release of or use of nuclear weapons. This point caused the Congress of the United States to initiate hearings and to introduce resolutions calling for Congressional approval before the President can release nuclear weapons.[16] Much has been made of the delegation of authority for the use of such weapons, with considerable publicity over the years about the Commander of the North American Defense Command (NORAD) holding such delegated authority.[17] The constraints on that authority have, however, been considerable. With the increasing pressure for tighter control over release of nuclear weapons, it is highly doubtful that the NORAD commander still retains such delegated authority.

Much is also made of the notion that the President of the United States can release the weapons by pushing a single button – that he has absolute authority and complete control over release procedures. It is true that no US weapon can be released without his authority, but it is also true that he cannot commit release by himself. Obviously this is a very sensitive matter. Over the years various legal judgments have all cited the constitutional powers of the President as Commander-in-Chief and the Atomic Energy Act as the basis for this authority. It would seem that the President's authority is firmly established in statute and that it is an imperative and vital element to the defence of the United States and the deterrence of war. But what about constraints on the President?

The entire system of procedures that prevents unauthorized or accidental use of nuclear weapons begins with the President himself. Since only the President can authorize the use of nuclear weapons,[18] he must give the command to do so to the Secretary of Defense (SecDef) who, in turn, directs that the Chairman of the Joint Chiefs of Staff (CJCS) execute the strike plan selected. But the President cannot do this without conferring with the SecDef and the CJCS. Because of the mechanics involved in authenticating the order from the President, as well as in releasing Permissive Action Link (PAL) codes to unlock weapons, it is not possible for the President to authorize the expenditure of nuclear weapons without the SecDef and CJCS being totally involved in the decision.

And what happens should the President and the Secretary of Defense not be available or be the first casualties in a nuclear incident? What is the succession of command? Dr James Wade, acting as a Department of Defense witness, responded to that question during Congressional hearings in March 1976 as follows:

'3 U.S.C. 19 provides for the order of succession if there is neither a President nor Vice President to discharge the powers of and duties of the Office of President.

'As for civilian authority in the Department of Defense, the Reorganization Act of 1958 (10 U.S.A. 124), provides that the chain of command flows directly from the President to the Secretary of Defense, and thence through the Joint Chiefs of Staff to the unified and specified combatant commanders. Thus only the Secretary of Defense is involved in the chain of command; however, in the event of death, disability or absence of the Secretary of Defense, the following designated officers in the Department of Defense shall succeed to the position and act as Secretary of Defense in the order listed:

(a) Deputy Secretary of Defense.

(b) Deputy Secretary of Defense (note: there were two deputies at the time).

(c) Secretary of the Army.

(d) Secretary of the Navy.

(e) Secretary of the Air Force.

(f) Director of Defense Research and Engineering.

(g) Assistant Secretaries of Defense ...

(h) Under Secretaries of the Army, Navy, and Air Force ...

(i) Assistant Secretaries of the Army, Navy, and Air Force.

'Should succession occur, the chain of command would remain unaltered; the civilian successor's authority in relationship to the military hierarchy would be as that of the Secretary of Defense.'[19]

The execution order of a strike plan then, begins with the President and through the SecDef and CJCS is transformed into a message that is transmitted to the appropriate commander of nuclear capable forces.

Within the nuclear forces, highly qualified and reliable crew members are in continual attendance and a single individual is never left alone with these weapons. There are always at least two people present (the so-called two-man rule), so that no lone person can take any nuclear weapons action without the other being aware of it. Further, these crew members are in constant communication with command centres through redundant and highly reliable communication networks and cannot take any actions to prepare the nuclear weapons for use until they receive the proper message referred to above. An authentication process is also incorporated in the system. Following these procedures are the PALs, which must be actuated to arm the nuclear weapons for use.

Some of the nuclear delivery systems in Europe are manned by the NATO allies of the United States. The legal basis for this action is contained in Section 144b. of the Atomic Energy Act of 1954, which states:

'The President may authorize the Department of Defense, with the assistance of the Commission, to cooperate with another nation or with a regional defense organization to which the United States is a party, and to communicate to that nation or organization such Restricted Data (including design information) as is necessary to –

(1) the development of defense plans;

(2) the training of personnel in the employment of and defense against atomic weapons and other military applications of atomic energy;

(3) the evaluation of the capabilities of potential enemies in the employment of atomic weapons and other military applications of atomic energy; and

(4) the development of compatible delivery systems for atomic weapons;'[20]

The procedures for the release of these weapons have been described by former Secretary of Defense Schlesinger as follows:

'Procedures for release of US nuclear weapons in Europe, while complex in detail, are simple in concept, as shown in Figure 1 (this figure depicts only release procedures and not the more general command relationships). Once the US President had released nuclear weapons for use by SACEUR [Strategic Air Command Europe] the release authorization would be transmitted through USCINCEUR [US Commander-in-Chief Europe] to US delivery units and US custodial units supporting Allied forces. The United States would simultaneously notify the other NATO governments of its decision. At the same time the President would authorize a major NATO commander, e.g., SACEUR (same individual as USCINCEUR, but with an Allied staff and command post facilities separate from those of USCINCEUR), to use the weapons, who would in turn signal authorization to the executing commanders via NATO communications channels.'[21]

One interesting aspect of the release procedure is the time involved in acquiring release authority. The many steps involved serve to guard against inadvertent release, but at the same time they can serve to jeopardize the responsiveness of the military commander in the field who has an urgent need for the use of nuclear weapons. For example, as long as 24 hours may be required for release authority to be granted to a NATO field unit.[22]

It should be apparent that there are ample restraints on inadvertent release or use of United States nuclear weapons. These restraints form part of the established command and control machinery and start with the President of the United States. Continued pressure for more civilian control over the military and the growing concern over the proliferation of nuclear weapons suggests that the future will see more constraints, not less, at least as far as the United States and its allies are concerned. In fact, the real danger may be that so many checks, constraints, and verification procedures are established that the United States will actually be unable to release and launch a nuclear weapon or weapons if it decided to do so, even with the civilian hierarchy intact, in full control of their faculties and all communications systems in full working order. The imposition of Congressional approval before the President is authorized to release nuclear weapons seems to be unnecessary, at least at this time in the evolution of nuclear capabilities.

SECURITY AND RELIABILITY

It appears wise to have adequate hardware and superior control procedures in the command and control system, but if security and reliability are weak the entire process may contribute to the initiation of nuclear warfare. What of the security and reliability of United States command and control systems?

Secretary of Defense Schlesinger reported on the political control of NATO nuclear weapons:

'The United States maintains positive control in peace and war over all NATO nuclear weapons except those belonging to the United Kingdom and France. The US President alone can release US nuclear weapons in Europe for use, following appropriate consultation with Allies. Weapons for both US and Allied forces are maintained under the positive, two-man control of US personnel until released by the US President. Additionally, all US nuclear weapons deployed in Europe are locked with coded devices (Permissive Action Links – PAL's) which physically enforce this US control.'[23]

The following quotation from the Congressional Record also bears on the subject of security and reliability: 'The command and control systems for the control of U.S. nuclear-capable forces are an integral part of our Worldwide Military Command and Control System (WWMCCS). These systems are designed to assure communications between the National Command Authority (the President and the Secretary of Defense), the Joint Chiefs of Staff, and the nuclear forces in the field, thereby ensuring that rational political as well as military decisions are transmitted.

'Special features for security and reliability are incorporated in those parts of the system relating to nuclear forces. These features include physical hardening of the telecommunications systems and the ability to operate in a jamming environment. An Alternate National Military Command Center (ANMCC) as well as a network of airborne command posts are included to provide redundancy, reliability, and survivability.

'Frequent tests and monitoring of the system are conducted to maintain a high readiness condition of the system, including the personnel involved.

'Improved survivability and reliability of the system are constant objectives. Toward this end, an increasing role for satellites and extremely low frequency communications is being considered or incorporated, or both.

'Command and control systems contain checks and balances which are designed to eliminate the capability for misuse of nuclear weapons.

'Physical safeguards are designed to prevent unauthorized use are several and varied, depending on the nature of the weapon, its delivery system, and its location. ...

'As strategies change and plans are modified accordingly, constant attention is paid to the command and control systems, in order to assure that they keep pace with the dynamics involved. Full-time professional personnel manage the systems and constantly take action to update their security and responsiveness to appropriate authority.'[24]

What about the physical vulnerability of control sites under conditions of nuclear attack? The protection or hardness of both US and Soviet command centres seems to defy destruction, at least to the point that some residual capability would persist. This was a significant point of concern for some time, so much so that concepts were advanced according to which an opponent's command and control centres should not be subjected to attack, particularly in limited war scenarios, so that the opposition would be able to communicate with and control its residual nuclear forces and terminate a launch. Recent redundancy and up-grading of communications facilities seems to have minimized this concern and to have engendered a feeling that plenty of capability exists to survive, even with the improved warhead yields and accuracies of modern nuclear weapons. Of course, physical security programs will have to keep pace with any improvements in the offensive capability of attacking weapons.

In reference to communications failures, Dr James Wade, the Department of Defense witness for Congressional hearings in March of 1976, discussed communication failures and reliability as follows:

'Mr. Ottinger. How many situations have there been in which there have been serious communication failures, can you describe them for us with respect to the communication systems which protect the use of weapons?

'Mr. Wade. Mr. Ottinger, we have many redundant sensors. I would like to provide an answer for the record. That is the kind of question that takes some time to properly answer.

'(The following was subsequently submitted for the record:)

'Redundant communications systems are used to maintain positive command and control of forces that either are equipped with or which store nuclear weapons. The focal point of control is the National Military Command System (NMCS) which consists of the National Military Command Center in the Pentagon; the Alternate National Military Center near Fort Ritchie, Maryland; and the National Emergency Airborne Command Post based at Andrews Air Force Base, Maryland. The National Military Command Center and the Alternate National Military Command Center are equipped with direct secure and nonsecure telephone systems and direct secure teletype circuits to the command centers of the unified and specified commands and the military services. The National Military Command Center and The Alternate National Military Command Center also have multiple communications which link them with other governmental agencies including the White House. Additionally, the Defense Communications System including AUTOVON (DOD telephone) and AUTODIN (DOD teletype) provide communications to all U.S. Forces. When airborne the National Emergency Airborne Command Post is provided secure and nonsecure telephone communications with the command centers of the unified and specified commands and the military services through ground entry points into landline systems. The airborne command post is also equipped with low frequency/very low frequency, high frequency, and ultra-high frequency radio systems for communications connectivity with command centers and forces of the unified and specified commands.

'A catastrophic failure of all systems described above has not occurred and is not expected to occur barring a nuclear attack. Temporary failures of single systems have been experienced at individual command centers; however alternate communications have always been available. If land based communications are denied in a nuclear war, the worldwide airborne command post radio net would provide serviceable communications with strategic nuclear forces.'[25]

As to the security of the weapons themselves, the following from the *Congressional Record* is of some relevance: 'All nuclear weapons have some type of command and control mechanism which is designed to preclude unauthorized use, and all nuclear weapons are equipped with safety devices that meet rigid standards. In addition to the devices installed on nuclear weapons to insure their safety and security, there are two-man rules and control which require that no one person is permitted alone near a nuclear weapon without a companion who is qualified in the same specialty, e.g., an electrician must accompany another electrician when performing maintenance or inspection on a nuclear weapon. With regard to enemy capture of a nuclear weapon, similar safety and security devices thwart the arming, fuzing, and firing of the weapon, particularly if the enemy has little or no knowledge of the mechanical or electro-mechanical operation of the protective device. It is possible, however, that these mechanisms can be defeated by a sophisticated enemy over a period of time. Thus, emergency destruction devices and procedures have been developed so that nuclear weapons may be destroyed without producing a nuclear yield in the event that enemy capture is threatened.'[26]

Perhaps one of the most significant and logical constraints imposed on unauthorized use of US nuclear weapons and one which contributes to the security and reliability of command and control systems, is the screening and security check process which is required for those in a position to guard, transport, deliver, administer, or supervise the use of nuclear weapons. It is called the Personnel Reliability Program (PRP). This program provides a careful screening of personnel before they are allowed to per-form duty associated with nuclear weapons, and a continuing evaluation of each person to ensure their stability, reliability, and suitability for con-tinued performance of duty in this critical area. Inspection teams, from various commands independent of the unit involved, conduct periodic inspections to ensure that the PRP is followed and effective. Over the years, this program has been extremely successful in detecting and elimi-nating personnel who for one reason or another (drug or alcohol abuse, marital problems, financial problems, etc.) are no longer fit to be assigned in this extremely sensitive area. Additionally there are courses of instruc-tion, refresher and otherwise, plus numerous training drills, to keep hardware peaked and personnel up-to-date for maximum performance. Commanders and staffs in the field, both US and NATO alike, attend specific courses of instruction on release procedures. Periodic review of procedures and frequent simulation exercises refresh and test the under-standing level of those responsible for execution of war plans. All of this training contributes to the security and reliability of command and con-trol systems.

OTHERS' SYSTEMS

Probably one of the best sources of information on command and control systems used by other major nuclear powers is a document prepared for the House Subcommittee on International Security and Scientific Affairs, as part of that Subcommittee's preparation for hearings on the issue of control of nuclear weapons.[27] Much of the following information comes from this source.

In the United Kingdom, many of the nuclear weapons and systems are subject to United States control, but apparently there are some weapons, carried by British aircraft, that are free of a US veto. Final authority for the release and use of nuclear weapons in the United Kingdom rests in the Parliament, in practice with the Prime Minister, advised by the Cabinet. In response to a query, the British government through its Embassy in Washington, made the following statement about authority in Great Britain over the use of nuclear weapons:

'The Secretary of State for Defence said in Parliament in July 1974 that the whole of the United Kingdom's nuclear capability is committed to NATO and that our weapons remain subject to political control through alliance consultation procedures and could in no circumstances be used without the consent of British ministers. The statement applies to the British Polaris force and to U.S. weapons stored in the United Kingdom for United Kingdom use. The final decision about their use rests solely with the British Prime Minister.'[28]

Despite the above statement, it is still possible that secret contingency plans may exist which would, in extreme circumstances, allow military commanders to initiate the use of nuclear weapons. Authority for release, however, seems to rest solely with the Prime Minister.

In France, under the constitution of the French Fifth Republic, the President is Commander of the Armed Forces. As such, and by subsequent decree, he commands both the strategic and tactical nuclear forces, and a decision to employ either requires his explicit approval. There are at present no treaties or external obligations which limit the authority of the French government over the initial use of nuclear weapons.[29] Also, France has provided for continuing civilian control over nuclear weapons during conflict. Detailed war plans apparently exist to send aircraft first to points over friendly or neutral countries for aerial refuelling, before they proceed to pre-selected Soviet targets. Also, aircraft are equipped with 'black boxes' that can be activated to neutralize the nuclear weapons – an added safety measure.[30]

It would be most interesting to read a Soviet paper on existing command and control systems as they relate to the dangers of nuclear war. Little open literature appears on the subject, and for the most part analysis must be made on the basis of supposition.

While Soviet strategy calls for a capability not only to deter potential enemies from attacking, but to wage a nuclear war and win it, there seems to be considerable question about the delegation of authority for the use of such weapons. Western experts on Soviet military affairs believe that the power for the release and use of such weapons rests in the Communist Party's Politburo, with the key figure being the Communist Party's General Secretary.[31] Some experts believe that special troops of the Committee on State Security (KGB) guard and control the Soviet stockpiles of nuclear weapons, which makes such troops a significant factor in the nuclear command and control process.[32]

Western intelligence experts insist that the Soviets have constructed a most redundant and physically hardened (secure) command and control system; that they practise the use of the system a great deal; that at least a significant part will survive a major nuclear attack, and that it is under top-echelon control. From the foregoing discussion of satellites, it is obvious also that these systems play a large role in the Soviet command and control process.

The armed forces of the People's Republic of China are controlled by the Communist Party of China, and the state constitution designates the Chairman of the Central Committee of the Party as the commander of the armed forces. It is likely that a decision regarding the use of nuclear weapons would be made only by the Chairman. If circumstances prevented a quick decision by the entire Politburo, it seems probable that alternative arrangements have been made for a decision by the Politburo's Standing Committee, or through some alternate headquarters. It is reasonable to expect, however, that authority to use nuclear weapons in exceptional circumstances under carefully prescribed regulations may have been delegated to military leaders. Peking does not discuss its nuclear weapons strategy or tactics except in political terms. It has declared it will never be the first to use nuclear weapons.

It would seem that some formal, if not legal, procedure would be instituted, with adequate safeguards, to ensure that the authority to order the initial use of nuclear weapons would be held tightly. It would also seem likely that the Chinese have formulated contingency plans to consider alternative uses of nuclear weapons in case of crisis. These problems, and the dispersal of such weapons to avoid their being destroyed by surprise attack, would seem to present difficult problems of command and control.[33] Further, in view of the extensive steps the Chinese have taken to harden their missile sites, it is reasonable to assume that their command and control sites are equally hardened and capable of survival in time of crisis.

CONCLUSION

It seems doubtful that command and control systems will contribute much to the danger of nuclear war between now and the year 2000, at least among the major nuclear powers. The trend over the years has been toward tighter controls, particularly in those countries where delegation of authority might have existed in the past. As the nature of nuclear conflict becomes more awesome, the attention to command and control increases, more constraints are imposed, more redundancy is created, and physical hardening is increased. The real danger may lie in too much constraint. But at least it is hard to imagine an inadvertent release of a nuclear weapon or weapons under the systems used by the US and its allies, or by the Soviet Union or China.

If there is any danger in the command and control area, it will probably emanate from systems installed in less developed countries, should they achieve a nuclear weapons capability. Rather than contributing to the initiation of a nuclear war, command and control systems should act as measures to prevent such a war.

NOTES

1   *Bulletin of Atomic Scientists*, March 1976, 53
2   *Hearings*, The Subcommittee on International Security and Scientific Affairs of the Committee on International Relations, US House of Representatives, Ninety-Fourth Congress, Second Session, 16, 18, 23, and 25 March 1976 (US Government Printing Office, 1976)
3   Ibid., 61; Dr Herbert York
4   Ibid., 93
5   *Aerospace Daily*, 89, no. 3, (5 January 1978) and no. 7, (11 January 1978)
6   2 February 1978
7   Bernard Weintraub, *New York Times*, 4 October 1977, A-11
8   US Navy *Newsgram Summary*, August 1977
9   Ibid., May 1977
10 *Aerospace Daily*, 1 February 1978, 166
11 Ibid., 6 February 1978, 192-3
12 *New York Times*, 'Transcript of President's Press Conference,' Question 12, 31 January 1978
13 *Aerospace Daily*, 6 February 1978, 192-3
14 Ibid., 3 February 1978, 178

15 *Hearings*, Secretary of Defense Schlesinger, Section VII, Statement before Senate Armed Services Committee on 1975 Defense Budget, 5 February 1974

16 *Hearings*, 16, 18, 23, and 25 March 1976

17 John W. Finney, *New York Times*, 19 March 1976

18 *Authority to Order the Use of Nuclear Weapons*, Committee Print, prepared for the Subcommittee on International Security and Scientific Affairs of the Committee on International Relations by the Congressional Research Service, US Library of Congress, 1 December 1975, 1

19 *Hearings*, 185

20 *Atomic Energy Legislation* through 94th Congress, 1st Session, Joint Committee on Atomic Energy, Congress of the United States (US Government Printing Office, March 1976), 49

21 'The Theater Nuclear Force Posture in Europe', A Report to the United States Congress in compliance with Public Law 93-365 (undated), 7

22 Headquarters, Department of the Army, *Field Manual* no. 100-5 (FM100-5), 1 July 1976, 10-19

23 'Nuclear Force Posture in Europe', 7

24 *Hearings*, March 1976, 56-7

25 Ibid., 182

26 Ibid., 93

27 *Authority to Order the Use of Nuclear Weapons*

28 Ibid., 11

29 Ibid., 15

30 Ibid., 17

31 Ibid., 18

32 Ibid., 20

33 Ibid., 23-6

5

The Achievements of Arms Control

GEORGE IGNATIEFF

A discussion of the achievements of arms control, however modest these may have been, is relevant to an assessment of the dangers of nuclear war. While arms control or arms regulation measures cannot of themselves assure peace, their connections with the whole diplomatic process known as détente makes them an important aspect of any speculation about the dangers of nuclear war.

Indeed, arms control talks have largely reflected the efforts of the super-powers to moderate their enmity in the interests of survival in the nuclear age. The resulting measures, as will be seen, come closer to 'crisis management' than to 'arms control'. The word 'control' may be taken to imply an international authority exercising the powers of verification and inspection. Such a body does not exist except in the limited function of the International Atomic Energy Agency with the consent of the state to be inspected. This semantic problem with the use of the word 'control' has provided a fertile field for misunderstanding in all disarmament debates. There has been very little progress towards disarmament and the Soviet Union, for one, denounces in principle the idea of control being exercised over armaments and will accept control only over measures of disarmament.

Arms control in effect has as much to do with political relationships as with strategic-military relationships. This holds true particularly between the nuclear-weapon powers, whether the discussion is bilateral as in the Strategic Arms Limitation Talks (SALT) or multilateral as at the Geneva Disarmament Conference or the United Nations.

At the dawn of the nuclear age some of the best minds believed that if this supertechnology were applied to war it would produce such catastrophic results that all preparations for war would be rendered utterly obsolete. This belief has not prevailed. Instead, the relationship between the super-powers has proceeded on the assumption that the military-political-economic survival of the US, USSR, and other nuclear-weapons states requires a capability to survive a nuclear first strike and to inflict unacceptable damage on the attacker in retaliation. This doctrine is put forward on both sides as justification for the continuing reliance on deterrence, rather than disarmament, to ensure security.

PROPOSALS FOR THE ELIMINATION
OF NUCLEAR WEAPONS

Within months of the dropping of the only two atomic bombs used in war, an imaginative proposal was put forward by the US for the elimination of nuclear weapons from the armoury of nations. In 1946, Dean Acheson, then American Under-Secretary of State, in association with David Lilienthal, head of the Tennessee Valley Authority, proposed 'a plan under which no nation would make atomic bombs or the material for them. All dangerous activities would be carried on – not merely inspected – by a live, functioning international authority.'[1]

The Baruch Plan, as it came to be known when Bernard Baruch presented it to the Atomic Energy Commission of the United Nations, represented a far-reaching disarmament as well as arms control proposal. It would have eliminated the atomic bomb monopoly then enjoyed by the US and it would also have transferred all national privileges in the field of atomic energy to the control of an international authority. It included Baruch's controversial proposal that there should be 'condign punishment' for violation of a UN treaty banning atomic weapons and controlling the production and use of fissionable materials.

This plan proved too much to accept even in the aftermath of the most destructive war yet experienced by mankind. The Soviet counter-proposal took the form of a draft convention simply calling for a ban on the production and use of atomic weapons within three months of the entry into force of the convention, and for the destruction of existing stockpiles. The US was not willing to give up its monopoly in atomic weapons without the adoption of its proposed far-reaching assurances against the danger that these weapons would be developed by its rival.

The question of the elimination or even the reduction of nuclear weapons has remained ever since on the agenda of all arms control discussions, both bilateral and multilateral, without coming any closer to a solution. This failure meant that nuclear weapon proliferation, with all its attendant risks, was not contained at a time when there was only one stockpile to eliminate, that of the US. Since then, the USSR, the UK, France, China, and more recently India have been added to the list of those possessing a capability of nuclear or thermonuclear fission for military purposes.

In these circumstances, those involved in the negotiations for the elimination of nuclear weapons began to devote their efforts to the reduction of the threat of nuclear war, especially of surprise attack. General McNaughton, then Canada's representative on the UN Atomic Energy Commission, focused on this danger: 'I think the members of the United Nations Atomic Energy Commission now clearly recognize the validity of the suggestion first given in the Acheson-Lilienthal Report, that in a war of long duration it would probably not be possible to prevent the use of atomic weapons; that the worst danger to be feared is the surprise use of these terrible contrivances and in consequence, that the real objective to be sought is to free the world from secrecy in atomic matters and to allay suspicions giving a certainty of warning, if any nations should start to prepare for atomic war.'[2]

The main issue in assessing the dangers of nuclear war could not be more clearly stated. Efforts to allay this fear of a surprise attack or of a 'pre-emptive strike' occupied the attention of all those concerned with nuclear arms control until the advent of surveillance satellites in the 1960s which made possible the detection by 'national technical means' of preparations for launching a nuclear strike. Efforts to prevent a surprise attack were succeeded by efforts to place international restraints upon nuclear proliferation, especially through the Non-Proliferation Treaty and the international safeguards system of the International Atomic Energy Authority.

REDUCTION OF THE POSSIBILITY OF INADVERTENT WAR

In the early 1960s, progress was made in reducing the risk of nuclear war by accident, miscalculation, or failure of communication. As one means of accomplishing this objective, the establishment of rapid communications by direct link in case of emergency was proposed and accepted. A memorandum of understanding (the 'hot-line' agreement) was signed by the US and the USSR in June 1963. This was updated by the 'accidents measures' agreement of 1971 and the 'hot-line' modernization agreement as well as by 'hot-line' agreements between the USSR and France, as well as the USSR and the UK. Thus crisis management became essential in reducing the risk of nuclear war by the super-powers.

But the acceptance of the necessity of crisis management carries the disquieting connotation that the nuclear arms race continues, and that there will be crises. It is important to recognize the limitation as well as the potential of such arms control measures. The potential includes diplomatic contact and communication at all levels. Since the root causes of war lie in international anarchy, that is to say the prevalence of national sovereignty and interests over the common interest and international law, the development of lines of communication was critical.

In addition to communication between the super-powers over crises such as the successive confrontations over Berlin, the Cuban Missile crisis, and the Middle East, we have had the European Security Conference which culminated in the Helsinki agreement of 1975 and the on-going Conference in Vienna on the Mutual Reduction of Forces and Armaments and Associated Measures in Central Europe. These are multilateral negotiations involving the participation of all those powers concerned with the security of Europe, including Canada and the US. The Helsinki Declaration, signed in the summer of 1975, in particular represented a kind of codification of the various ideas embodied in détente, including such arms control measures as reciprocal observation of manoeuvres by representatives of NATO and the Warsaw Pact to reduce the possibilities of war by miscalculation.

Détente, however, has not led to a reversal or even a slowing down of the arms race. Moreover, it is largely confined to understandings about the reduction of the possibility of nuclear war in Europe. There, the NATO doctrine of 'flexible response' assumes the use of tactical nuclear weapons in response to Soviet attack with conventional weapons, without Soviet prior agreement to refrain from escalating hostilities to total war. Those who have been left out of the super-power consultative process have denounced détente as an exercise by the super-powers in hegemony. China, indeed, has insisted that a pledge of no 'first use' of nuclear weapons by the US and USSR is a condition of its participation in any arms control negotiations. Furthermore, when the north-south confrontation intersects with the east-west confrontation, détente has not prevented super-power intervention in local wars in Indochina, Angola, or the Middle East and other local wars which also involve the risk of nuclear confrontation.

Newly independent and economically underdeveloped countries have increasingly been drawn into the orbit of super-power hegemony and away from their traditional 'un-committed' role in world affairs. The super-powers and their allies are involved in the supply of weapons, training, and other military assistance, tending to add fuel to the arms race and increasing the risk of limited nuclear conflict. Thus General Alexander Haig made this revealing statement in an interview granted to *Newsweek* on the occasion of President Carter's visit to NATO in January 1978: 'We are faced with a tremendous modernization effort on land, sea and air. The Soviets have built up 45 divisions on the Chinese front without diversion from the European theatre. And all this leaves a large residue of weaponry to answer Third World calls. Arms are the cutting edge of their influence in the Third World – a key factor in our own assessment of the relentless growth of Soviet military power.'[3]

This statement by the Supreme Commander of NATO and similar charges by Soviet leaders suggest that the arms control measures so far undertaken to reduce the possibility of war have hardly had the desired effect. Instead, they have added fuel to the arms race between the US and the USSR and their respective allies and have involved them in Third World problems. Those who believe that deterrence with its costs and risks cannot match the advantages which might be obtained in improved collective security and reduced expenditures on defence as a result of real disarmament argue that the arms control measures associated with détente have in fact institutionalized the arms race.

The case made by these critics of arms control is persuasive, especially when one considers the problem of overcapacities for fighting a war of 'overkill'. Bringing the nuclear capacities of the super-powers down to a minimum necessary to deter war is a reasonable objective, but one which has certainly so far not been brought any nearer to realization by SALT.

There are certain aspects of SALT and other bilateral contacts and negotiations that undoubtedly are of value. For one thing, the capabilities of the nuclear arsenals of the super-powers are no longer secret, even though secrecy shrouds plans for their use. Knowledge of the circumstances under which they would be prepared to use nuclear weapons would provide the key to assessing the dangers of nuclear war.

Another benefit of SALT, as of other methods of communicating between the super-powers, is the machinery of constant contact and negotiation which to a considerable extent reduces the risk of nuclear war by design or intention. SALT has proven a certain measure of effectiveness in arriving at agreements to restrict the building of defences against ballistic missiles and in dealing with the nuclear equation by which nuclear parity is determined.

The negative result of institutionalizing the arms race is that the super-powers have become prisoners of their own various industrial, military, and scientific interests and of their tendency to match every move of the adversary, as essential to parity and ultimately to survival. It should be noted that, so far, all tactical nuclear weapons remain totally outside the regulations of arms control agreements and that delivery vehicles that can be used for conventional (as well as nuclear) weapons are also regulation-free.

The risk inherent in the present open-ended competition between the super-powers is evident. Even what has been agreed to date does not provide any barrier against qualitative improvements of existing nuclear-weapons systems, nor against innovations introduced to keep pace with advancing technology through research and testing. Experts dispute, for example, whether the new generations of weapons systems – the improvements in bombs (like the neutron bomb) or in the means of delivery (like the American long-range Cruise missile or the Soviet ss20) – represent a legitimate development of new capabilities to keep pace with advancing technology, or whether they have a destabilizing effect which increases the risk of nuclear war.

There can be no doubt that, unless some new approach to arms control is attempted, the present dynamic elements in the situation will promote an ever-increasing overkill capacity, as each side strives to retain what is considered to be a 'safe margin' of parity. Such a new approach must at the very least include the total prohibition of nuclear testing and of flight testing of delivery vehicles as the first steps in an effort to scale down to some agreed minimum deterrent. A further exchange of information should be possible now that the governments of the two super-powers have derived sufficient knowledge of each other's capabilities from satellite surveillance. With the reduction of the barriers of secrecy, one could see arms control measures serving to reduce the possibilities of nuclear war.

GENERAL AND COMPLETE DISARMAMENT

While all the wars waged since the Second World War have been local wars fought with conventional weapons, almost all the discussion and all the measures of arms control agreed to have related to nuclear weapons. This preoccupation is understandable since the use of nuclear weapons constitutes a threat to civilization and even to human survival.

But from the outset, the aims of arms control were defined at the UN in comprehensive terms, inclusive of all arms and armed forces. The Charter of the United Nations gave primary responsibility for the maintenance of

international security to the Security Council, which was to act on behalf
of the world community in dealing with international disputes and any
threats to the peace. National armaments and armed forces were to be
subordinate to the authority of the Security Council, through agreements
to be negotiated with that body, and all arms were to be subject to regulation, i.e., arms control. The permanent members of the Security Council
were the super-powers and when their wartime alliances broke down the
basis of the world security system collapsed. Consequently, the agreements which were to have subordinated national armaments and armed
forces to the world organization fell by the board and the Security Council in effect ceased to exercise any jurisdiction in the matter of arms
control.

When the General Assembly of the United Nations took over the responsibility for providing a forum for the discussion of disarmament and
arms control in 1959, it set general and complete disarmament as the goal
to be pursued. In the course of resuming negotiations on disarmament, the
Soviet Union and the United States agreed to a set of principles as a basis
for renewed negotiations. These principles specifically related the problem of disarmament to the problem of preventing war. Thus, the goals of
the negotiations were stated to be:

(a) That disarmament is general and complete and war is no longer an
instrument for settling international problems; and

(b) That such disarmament is accompanied by the establishment of reliable procedures for the peaceful settlement of disputes and effective
arrangements for the maintenance of peace in accordance with the principles of the Charter.[4]

Although in the prior negotiations both sides had submitted the outlines
of draft treaties on general and complete disarmament, the two super-
powers soon disagreed on the important, substantive issue of whether
nuclear delivery weapons should be eliminated in the first stage as
desired by the Soviet Union, or retained for later disposal as preferred by
the United States. In other words, differences over the strategic balance
between the super-powers prejudiced the possibility of progress in any
comprehensive approach towards disarmament. In order to escape from
this impasse which threatened to bring disarmament talks to a standstill,
the negotiations turned to consideration of partial or collateral arms
control measures.

Meanwhile, the winds of change of decolonization were blowing away
the remnants of empire in the West. Scores of countries in Africa and
Asia had found independence under conditions that involved them or

their previous colonizers in a series of wars. The proliferation of states and of weapons went hand in hand. The fact that they were conventional weapons seemed to have made them exempt from any restraints except those that might be adopted by individual exporting countries. The question of restrictions on the sale of conventional arms remains an important item on the agenda of any conference attempting to curb the danger of nuclear war, especially with the growing automaticity, lethality, and sophistication of conventional weapons.

The concern that local wars fought with conventional weapons might turn into nuclear confrontation arises from the fact that the nuclear-weapon powers, especially the super-powers, have all at one time or another intervened in the affairs of Third World countries. In this way, the north-south confrontation tends to intersect with the east-west, and local wars if allowed to spread could get out of hand, risking the threat of nuclear war. In order to reduce that risk, consideration needs to be given to measures of arms control of conventional weapons. Such measures would include indirect methods, such as publishing and monitoring military expenditures and international arms sales, and direct methods, such as prohibiting export of certain categories of weapons to areas of conflict, as well as strengthening the peace-keeping and peace-making capacities of the United Nations.

COLLATERAL MEASURES OF ARMS CONTROL

After the failure of talks on general and complete disarmament, the Geneva Disarmament Conference wanted to avoid a similar breakdown in negotiations. To this end, it introduced the consideration of various ways of lowering international tensions, building up confidence, and preventing the extension of the arms race to new environments. The discussion of such measures was not intended to prejudice the negotiation of agreements on conventional or nuclear disarmament, nor any confidence-building arrangements discussed bilaterally, such as the 'hot line' between Washington DC and Moscow. In fact, these collateral measures have proved to be the only area in which some progress was registered at Geneva in the sixties and early seventies.

Among the collateral measures favoured by the Soviet Union and its allies have been: the reduction of military budgets; a non-aggression pact between NATO and the Warsaw Pact powers; the prohibition of the use of nuclear weapons; the establishment of nuclear-free zones; the reciprocal withdrawal of foreign troops from the territories of other countries; the elimination of foreign military bases and the reduction in the number of armed forces; the partial test ban; and the non-proliferation treaty.

The United States and its allies, for their part, singled out the most urgent arms control measures relating to nuclear activities, particularly the test ban and the issue of non-proliferation. They have also given priority to the cessation (cut-off) or limitation (cut-back) in the production of fissionable material, the transfer of agreed stocks to peaceful uses, a freeze on strategic delivery vehicles, and the reduction of bombers.

At the height of the Sputnik period when the US and the USSR were competing as to who would put the first man on the moon, Canada, supported by Italy and Mexico, had pressed for a commitment to ensure the peaceful uses of outer space. Nuclear weapons and other weapons of mass destruction were subsequently banned from outer space on the recommendation of the General Assembly in 1963, and by a Treaty signed by the US and the USSR in 1967.

The most important collateral measures to date have, however, been the Partial Test Ban of 1963 and the Non-Proliferation Treaty of 1968. These were addressed to vertical and horizontal nuclear proliferation, respectively. The partial test ban, by putting restraints on the environment in which testing could take place and limiting testing to underground explosions, was intended to restrict the development of new weapons by the nuclear powers. In effect, since the signing of the treaty, testing has steadily increased both in the US and USSR, while China and France have so far refused to accept this restraint. The most that can be said about this agreement is that it has become a sort of environmental measure, reducing the fall-out effects of massive explosions that the two super-powers indulged in on land and at sea before the ban went into effect.

The Non-Proliferation Treaty (NPT) was intended to prevent the spread of nuclear weapons to non-nuclear countries; however, the obligations of this treaty proved unbalanced. The nuclear powers undertook to negotiate, in good faith, the cessation of the nuclear arms race. This they have failed to carry out – or, if they have, there is little to show for it! The non-nuclear powers were obliged to accept international controls over their nuclear fuel and installations, and the International Atomic Energy Agency (IAEA) and its safeguards were used to implement this undertaking.

The weakness in mutuality and balance was noted when the General Assembly voted in June 1968 to recommend the conclusion of the NPT. France and a number of potential nuclear countries abstained, including Argentina, Brazil, Pakistan, Israel, Spain, Switzerland, South Africa, India, and several other African countries. India flatly refused to join the NPT during the negotiations, arguing that the treaty was discriminatory. India's acquisition of a plutonium separation plant, leading subsequently to a test explosion, points up the inevitable conclusion that what is needed now is not another 'paper' arms control measure dependent upon good faith for its implementation. Rather, we need agreement on comprehensive, universal, and vigilant controls, especially of the critical elements in the fuel cycle.

In order to obtain agreement to these kinds of controls from countries like India, it may be necessary for the nuclear-weapons powers to carry out their previous pledge at least to begin to cease and reverse the arms race, and to submit their non-military nuclear facilities to inspection and verification by the IAEA.

This kind of mutuality of commitment might then open the door to better understanding with non-nuclear countries with regard to the supply of nuclear technology and materials. It must be recognized that the developing countries' seeking of nuclear sources of energy is an integral part of their demands for a fair share of the world's resources in order to raise the standard of living of their peoples. Thus, to control nuclear proliferation, measures preventing the diversion from peaceful uses to nuclear weapons or other nuclear explosive devices must be improved. In order to achieve this goal of peaceful nuclear development, however, there must also be *inducements* to join the NPT and to accept a universally acceptable system of safeguards under the IAEA. To provide such inducements, the nuclear-developed countries must be ready to accept the same controls as those seeking development, and they must be willing to transfer nuclear technology and materials to developing countries.

The remaining collateral measures agreed to at Geneva and elsewhere were the Biological Weapons Convention of 1971, outlawing germ warfare and eliminating toxic weapons; the Treaty of Tlatelolco, prohibiting nuclear weapons in Latin America; the Sea-Bed Treaty of 1972, prohibiting the emplacement of nuclear weapons and other weapons of mass destruction on the sea-bed or ocean floor; and the Environmental Modification Treaty, prohibiting some forms of environmental warfare. These measures of arms control are even more marginal in their impact on the possibilities of nuclear war than the other measures we have considered.

The Biological Weapons Convention at least can be said to be the only measure of actual disarmament agreed to since the Second World War, since it involved the destruction of existing stockpiles. In any case, bacteriological and biological weapons as well as environmental warfare must surely be the least significant addition to the military capabilities of any powers large or small. No adequate control provisions were adopted and the convention simply amended the Geneva Protocol of 1925, outlawing chemical warfare by adding another group of noxious and lethal agents to the ban. Moreover, ambiguities remain regarding the precise definition of prohibition by the Geneva Convention and the negotiation of an effective total ban on the use of chemical and biological weapons remains on the agenda.

The Treaty of Tlatelolco was in large part due to Mexico's reaction to the Cuban missile crisis, and was an attempt to keep nuclear weapons out of Latin America. It also debarred the testing, use, manufacture, production, or acquisition of nuclear weapons by its signatories. Unfortunately, the treaty is not yet in force. Three important nations of the hemisphere – Argentina, Brazil, and Chile – have signed but not ratified the treaty, while Cuba has not even signed it. Despite these gaps in its implementation, the treaty is a first step towards the denuclearization of the area and provides a possible model for the denuclearization of other areas in the world where the possibilities of war are more evident, like the Middle East or South-East Asia.

The most that can be said about the Sea-Bed Arms Control Convention is that it bars the establishment on the sea-bed or ocean floor of stationary bombardment systems armed with nuclear weapons, in the event that any power should wish to resort to this method for purposes of concealment. What the sea-bed treaty is supposed to prevent, however, has never been of military interest. In any case, submarines do a better job of providing under-water cover for the discharge of nuclear weapons. This arms control measure did keep the Geneva disarmament negotiators busier for a while than they would have been otherwise, but it did not really contribute to what is a desirable objective: the complete demilitarization of the oceans to permit their unrestricted economic development and exploitation. This question is now engaging the attention of the Law of the Sea Conference at the United Nations. The Sea-Bed Arms Control Convention was a 'non-armament' measure, extremely difficult to control, and its signing might be termed a 'non-event'.

THE URGENT NEED FOR PROGRESS

From this discussion of 'achievements' in arms control to date, it is obvious why there is a growing demand for some dramatic happening to highlight public concern about the lack of progress towards disarmament. At the United Nations, this clamour has found expression in the form of support for a special session of the General Assembly, which took place in 1978, or of a World Disarmament Conference. The latter would direct attention to disarmament as urgent and essential, if we are to reduce the possibility of war and husband scarce resources for peaceful uses.

Progress toward disarmament has been virtually nil. None the less, some progress in measures of partial arms control has been achieved, especially in areas where the two super-powers and their respective allies have tried to reduce the possibilities of surprise attack by improving communications to facilitate crisis management, increasing contacts at all levels of government, and exchanging more information. It can be argued that these kinds of measures, including satellite surveillance, have had the effect of reducing the possibility of nuclear war by increasing the ability to detect preparations for such war in advance.

The possibility of nuclear war through accident or miscalculation is not, however, ruled out. Especially dangerous is the potential for escalation of violence arising from a limited war, and the proliferation of nuclear capabilities to still further countries. These will not have the benefit of an invulnerable retaliatory capacity for deterrence, and among them conventions of communication and reciprocity in matters of crisis management either will not exist, or will not be as elaborate as those between NATO and the Warsaw Pact. The most promising motivation for more effective action in the field of arms control and disarmament is the widespread, virtually universal, craving for peace in a world in which there are relatively few nations that have not in recent years experienced the ravages of war.

In order to give expression to this craving and clamour for effective action, it is essential to avoid the impasse of all or nothing which was the fate of the discussion of general and complete disarmament based upon the Zorin-McCloy Principles in the 1960s. Crucial to any progress in reducing the possibilities of nuclear war are: a / certain prior agreements among the super-powers; b / agreements by the other nuclear-weapons powers; and c / curbs on non-nuclear weapons.

Agreements among the super-powers
In order to reduce the possibility of nuclear war and open the way for China to enter into commitments similar to the arms control measures accepted by the super-powers, the US and USSR should first be prepared to moderate their nuclear hegemony by an unconditional pledge not to be the first to initiate any act of nuclear warfare – i.e., to renounce the option of 'first use'.

The other commitment which the super-powers should undertake is not to attack any nuclear-weapons-free country with nuclear weapons. The resolution passed by the Security Council on this matter in 1968 took the form of offering assistance in the event of attack. What is needed is the outlawing of any attack with nuclear weapons on a nuclear-weapons-free country.

The super-powers should also make a special effort to stop and reverse the gushing stream of nuclear overkill. This goal could be achieved by following up the SALT I and Vladivostok agreements not only with quantitative reductions, but also with an agreement curbing qualitative competition, by not seeking to develop new nuclear weapons or new generations of existing weapons systems. Unless both stop the development of new weapons, the game of 'catch-up' will never stop.

Agreements by other nuclear weapon powers
It behooves all nuclear-capable powers, which are supplying non-nuclear-capable countries with nuclear fuel and technology, to agree on ways of strengthening international safeguards under IAEA. The processing and distribution of nuclear fuels and reactors must be regulated so that competition does not contribute to nuclear proliferation.

All nuclear-weapons powers should be urged to participate in arms control and disarmament negotiations. The first agreement that should be sought is for the banning of all nuclear weapons tests. Previously, those nuclear powers who have participated in arms control negotiations have argued that it would be prejudicial to their security if a comprehensive test ban went into effect but were not accepted by all nuclear weapons powers. This vicious circle has to be broken. Moreover, arguments that control of a test ban is impossible no longer hold water since sensitive seismological instruments, as well as satellite surveillance, now provide adequate means of verification.

Once a way is found to curb nuclear weapon development, by a comprehensive test ban and by stopping flight testing of new delivery vehicles, attention should be focused on trying to fix the parameters and rules for a minimum deterrent. It is difficult to conceive of the nuclear powers agreeing to a gradual scaling down of their respective capabilities unless they know what the size and composition of a minimum deterrent force might be at the end of the process. It is also difficult to conceive that the nuclear powers will not insist on retaining some 'nuclear shield', so long as they remain dependent for their security on national armaments and armed forces, rather than upon international authority backed by forces like the United Nations.

Curbs on non-nuclear weapons

We have already noted that the issue of curbing the proliferation of conventional arms has been overshadowed by the discussion of nuclear arms control. Because conventional weapons have a relatively limited range of threat and their effects are less destructive, they have been used in innumerable wars, while nuclear weapons have only been stockpiled. It is recognized, however, that wars starting with conventional weapons could possibly escalate to nuclear war, if the confrontation of nuclear-weapons powers were involved. Such a threat has been considered more likely in Europe where super-power confrontation arises from treaty obligations, but it could conceivably occur elsewhere by accident or miscalculation.

The other factor bearing upon the control of conventional weapons is that only the two super-powers are entirely self-sufficient in arms production. All other countries are more or less dependent on imports of certain weapons, parts, and equipment, or on licences needed for the domestic production of arms, especially as these become even more automatic, lethal, and sophisticated. This dependence applies to industrially advanced countries; conventional arms sale are even more important for the developing countries. International transfer of conventional weapons is constantly increasing.

In order to institute curbs on the sale of conventional arms, the first step is to lay bare the facts. Arms control measures might then be sought, either indirectly or directly. Indirectly, one way of curbing conventional arms production and transfer would be to curb military expenditures by international agreement. Military expenditures might be required to be reported to a United Nations agency and monitored by it. Registration of weapons production or transfer might also be required.

A more direct approach might involve invoking the Hague Convention of 1907 prohibiting the transfer of arms from outside states, presumed to be neutral, to any state taking part in warfare. The fact that such transfers take place and are not discussed at the United Nations, points to a need to focus on the problem.

In addition to curbing the transfer or sale of conventional arms to certain areas of hostility, it should be possible to outlaw or curb the production and transfer of certain non-nuclear mass destruction weapons, such as the biological and chemical, whose use is already supposed to be curbed by the Geneva Convention and the Biological Weapons Convention. As conventional weapons become increasingly automatic, lethal, and sophisticated, consideration should also be given to placing restraints on the production and transfer of specific arms more suited to total war (leading to the use of nuclear weapons) than to purely defensive purposes.

Further efforts are also required for regional arms control and disarmament arrangements. A case in point is the proposal which has been under consideration for some time at the United Nations for an agreement to limit military activity in the Indian Ocean. By the same token, an essential element of any Middle East settlement must surely be to provide local restraints on military activity as well as guarantees for the observance of the settlement from outside powers. In this way, beginning with joint efforts to restrain the possibility of nuclear-weapons proliferation (on the model of the Tlatelolco Treaty) wider demilitarization could be built up in regions where neighbouring countries have an obvious mutual interest in arms limitation as a means of promoting confidence and peace.

CONCLUSION

Finally, it must be admitted that the 'achievements of arms control' to date have yet to come to grips with the central and basic problem of drastic reductions in nuclear weapons and systems, and an effective cessation of the technological or qualitative arms race. All that is necessary to prove this is the continuing escalation of military expenditures by the super-powers and the development of new weapons. It can be argued that international anarchy, as it prevails today despite the United Nations and its charter, is the root cause of the possibility of war. The strengthening of international organization and the building up of a respect for international law, to which all countries must contribute, has to go hand in hand with arms control, if we are truly to reduce the possibilities of war.

Whether the countries possessing or capable of developing a nuclear capability decide to exercise it within the next few years will depend mainly on consideration in each country of its security requirements as well as the international climate affecting international co-operation. The workability of arms control depends on the example and the standard of international relations set by the two super-powers who at present set the pace in the arms race. Only by their leadership and example can we hope to succeed in having any de-escalation of the arms race and any control of the proliferation of nuclear weapons.

If the US and the USSR continue to set the pace in militarization in both nuclear and conventional weapons, relying on national armaments rather than international peace-keeping forces for the maintenance of national peace and security, it cannot be expected that other countries will accept the legitimacy of nuclear restraint and arms control. If the nuclear-weapons states should ratify agreement on SALT II and accept nuclear restraint and live up to their obligations and commitments undertaken under the Non-Proliferation Treaty, then there is a chance that this Treaty can be strengthened and revived and with it the safeguards administered under the International Atomic Agency. Developing countries who place their hope for future economic development on the application of nuclear energy will only respond to effective negotiations on arms control if they see signs that the super-powers are willing to live up to their commitments to stop nuclear proliferation. The problem of the developing countries, moreover, cannot be resolved by the transfer of nuclear technology. They are demanding a more equitable share of the world's wealth and this involves more effective programs in the north-south dialogue, especially those related to the New International Order.

The third area where progress must be made is with international organizations. There is no feasible alternative to the United Nations. Its authority and prestige must not only be strengthened generally, but the machinery for the negotiation of arms control agreements must be improved by taking the chairmanship away from the two super-powers and substituting an elected chairman, making the body more representative of all the countries with a military capability, both nuclear and conventional, and by striving in the direction of taking decisions by a general consensus rather than by vote so as to ensure that the decisions on arms control are broadly acceptable and will be carried out.

NOTES

1 Dean Acheson, *Present at the Creation* (W. W. Norton & Co., 1969) 153
2 In a speech on 31 March 1950 in Hamilton, Ontario
3 *Newsweek*, 2 January 1978, 'Carter's New Year's Whirl', 15
4 Zorin-McCloy principles

Future Developments as They Affect the Threat of Nuclear War

6

A World of Many Nuclear Powers

WALTER SCHÜTZE

During the sixties, the major effort at non-proliferation was mainly, if not exclusively, aimed at preventing the two foes of the Second World War, Germany and Japan, from acquiring nuclear weapons of their own. This objective was indeed achieved by the NPT. It might, however, be said that, contrary to the situation of today in countries on the threshold of nuclear-weapons status, there was never any real desire on the part of the Germans or the Japanese to build their own bomb. The integration of these two countries into the American security system and the subsequent presence of American forces on their soil had not only diminished the incentives for such an independent course, but also provided sufficient opportunity for the United States to make them toe the line.

The conditions of enforced stability along the east-west axis do not exist in the rest of the world today. The emerging potential medium powers outside the US alliance system and the Soviet-dominated sphere are likely to conclude that the outcome of the first non-proliferation debate in the northern hemisphere proves the need of staying clear of too stringent military commitments to the big powers. In any event, the whole character of the non-proliferation problem has changed markedly since the beginning of the seventies. We are faced with what might be called a 'nuclear drift' away from the industrialized countries of the north to the other regions of the world – to countries that lack the economic and technological base of Europe, Japan, Australia, and New Zealand, but which enjoy a greater margin of independent action, and also feel less secure.

NEW NUCLEAR POWERS: HOW MANY AND WHEN?

Before examining the constraints on proliferation, let us first consider the capabilities and incentives of the non-nuclear-weapons states. The spread of civil nuclear technology and of power reactors is most relevant here. It is generally admitted that a direct link exists between the world-wide diffusion of nuclear 'know-how' and the dangers of proliferation. As a former director of the US Arms Control and Disarmament Agency (ACDA) has pointed out,[1] by the mid-1980s some 35 countries will have accumulated enough plutonium to make several dozen nuclear weapons. The Stockholm International Peace Research Institute (SIPRI)[2] lists 15 non-nuclear weapons countries which, at the end of 1976, were theoretically capable of making atomic bombs. By the end of 1980, the number of these threshold states will have increased to 23, and again to probably 28 by the mid-1980s. By this time, the SIPRI study suggests, these countries will have nuclear power reactors with a potential annual plutonium production rate of about 30 000kg. Theoretically, this would allow them to build ten 20KT atomic bombs per day, if one assumed that they also possessed the technical capacity to separate plutonium from the spent fuel elements of their reactors. If the development of 'conventional' light-water reactors continues at this rate, the number of civil nuclear countries might be expected to reach 50 by the end of the century, although the scarcity of uranium will be a very serious handicap from the 1990s onward.

Whatever the course chosen by potential civil and military nuclear powers in developing their capabilities, it should be apparent that not only 'demand-pull' from recipients but 'supply-push' from sellers will be at work in the world-wide diffusion of nuclear technology.[3] At least two of the most important suppliers, France and West Germany, are offering to sell facilities covering the whole range of the nuclear fuel cycle in order to remain in a very competitive market, when their domestic needs are inadequate to maintain fully their own nuclear industries. We need not go into the political controversies here. But we must note that this form of technology transfer, leading to the creation of a complete scientific and technical nuclear infrastructure in countries of the Third World, is in itself very clearly an element of proliferation. In the medium term and certainly by the year 2000, it will lessen the strong dependence of less developed countries on the industrialized nations, and will therefore seriously limit the latters' means of action.

How many nuclear weapons states will there be around the turn of the century? The answer must remain highly conjectural, as both capabilities and intentions are involved and interconnected. The existing means and resources – including a national uranium supply – might prompt a decision to go nuclear, and the will to do so might in turn prompt a military crash program.

There exists, on available evidence, a first category of immediate threshold countries. This category excludes India, which is in a very ambiguous position, as she has the explosives but has pledged not to use them for military purposes. It includes Israel and South Africa who are already 'covert' nuclear powers in that they could very soon explode a nuclear device if they choose to do so.

The second category comprises what one could call the critical nth countries, who have also refused to sign the NPT and have at least admitted a strong interest in the nuclear option: Argentina, Brazil, and Pakistan. To these should be added signatories of the NPT who are not willing to proceed with ratification, and who have made it clear that they intend to review their security requirements in the light of international developments: Egypt and Indonesia.

The third category consists of countries who have ratified the NPT but maintain their reservations and pursue a policy which would enable them to go nuclear within some years: Iran, Iraq, Libya, South Korea, and possibly Taiwan.

A fourth category of states comprises countries which, independent of their NPT status, could be 'triggered' into a policy of nuclear armament by critical developments within their regions: Algeria, the Philippines, Nigeria, Zaire, Syria, and possibly Chile.

It is significant that this approximate list of the most likely nuclear candidates excludes countries of Western Europe and communist regimes. Though Spain and Portugal have not signed the NPT and Turkey has gone only so far as to become a signatory, there seems to be little point in putting them in a category of nth countries. As for the communist countries, North Korea and Vietnam could be listed as candidates for the later 1980s, if Soviet influence were eroded and grave tension developed in their relationship with China.

Again it must be stressed that these projections are extremely hazardous and wholly dependent on what kind of scenario one adopts for the course of world events during the next decade. It would seem unjustified to include, as do recent studies of the Hudson Institute,[4] West Germany and Japan among the group of critical nth countries, although there are some incentives for proliferation in this quarter.

As mentioned before, the 'firebreaks' against the horizontal proliferation of nuclear weapons erected during the 1960s and strengthened as a consequence of the Indian explosion have proved their value – despite the expectations of many who believed that the critical point would be the emergence of the sixth nuclear power. In this respect, the Indian decision of 1974 indeed opened an avenue for nth countries wishing to bypass the military issue by claiming that they intended to use the atomic device for peaceful purposes only (the case of Brazil, in particular). As for the alleged South African preparations for a nuclear test in August 1977, such a development might indeed have triggered off a wave of proliferation. This may explain why the super-powers took such strong joint action to prevent a test by the government in Pretoria.

The experience of the past suggests that, assuming a continuation of the 'normal' course of events in world politics, even the critical nth countries will prefer their present ambivalent attitude to an openly declared nuclear weapons option. This may be, of course, because the most immediately concerned states have not quite reached the take-off stage. And yet an international climate not marked by extreme alarm certainly inhibits governments as well. It seems therefore that the timetable of actual weapons proliferation will be determined primarily by what is happening on the world scene. A breakdown of east-west détente on a large scale and a complete collapse of arms-control policy would evidently have a triggering effect. And even without such extreme scenarios, the outbreak of local wars – a renewed Israeli-Arab conflict or a dramatic heightening of tensions in southern Africa – could have somewhat similar consequences at least on a regional scale. What one cannot take for granted is that within the next decade or so the nuclear *status quo* will be maintained. Nor can it be assumed that by the year 2000 there will not be around 35 states possessing their own nuclear arsenals as a consequence of varying combinations of concern for national security, international status, and internal political and bureaucratic pressure to assert the national interest through reliance on nuclear weapons.

CONSTRAINTS TO WEAPONS PROLIFERATION

The very strong line taken by the Carter administration on the issue of non-proliferation has again raised the question of whether the international community is able to find ways and means to stop this trend. In recent years the debate has centred around the problem of institutional constraints, or the strengthening of safeguards to prevent the diversion of fissile material for military purposes. There is a real danger, however, that American insistence on a policy of 'denial' – as opposed to a policy of 'controlled cooperation' advocated by some European suppliers (notably France and Western Germany) – will be seen by nth countries in the Third World as an attempt to discriminate against them (a point alluded to in the previous chapter). If so, it will in the end serve to increase the risks of a north-south conflict over the use of nuclear energy.

The French president, Giscard d'Estaing, once said that the best way of preventing proliferation would be to convince the countries concerned that it is not in their interest to possess a bomb of their own, and he advocated self-restraint on the part of the nuclear powers. But his pledge not to use these weapons against non-nuclear countries is clearly not sufficient, as such a use must be considered to be very unlikely, if not downright impossible. On the other hand, a nuclear-weapons states' guarantee of nth countries against aggression, as discussed in the United States in the 1950s, is not credible any more, if it ever was, in the absence of firm alliance commitments.

As far as self-constraint on the part of the nuclear powers is concerned, the pledge of Article 6 of the NPT to stop the nuclear arms race and speedily to engage in negotiations for universal and total disarmament has still to be fulfilled – to put it mildly. It is doubtful whether the nth countries will be satisfied with the eventual conclusion of SALT II and subsequent agreements to limit the strategic arms race as really opening the way to an actual reduction of the arsenals of the super-powers (see Chapter 5). There is no need here to emphasize the very important link between vertical (upwards among existing nuclear-weapons states) and horizontal (outwards to embrace nth countries) proliferation. The mounting disappointment of the non-nuclear powers with the achievements of arms control policy (including the negotiations within the United Nations framework in Geneva, the European force reduction talks at Vienna, etc.) cannot but erode remaining constraints on selection of the nuclear option. Lack of sufficient progress in these fields will provide some critical nth countries with an excuse for proliferation.

Furthermore, the growing 'militarization' of international politics and the continued diffusion of ever more sophisticated conventional weapons systems in the countries of the Third World and particularly in the Middle East are bound to affect the attitude of prospective candidates to nuclear status. To obtain delivery vehicles on the international market is not a serious obstacle any more, as even relatively simple airplanes, like the F-5, the Mirage III, and tactical missiles are able to carry a nuclear warhead. An agreement by the major arms suppliers of East and West to limit arms transfers, eventually leading to a comprehensive embargo, would help to stop this trend. But here again the prospects for a joint demonstration of self-restraint look rather dim at present.

A more promising way of reducing the incentives to go nuclear is to be found in current efforts to achieve a comprehensive test ban. The possibility of conducting underground tests even within the US-Soviet agreed maximum of 150KT yield is still a critical factor in determining the attitudes of nth countries. As atmospheric nuclear tests cannot be carried out in the threshold countries or their territorial waters (probably including Brazil), a comprehensive ban would be a strong disincentive to openly declared nuclear status. Quite simply, an explosion is necessary to demonstrate without doubt a newly acquired weapons capability. By the end of 1976, the number of parties to the limited nuclear test ban of 1963 was 108 (as compared with 101 for the NPT): these included Egypt and Israel, and Pakistan as signatories. New pressures and incentives towards a comprehensive test ban and universal compliance with other arms control measures would moreover make it easier to develop a system of political and economic sanctions against countries who proceeded with the explosion of a nuclear device.

This brings us to the question of institutional constraints, as embodied in the guidelines of the London 'suppliers club', and various safeguard agreements concluded under the auspices of the International Atomic Energy Agency. The international inspection of all civil nuclear facilities, provided it can be agreed upon and carried out effectively, would certainly inhibit unauthorized use. On the other hand, it could encourage nth countries to bypass such controls and to undertake a clandestine weapons program.

What is required is an agreed set of international sanctions, going beyond mere reproval, whereby a country tempted to go nuclear will be made aware of the political, economic, financial, and military risks incurred. This approach might look rather utopian and impractical, if the nth country to be deterred were, for example, a big oil producer. But there is much to be said for a non-proliferation philosophy based on the assumption that it is not in the self-interest of a given country to build the bomb.

MANAGING THE INTERNATIONAL SYSTEM
IN A MULTI-NUCLEAR WORLD

Assume that within the next decade or so several new nuclear powers emerge. As an initial consequence of a multi-nuclear setting, the ability of the two super-powers to manage a crisis in other regions of the globe would be seriously impaired. Familiar means of exerting influence and pressure in these regions might become inoperative. For example, conventional arms deals, including technical and logistic assistance, which today provide great leverage for the major powers would become much too risky vis-à-vis a nuclear power, and would have to be discontinued for fear of direct involvement in a nuclear conflict.

The relative isolation of new nuclear powers from the international community, arising from the need of the 'law breakers' for greater self-reliance and the ensuing reduction of interdependence, would in all likelihood tend to fragment the structure of inter-state relationships. The United Nations in particular would be in danger of total inadequacy, since the present status of the nuclear powers, permanent membership on the Security Council, could not be extended to newcomers.

Nor does the precedent of NATO, and the coexistence of several nuclear powers within an alliance, provide a way out. The NATO pattern cannot be repeated anywhere else in the world. The well-known thesis of General Gallois that a national nuclear force is incompatible with alliance commitments, proven wrong in the Atlantic case, would be validated by the emergence of new nuclear powers in the non-aligned world, the more so as these newcomers could well have to adopt a 'tous azimuts' strategy. The spread of national nuclear forces would in addition weaken and disrupt existing regional groupings like the Organization of American States, the Organization of African Unity, or the Association of South-East Asian Nations, leading to dangerous instabilities in those areas of tension where proliferation is most likely to occur.

A more optimistic assessment could be based on the view that the addition of several nuclear powers would not fundamentally alter the nature of the international system and would bring greater flexibility to balance-of-power exercises by making the established nuclear countries more cautious in their dealings with the new ones. Most probably, the east-west bipolar relationship, with China in the uncertain role of the third man, would persist in a new nuclear environment. Indeed, intra-alliance discipline as well as inter-alliance co-operation could be strengthened by the imperative need for crisis management. The real issue is, however, whether proliferation will split the world into a relatively stable and structured northern hemisphere and a more fragmented, and accident-prone southern hemisphere.

The charge of irresponsibility directed against the new nuclear states has since the end of 1950 overshadowed the non-proliferation debate and its racialist implications have been strongly resented in the Third World.[5] There appears to be no reason to make out an *a priori* case against all nth countries and to assume that only the old nuclear powers, which have learned to live with the bomb, can be expected to act wisely and exercise self-restraint in nuclear matters. The point is rather that there will be a greater mischief-making potential for 'maverick' candidates like Libya and other countries with unstable or downright paranoic leaders. Because of the inevitable weakening of political links (regional groupings) and economic solidarities, which would follow in the wake of widespread nuclear disarmament, we might witness again a gradual breakdown of the over-all system, like the one which occurred in the Middle Ages when the feudal lords became able to muster small but reliable armies and hence to defy their imperial masters. Feudalistic fragmentation, with much more serious consequences, is a prospect we may have to face over the next two decades.

Precedents and past experiences are sometimes helpful, but hardly conclusive in such a speculative area as this. They do not apply to the parts of the world where the bomb will probably spread first. This presentation, therefore, constitutes no more than a very summary and hazardous sketch – an attempt not so much to find answers as to pose questions.

NOTES

1 Statement by Fred Iklé before the Sub-Committee on International Security and Scientific Affairs of the Committee on International Relations, United States House of Representatives, Washington DC, 5 November 1975
2 SIPRI, World Armaments: The Nuclear Threat (Stockholm, June 1977)
3 Lewis A. Dunn, The Proliferation Policy Agenda: Taking Stock, Report of the World Peace Foundation Conference on Managing a Proliferation-Prone World, Endicott House, Dedham, Mass., December 9-11, 1977
4 Lewis A. Dunn and Hermann Kahn, Trends in Nuclear Proliferation, 1975-1995 (Hudson Institute, May 1976), and Lewis A. Dunn, Changing Dimensions of Proliferation Policy, 1975-1995 (Hudson Institute, February 1977)
5 See in particular the contribution of Sisir Gupta in Alastair Buchan ed., A World of Nuclear Powers (Englewood Cliffs NJ, The American Assembly, 1966).

7

Weapons Developments and the Threat of Nuclear War

RICHARD L. GARWIN

Many wars have been waged because of political goals, economic aspirations, racial hatred, and the like. The availability of novel weapons is not generally regarded as the proximate cause of war. However, old weapons used in a new way or weapons more recently acquired (hence more modern and perhaps more effective) may have persuaded some nations that they could actually win a war which they might not otherwise have started, because of poor prospects for the outcome. Thus the Second World War would probably not have been initiated if Germany had not acquired modern tank and aircraft forces.

CRISIS INSTABILITY

Certain weapons by virtue of their very capabilities can, however, lead to destructive war. This problem has been discussed for the last quarter-century in regard to strategic nuclear weapons under the rubric, 'crisis instability'. Put in its starkest form, if the strategic offensive forces of the United States and the Soviet Union consisted entirely of land-based, MIRVed ICBMs (intercontinental ballistic missiles equipped with multiple independently targeted nuclear warheads), each nation, as now, could destroy its opponent by launching its ICBMs at the population and industry of the other. Neither nation would do that if it were sure to bring about its own destruction. But under the assumed conditions of the existence of land-based ICBMs only, and setting aside submarine-launched ballistic missiles (SLBMs) and strategic bombers, if the number of MIRVed warheads on each missile were sufficiently large, and the accuracy and reliability of each of the warheads sufficiently good, then one side might consider attacking the missile silos of the other side with some fraction of its own ICBMs, in the hope of entirely disarming its opponent while retaining the power to destroy and hence to coerce the other side. Thus since the days of the strategic bomber, 'surprise attack' has been uppermost in the minds of national leaders and strategic planners. One response to this concern has been the development and deployment of the present, less vulnerable, strategic forces (SLBMs in nuclear submarines, ICBMs in hardened silos, warning systems and ground alert to enable the strategic bombers to take off before they can be destroyed).

The avoidance of crisis instability is a continuing concern because it could lead to the outbreak of destructive nuclear war motivated by self-preservation rather than by the malign intent to destroy the adversary. Thus one line of technological evolution must be avoided or compensated if it is not to have the most dangerous impact on national and world security. The MIRV itself, as is well known, has this unfortunate effect. An ICBM with a single warhead can destroy no more than one of the opponent's ICBMs, and by reason of imperfect accuracy and reliability, can do considerably less. But a force of MIRVs can in principle destroy a numerically equal or superior force of MIRVed missiles, thus leading to crisis instability.

No serious effort was made by the United States to obtain an arms control agreement with the Soviet Union at an early time to prevent the development and deployment of MIRVs; even so, crisis stability is maintained to the present time for many reasons:

the accuracy and reliability of individual MIRVs is not sufficient for a single-MIRV warhead attack on each silo to kill a sufficient fraction of the silos to constitute a disarming strike:

insufficient numbers of MIRVs are available on the two sides (except for the US Poseidon warheads) to constitute a disarming strike even if many warheads could be used to destroy each silo;

since warheads are less durable than silos, the explosion of one RV (reentry vehicle or nuclear warhead) near a silo puts very strong constraints on the timing and nature of attack by successive RVs if they are to explode and to contribute to the damage expectancy against the target silo;

there is no reason to believe that a nation will allow its ICBM force to be destroyed in its silos when it could launch the ICBMs during the thirty-minute flight time available after the launch of the enemy ICBM force; and in fact, the United States has many more warheads on its SLBMs and on its ICBMs, and has also a very substantial force of strategic bombers which can take off sufficiently rapidly to avoid destruction before launch.

Note that there is no such thing as 'crisis instability of the MIRVed ICBM force' when that force is embedded in a complex of other strategic offensive forces, launch-on warning options, and the like.

A crisis-unstable force is perhaps the least desirable of all strategic forces, since a responsible leader possessing only such a force would have to keep it on alert (ready to launch on warning) lest it be destroyed by the other side. Since the same applies for the other side itself, it is clear that the stage would be set for unwanted war.

THE PROBLEM OF STRATEGIC DEFENCE

Somewhat less hazardous would be the one-sided achievement of a capability or belief in the ability to defend the nation entirely or substantially against attack by ballistic missiles. In the abstract, a nation might thus feel secure against the ICBM and SLBM force of the other side, and could then coerce, bully, or destroy the other side as it desired. In truth, the absence of an effective anti-ballistic missile (ABM) system, the possibility of fighting and destroying even an apparently effective ABM, and the existence of the strategic bomber force all mitigate the worry about acquisition of ballistic missile defence by the other side. Still, the American-Soviet ABM treaty of 1972 plays a substantial role in committing the US and the USSR not to deploy or lay the basis for a deployment of an ABM defence of their territories; effectively it denies even credible localized defence, except perhaps of certain silo fields.

Although penetration of air defences by strategic aircraft flying at low altitude seems reasonably assured, the fact that ABM would counter two of the three arms of the strategic triad made it a threat to be taken very seriously. Thus, the SALT I treaty quenched a serious US-USSR arms race in ABM technology, which probably would not have led to effective ABM on either side but which would have wasted a lot of resources.

STRATEGIC WAR ARISING FROM SMALLER NUCLEAR POWERS

The outbreak of war elsewhere could lead to war between the US and the USSR. This paper is concerned with weapons developments as they affect the threat of war, and thus with the contribution of weapons developments to the initiation of war between lesser powers and its spread to the super-powers. Obviously, fledgeling nuclear forces in a small country (unprotected by great distance from its enemy, and not possessing adequate warning systems, buffer time, ultra-hard basing, and the like) may provide an attractive target for attack. Thus, the proliferation of nuclear weapons to additional countries can lead their neighbours and opponents to the acquisition of nuclear weapons and to an increasing rate of proliferation. In addition to the possible threat of their use by national governments, nuclear weapons may also be the object of military or other coups, with threatened or actual use.

THE ROLE OF THE CRUISE MISSILE

The renaissance of cruise missiles, with modern small jet engine technology and with the use of modern semi-conductor computers for control and guidance, has the potential for replacing vastly expensive modern tactical aircraft for the bombardment of ground targets. In the tactical theatre, radio guidance may be less costly and more precise than the terrain comparison (TERCOM) planned by the United States for its nuclear-armed air-launched strategic cruise missile, although the terrain information may in fact not be conveniently available or usable by one of the participants in the theatre.

Various incapacities of missile and electronics in early surface-to-air missile (SAM) systems required the missiles to be collocated with the radars and even forced the missiles to be on launchers which slewed with the radar. More recent systems allow vertical launch of the SAMs and guidance from wherever they happen to be to the target being tracked by the radar. Similarly, modern cruise missiles can be based remote from their guidance and command system and launched by radio control. This permits them to be based individually in such a way that they are not vulnerable to attack by nuclear or non-nuclear weapons and sufficiently remote from the battle area that they are not easily overrun.

Although cruise missiles can be used to attack fixed targets with an accuracy determined by their navigation system, they can also be used to deliver explosive payloads into the acquisition 'basket' of a laser target designator or other precision guidance system. Thus they can be used against moving targets as well as fixed targets. If effective reliable tactical cruise missiles of 1 000-pound high-explosive warhead and 500-mile range are widely available at a cost of $40 000 each, they will have an important impact on tactical war capabilities because they will remove a very large fixed cost of aircraft, maintenance, training, basing, and the like. There are many constituencies with an interest in making such a cruise missile system costly and few with an interest in making it affordable; it remains to be seen how soon and to what extent it will actually replace aircraft.

Cruise missiles with relatively short range may provide shore batteries, submarines, small boats, and aircraft with the capability effectively to deny access to large areas of the sea, even to advanced warships. Armour is an expensive counter and of dubious utility. The more likely contest will evolve in the measure-countermeasure field, in which the ships that are nominally the targets attempt to confuse or disable the cruise missile seeker (normally either radar or infra-red). There is also the possibility of employing anti-cruise missile weapons to destroy physically the cruise missile before it reaches the ship.

OTHER PATHS TO US-USSR STRATEGIC WAR

War between the US and the USSR would be a disaster for the rest of the world – the more so the larger the weapons and the greater their number. But it would be a far greater disaster for the two named countries. War might come from crisis instability, with neither side wishing that destruction. As indicated above, war might come from miscalculation of the effectiveness of one's weapons or even, possibly, from a correct calculation in the case where one side achieved a truly protective shield. Contributing to this, but not in itself a cause of war, would be an effective anti-submarine warfare (ASW) capability against the strategic ballistic missile launching submarines of the other side. If indeed one side could reveal in an instant the SLBMs of the other side in no matter what ocean of the world, could attack within seconds or a few minutes and effectively destroy them, and at the same time could 'pin down' the land-based missiles of the other side and eventually after some hours or days destroy them before they could be launched (and if the bombers could be countered or by sabotage prevented from taking off), that one side might hope to escape destruction. ASW in itself is not destabilizing or dangerous. The problem is that ASW development and the procurement of ASW forces goes on at least in part to counter tactical submarines, but the capability spills over into some, perhaps marginal, effectiveness against SLBMs, thus tending to erode deterrence.

THE CASE OF CHINA

We have sketched the possibility of super-power war arising from crisis instability, from the imagined negation of the strategic offensive force of the other side, and from spread of nuclear conflict initiated by lesser nuclear powers. Over the next twenty years (perhaps even more over the next few years), it is possible that the enmity between one of the super-powers and its contender for ideological leadership in the socialist world (the USSR and China) could lead to major nuclear war in which the United

States would have difficulty standing aside. It is hardly conceivable that China could hope to disarm the Soviet Union by a first strike against the USSR, in the hope of reducing damage to China in a nuclear war. It is not at all impossible (especially on the scale of plausibility involved in analyses of the US-USSR strategic confrontation) that the Soviet Union would launch a major nuclear strike against China in order to destroy her strategic nuclear capability as a prelude to coercion aimed at installing a government in China with beliefs and aims more compatible with those of the Soviet Union.

With a much smaller nuclear force than the United States, with no nuclear armed missiles or submarines, and with much less warning time for nuclear-armed aircraft or ICBMs, the Chinese are said to rely on camouflage and other techniques for the preservation of their missile force against the possibility of Soviet nuclear strike. Furthermore, even large numbers of warheads cannot be used against individual silos because of fratricide considerations (the disabling of one warhead by blast and radiation effects produced by another). Accordingly, the Soviet Union may not be confident of its ability to destroy even a modest Chinese ICBM force. No doubt the existence of the massive US strategic offensive force further reduces the probability of a Soviet attack on the People's Republic of China.

ARMS CONTROL VERSUS DEFENCE MANAGEMENT

In a logical world with defence leadership and industry subservient to political leadership and national goals, a strong capability for defence management would achieve effective defence at minimal cost. It would also incorporate the important goals of arms control – reducing the probability of war, reducing the damage if war comes, reducing the cost of preparing for war. Priorities among these three arms control goals have always been troublesome; thus, the first (and to my mind vastly most important) can be eroded by insufficient expenditures. Similarly, vast forces which by their deterrent effect very greatly reduce the probability of a particular mode of initiation of war, may, even so, guarantee substantial destruction if war comes.

From recent US history, two major strategic initiatives, the B-1 bomber program and the Trident submarine program, are enormously expensive but seem entirely innocuous from the point of view of arms control. In the super-power deterrent context, they added nothing more than a greater guarantee of assured destruction in comparison with their predecessors, the B-52 penetrating aircraft and the Poseidon submarine. In his over-all interests as a US citizen, the author has opposed these programs, favouring the air-launched cruise missile on the B-52 (or successor cargo-type aircraft), and the retrofit of the Trident I missile into the Poseidon submarines. His reasons are in part to achieve the stated goals of these weapon systems more quickly and at very considerably smaller cost, but primarily to avoid the confusion and self-delusion in the US military-related sector which arises when exaggerated and specious arguments are used to support the choice of a clearly inferior approach to defence capability – the B-1 and the Trident submarine. From the arms control point of view, the problem is one of procedure and not of substance. Successfully used to win expensive, less-effective, but innocuous systems from an arms control viewpoint, such specious arguments can next be used to obtain systems which are highly dangerous in their implications for arms control and the outbreak of war.

When this paper was presented, in May 1978, the US B-1 program was dead, replaced by the program for mounting air-launched cruise missiles on B-52G bombers or their successors. The air-launched cruise missile (ALCM) is innocuous in its primary role to the arms controller, but it does introduce difficulties in the conclusion of a SALT agreement and through the fact that it provides more effective non-nuclear delivery capabilities for other nations.

THE NEUTRON BOMB

Out of all proportion to its military effectiveness or arms control impact, the neutron bomb re-emerged upon the public consciousness in summer 1977. The effects and utility of the neutron bomb can most readily be assessed by making the extreme assumption that all of its energy comes from the fusion of deuterium and tritium, with 80 per cent of the energy emerging in the form of 14 Mev (i.e., high energy) neutrons. Because of the exponential absorption in air of bomb neutrons, a factor 8 increase in bomb yield (energy release) increases only by a fixed amount the distance to which people receive a lethal dose of radiation. But a factor 8 increase in yield corresponds at any yield to a factor 2 extension in the distance to which lethal overpressure is reached for any class of target. Thus, an 'ideal' 1 kiloton neutron bomb will destroy structures by blast only over an area about one-quarter as large as an 8 kiloton nuclear explosive (whether neutron bomb or plain old fission bomb). But for a small class of military targets resistant to blast but vulnerable to radiation (tank crews or soldiers in open foxholes), the lethal area is about the same. Since a 1 kiloton neutron bomb is almost certain to cost considerably more than a 10 kiloton fission bomb, its 'advantage' stems not from any increase in military effectiveness but from the possible benefits of reduced lethality. Unfortunately, although radiation in doses above 5,000rem not only kills tank crews but also incapacitates them in a matter of minutes, exposures of only 400rem under wartime conditions (i.e., doses received over a brief interval of time) will kill military or civilians after a delay of a week or so.

From the arms control point of view, the neutron bomb is a more expensive way to get less destruction and should be opposed by arms controllers only if it is believed substantially and irresponsibly to increase the risk of war. Certainly, NATO military planners should welcome the 'threat' of the Soviet Union to develop and deploy neutron bombs if the United States introduced them into the NATO armamentarium.

THE 'CAPTOR' MINE: A NOVEL ANTI-SUBMARINE WEAPON

The United States is equipping its anti-submarine forces with the CAPTOR ASW mine, which consists of an encapsulated Mk-46 torpedo, capable of mooring in deep water and deliverable by aircraft, surface ship, or submarine. After a long period of development and tests, CAPTOR has been demonstrated incapable of firing at surface ships and to have a good probability of destroying submarines at any currently achievable depth which come within the acquisition range of the mine. A CAPTOR barrier could secure the Greenland-Iceland-United Kingdom gap of some 700 miles. Some 300 mines might provide 30 per cent attrition of Soviet submarines making a round trip from their bases into the North Atlantic and back. Such a mine barrier has an effective life of at least six months, with an investment cost only a small fraction of that for a nuclear attack submarine force which might provide similar attrition over the same barrier length. Enough CAPTOR to mount some 30 such barriers could be bought for a billion dollars, the cost of only four or five nuclear attack submarines.

The utility of nuclear attack submarines to destroy merchant shipping will also be substantially impaired in the future by the very high cost of nuclear-powered attack submarines (SSNs) and by their relatively small load of torpedoes or anti-shipping cruise missiles. Modern container ships make 25 knots, and such a speed requires a nuclear submarine to produce a lot of noise in order to get into firing position. Furthermore, the United States has begun development of a set of weapons (Arapahoe) which are to be put into standard containers and deck-mounted on merchant ships, either for self-protection or to offer a readily augmented force. The latter could include, for instance, ASW helicopter capability, ASROC (anti-submarine rocket) launchers, towed acoustic sensors, and the like, which would pose a very serious threat to a submarine within torpedo range of a merchant ship.

NEW STRATEGIC BASING CONCEPTS

Although there has been much discussion of land-based mobile missiles, of covered trenches for deceptive basing, of multiple aim-point basing, a particularly good augmentation or supplement to the US strategic force could be small submersible vehicles deployed within 200 miles of the US coasts, each vehicle carrying perhaps two encapsulated ICBMs. Missiles carrying some 11 large (Mk-12A) warheads seem possible, with a responsiveness and accuracy entirely comparable with that which could be obtained from missiles based in silos. The near-shore basing could result in short tours of duty for the sailors (one month), non-nuclear propulsion (fuel cells), and an over-all displacement for the vessel (including two missiles) of about 700 tons. External carriage of the missiles should achieve a 95 per cent at-sea record, with an over-all investment per missile in the range of $20 million, including the submarine vessel. If 400 such missiles were deployed, with perhaps 4 000 ready MIRV warheads, the Soviet Union might have good cause to regard this as a substantial threat against its ICBM silos. Soviet ability to deploy a comparable system is impeded by her lack of coastline comparable with that of the U.S., and systems of similar survivability might have considerably higher cost for the Soviet Union.

NAVAL CRUISE MISSILES

A ship is so obvious on the ocean and such a valuable target that not only the Soviet Union but also Third World nations possess and will soon possess much more capable anti-ship forces based on land, in submarines, or on small surface ships. The defence against such cruise missile attack is likely to be a point defence from the target ship. It is unlikely that the few US aircraft carriers would be able to survive massive cruise attack from Soviet forces in a large-scale war. The aircraft carrier is likely to be replaced by ships and capabilities bearing a closer relation to a more narrowly defined set of missions for the Navy.

Contributing very substantially to naval capabilities will be ocean surveillance by radar satellites like the Soviet satellite which fell on Canadian territory in January 1978.

'NAVSTAR': HIGH PRECISION GUIDANCE
OF WEAPONRY, USING SATELLITES

The United States is now deploying a second-generation military (and civilian) navigation and guidance satellite system, which promises 25-foot accuracy in three dimensions the world over, with updates at 0.1 second intervals. Such a system can revolutionize the accuracy and cost of munitions, guiding tactical munitions all the way to their targets with an accuracy of 20 feet or so if the target (bridge, radar, silo, aircraft shelter, or the like) has been located in the common NAVSTAR grid. Furthermore, such accuracy will be attainable with a receiver/computer costing about $1000 or, alternatively, with a simple transceiver on the weapon, with processing in some mother vehicle or direction centre. Such capabilities will put a major premium on precision target location in the same system, on battlefield observation by small drone aircraft, and on the capability to jam (and to counter the jamming of) NAVSTAR signals.

If the NAVSTAR satellites were the only source of accurate guidance data for such weapons, the NAVSTAR constellation would be put into jeopardy of destruction by the Soviet Union. Fortunately, in any tactical theatre, the satellites could be supplemented with or replaced by a set of airborne (and balloon-borne or rocket-launched) transmitters, which could provide significant anti-jam margin as well as fully replacing the NAVSTAR satellites locally.

Can these very high accuracies be used to threaten strategic missile silos by means of a high-explosive attacking force? No, because there are both active and passive defences which can easily protect a hard concrete silo against a few hundred pounds of high explosive. For instance, simply providing a steel 'blasting net' such as used to cover rocks in a city (while dynamite is detonated on the rocks) around the silo can effectively prevent access by cruise missiles to the silo. Furthermore, even nuclear-armed cruise missiles can have considerable trouble getting within a required 300m of a silo if it is defended by means of an effective SAM system mounted essentially on the silo cover. Of course, if the kill radius against the silo is 200m, the kill radius against an ordinary SAM of 10psi hardness might be about 1.2km, so several successive nuclear-armed cruise missiles could well attack the silo.

IMPROVED AIR DEFENCES

The United States has essentially no air defence against strategic attack, just as it has no ABM system. The Soviet Union has continued to emphasize air defence, although the US Defense Department is confident of the penetration capability of even the subsonic B-52 in its planned and practised low-altitude role. Supporters of the B-1 have said that the introduction of ALCM on the B-52 will lead the Soviet Union to develop and to deploy long-range airborne-warning-and-control (AWAC) aircraft off the shores of the Soviet Union, together with long-range interceptors capable of destroying the B-52 before it launches its cruise missiles. While there may be some plausibility in this threat, there is no logic, since it would have been at least as valuable to the Soviet Union to develop and to deploy such capabilities against the B-52 itself, which had to penetrate not only to the anticipated ALCM launch line but to the shores themselves of the Soviet Union and across many hundreds of miles of Soviet territory to reach its target. Obviously, the Soviet Union would have deployed such a defence if it could have, considering the expected sorry performance of its interior SAM and fighter defences against the B-52.

Thus it is unlikely in the extreme that the ALCM itself will goad the Soviet Union to attack the much harder job of destroying the ALCM launcher (the B-52). Still, the progress of technology itself could make such an outreach defence preferable to area defence within the Soviet Union. How would such a race turn out? It seems that the advantage is all on the side of the offence, since the defence must perforce depend upon high-power radars carried by large vulnerable aircraft. Among the dozens of missiles which could be carried by the advancing offensive force a few could be nuclear-armed anti-AWAC missiles which could progress at subsonic or supersonic speed and be directed to, or home on, the AWAC vehicle.

EXOTIC WEAPONS

'Directed energy weapons' such as damage-producing lasers and charged-particle beams receive a lot of attention in the press and considerable budgets for exploration. They are less promising when one realizes that they must have some base, they must be used against some specific targets, and that they are in competition with existing and novel means of achieving the same goals. In general, their use may be evaluated in regard to the ability of the potential enemy to *defend* (largely passively) against them, to *destroy* them, or to *deter* their use (for instance by attack on the corresponding target complex, whether by directed energy weapon or more conventional or nuclear means). In this regard, satellites in peacetime are physically subject to damage by ground-based high-energy lasers. All three approaches to protection of the satellites are important, but an additional layer of defence can be sought in bilateral or international treaties protecting satellites in peacetime against damage or destruction.

Enough hundreds of millions of dollars spent on damage-causing lasers or charged-particle beams may well provide capabilities that some faction in the Soviet Union or in the US has a vested interest in trying out. Even if, as I believe, such devices are inferior to improved guided missiles and other systems, they may create substantial impediments to the rationalization of military forces and to the establishment of an otherwise desirable arms control regime.

THE IMPORTANCE OF DOCTRINE

Secretary of Defense Schlesinger proposed in 1975 the development by the United States of a 'hard-target killer', and he also espoused 'limited nuclear options'. Of course, the United States had long had the capability to use its strategic nuclear weapons in other than a total destructive strike, so that the emphasis on limited nuclear options was puzzling. Even more puzzling was the formal testimony by Schlesinger's office to the US Congress that the Soviet Union might launch an attack on the US strategic force and kill as few as 800 000 US citizens, a number which, in the view of the Secretary, apparently would not guarantee a nuclear response by the US against the Soviet Union. Obviously if such views were current on the Soviet side as well, nuclear war would not only be thinkable but even possible as a diversion, a flexing of muscles.

Elsewhere, I have emphasized the stabilizing aspect of strategic nuclear forces if they are given the job to do which they cannot avoid doing well – to attack population, industry, and soft military targets.[1] In addition to the robust capability to carry out such an attack (including command and control systems), the United States (and the Soviet Union) need a doctrine and a declaratory policy for the use of these weapons. In the reference, I propose such policies (including no first use against non-nuclear-weapons states), which not only provide for strategic stability in the avoidance of strategic nuclear war, but also should enhance the reluctance of non-nuclear states to acquire nuclear weapons.

If nations with nuclear weapons want to start nuclear war, there is no way of stopping them. 'Crisis instability' is not just a term; it is nuclear holocaust in the making.

NUCLEAR WEAPONS POSSESSED BY SMALLER POWERS

Nuclear capabilities of smaller states are quite likely to result in substantial destruction of those states or their neighbours. They will surely result also in preparations by the major nuclear-weapons states for pre-emptive or punitive attack on the smaller nuclear-weapons states. Unfortunately for the tidiness of the situation, nuclear weapons of smaller states may be more subject to theft and to use or threatened use by non-national groups, perhaps provoking large-scale police-type actions.

Perhaps the greatest threat leading to nuclear war would be a loss of faith by a substantial fraction of the people in the United States and the Soviet Union that the world was getting better. If that faith were largely replaced by a belief that the world would be a better place with a lot fewer people (even a lot fewer Americans or Soviets), a major barrier to nuclear war would be removed.

CONCLUSION

Weapons developments, as in the past, can be stabilizing or destabilizing. Strictly *nuclear* developments appear limited in potential and are relatively innocuous, except for the proliferation of nuclear weapons to additional states.

Among the two nations with the largest nuclear forces, it continues to be important to avoid developments or postures which lead to crisis instability and the unwanted initiation of nuclear war in a pre-emptive strike on vulnerable land-based missiles. The prospect of effective defences against massive nuclear attack would also be destabilizing, but of somewhat lesser concern. (A more thorough treatment of a prescription for security in a nuclear age is to be found in my 'Reducing Dependence on Nuclear Weapons'.)

So long as conflict and nuclear weapons exist, the world is not totally safe for its people. It does not seem to me, though, to be in the interests of humanity to ignore this salient fact and to attempt to make the world safe for war. No weapon, offensive or defensive, thus far proposed can plausibly remove the destructive capability of nuclear weapons against the wealth and population of nations. Why not let the other fellow spend his money on new technology to which we can later respond, rather than forcing him into fields which do not improve our own security?

The threat of war seems dominated not by weapons developments but by the behaviour of nations – their political goals, economic aspirations, hatreds, as well as by inept and irresponsible actions of government which can be very dangerous in an armed world.

NOTES

1 'Reducing Dependence on Nuclear Weapons: A Second Nuclear Regime', *Nuclear Weapons and World Politics* (New York: McGraw-Hill, 1977)

Nuclear War

8

Nuclear Terrorism and Nuclear War

WILLIAM EPSTEIN

In the period since the Second World War, violence on both the national and international levels has increased, is still increasing, and is not likely to diminish in the years ahead. During the past decade in particular the problem has taken on a new dimension. It is no longer simply a matter of individuals or small groups using acts of violence or the threat of violence to achieve their aims within some national entity. The problem has now taken on an international or transnational character that has become increasingly sophisticated, better organized, and more difficult to cope with.

The massacre at Tel Aviv's Lod Airport by the Japanese Red Army group on behalf of one of the Palestinian liberation groups in May 1972, followed by the attack by Palestinian terrorists on Israeli athletes at the Munich Olympics in September 1972, shocked the world into taking international terrorism seriously. For the purposes of this paper, it is not necessary to have a strict legal definition of terrorism. It is sufficient to describe terrorism as the threat or use of violence by individuals or groups intended to inspire fear (create terror) in order to achieve some objective. International terrorism is terrorism that has foreign or trans-national aspects or effects, contrary to the rules of international law, which usually has some political objective.[1]

The rapid growth in terrorist activities on both the national and inter-national levels in the past few years has been well documented. A 1974 study undertaken for the US Atomic Energy Commission identified more than 400 incidents of international terrorism across state borders or in-volving foreign countries by more than 50 well-armed and well-financed international terrorist groups in the preceding six years. Between January 1968 and January 1978, there were 1 019 incidents of international terrorism in which 1 017 persons were killed and 2 509 were wounded or injured.[2] The number of acts of domestic terrorism and violence by small national groups is much greater, and many of these national groups appear to have international links and to rely on foreign governments or organizations for assistance and asylum, so that a 'terrorist international' seems to be in the process of development. The international basis and connection of terrorist activities has increased their danger as well as the difficulties of controlling them.

A report prepared for the US Department of Justice in October 1977 stated: 'At root is the increasingly nihilistic character of transnational terrorist groups – they are well armed, trained and ruthless, and they have money and technical assets. ... There is no doubt that mass annihilation is feasible – and resourceful, technically oriented thugs are capable of doing it.'[3]

Since most terrorist groups, even well-organized ones with international connections, are relatively small and weak and must produce speedy results, their threats of violence must be all the more dramatic and shocking. The nature of terrorism is such that nuclear weapons and threats would seem to be the ideal and almost inevitable instruments for terrorists if they wish to achieve an extremely high and difficult objective such as the overthrow of a government or the reversal of its policies. By raising the level of horror to nuclear superterrorism, terrorists would raise the stakes and improve the chance of their achieving such a supreme goal as the destruction and replacement of a detested government. In some circumstances terrorism could become a form of total warfare, subject to no rules or restraints. Terrorists who are willing to die for their cause may succeed in acquiring both nuclear weapons and the nerve to utilize them, while less dedicated or more rational persons would hesitate to incur either the risks or the horrors involved in the venture.

There may, of course, be some self-imposed constraints that could prevent or inhibit groups from undertaking acts of nuclear superterrorism. In addition to their concern about the political risks, there could be moral, psychological, and humanitarian restraints that would keep some individuals or groups from embarking on a course of action that might result in cold-blooded mass murder. Revolutionary groups as well as national liberation movements – and their respective situations may differ greatly – might risk alienating the public and creating a backlash of revulsion instead of sympathy. By engaging in nuclear terrorism they might provoke a massive police crackdown and extreme reprisals that could frustrate or abort their efforts.

There is, however, little empirical evidence upon which to base any informed judgment on how terrorists might behave in any given situation. The only evidence from which we can attempt to draw any conclusions is from the field of conventional terrorism. While the mass slaughters engaged in by some of the more extremist Palestinian groups or African guerillas created revulsion among some foreign people, and perhaps also among some of their sympathizers, supporters of such groups or the movements they claimed to represent appeared to approve of the actions and to regard the perpetrators as heroes who had succeeded in advancing their cause.

Some people may regard the use of nuclear weapons at Hiroshima and Nagasaki as a form of unnecessary state terrorism, but it is probably correct to say that in 1945 the overwhelming reaction in the Allied world varied from approval to elation. On the basis of past experience, therefore, not only nihilistic or anarchistic terrorist groups but also those that purport to be part of mass movements that require public support may come to regard nuclear terrorism as providing greater advantages than disadvantages in furthering their aims.

If terrorists who have already demonstrated their capacity and willingness to strike say that they have planted a nuclear bomb in a city and would explode it unless their demands are met, there would be a strong likelihood of their blackmail succeeding. Their prospects would be enhanced if they could convince the authorities that they did, in fact, have a workable device; but even if there were some scepticism about their claim, the risks of not giving in to them might be too great. Who would dare to call their bluff and risk the death and devastation that would result from even a small portable crude bomb with a yield must less than that of the 15 kiloton bomb that destroyed Hiroshima?

There have been 44 nuclear threats in the United States since 1970, but none of these was credible and all failed.[4] Had any of these threats been credible, however, the outcome might have been the opposite. Within the next decade or two, it is highly probable that the threats will become increasingly credible.

TERRORISM AND NUCLEAR PROLIFERATION

It is generally accepted that, despite criticisms of nuclear power as a source of energy and indications of a slow-down or stretch-out in the building of nuclear power plants, there will be a huge upsurge in the use of nuclear power in the next decade or two. The proliferation of nuclear research and power reactors will mean the proliferation of the knowledge of nuclear technology. Even on a conservative estimate, within a decade the number of countries having direct access to nuclear materials and technology will certainly exceed fifty.[5]

This proliferation of peaceful nuclear energy and technology can be harmful in three ways of concern to us. First, it will open the way to such countries manufacturing their own nuclear weapons if they so choose. Despite all of the efforts devoted to prevent the further proliferation of nuclear weapons, most students of the problem appear to regard such proliferation as inevitable, although opinions differ as to the *rate* of proliferation. The number of nuclear weapons in the world today, including tactical ones, is in the tens of thousands. If, as is expected, additional countries do decide to go nuclear, not only will they add to the total number of nuclear weapons in existence, but these additional weapons will be small ones and in all likelihood not as well protected as are those of the more advanced nuclear powers. They will therefore present easier targets for theft or seizure by terrorists or competing military or political factions.

The second harmful effect of the proliferation of nuclear reactors and technology is that this will also result in the proliferation and availability of fissionable material, mainly Pu239. If the world moves into a plutonium economy, with plutonium recycling and fast breeder reactors (which produce more plutonium than the uranium fuel they consume), the amount of plutonium in nuclear facilities in the fuel cycle, in storage, and in transit will be very much greater. As is explained below, the theft or hijacking of plutonium by groups wishing to manufacture nuclear weapons is much easier, safer, and perhaps even more effective in terms of having a usable weapon than is the theft or seizure of an actual nuclear weapon.

Sir Brian Flowers, Chairman of the UK Royal Commission on Environmental Pollution, which reported on nuclear power and the environment stated in 1976: 'Because of its toxic and fissile properties, plutonium offers a unique and powerful weapon to those who are sufficiently determined to impose their will. In these circumstances I do not believe it is a question of *whether* someone will deliberately acquire it for purposes of terrorism or blackmail, but only of when and how often.'[6] With so much plutonium, worth more than \$10 000 per kilogram available in the world, it is also quite likely that a black market in plutonium will develop, so that terrorist groups will be able secretly to buy the plutonium they require.

Finally, as the proliferation of nuclear facilities, material and technology grows, the number of scientists, engineers, and trained personnel who are familiar with the technology of making a nuclear weapon will also increase. There are already in the world today tens of thousands of persons who have considerable expertise in nuclear technology, and in another decade or two they may number in the hundreds of thousands. Their knowledge and expertise will be available to all sorts of governments and the services of some of them will undoubtedly be available for hire also by non-governmental and terrorist groups. One can visualize circumstances where well-financed terrorist groups would arrange and pay for the training of some of their members in various fields of nuclear technology.

HOW TERRORISTS COULD OBTAIN NUCLEAR WEAPONS[7]

A terrorist group could obtain nuclear weapons in three ways – by stealing or seizing a weapon, by stealing or seizing the fissionable material required for a nuclear explosion, and by manufacturing their own bomb.

A terrorist group or political or military faction might regard stealing or hijacking a tactical nuclear weapon from some Armed Forces' storage bunker or in transit, as the best or easiest way of acquiring a nuclear bomb without having to go to all of the trouble of fashioning one. And such a stolen bomb could have a yield of considerable size, while that of a home-made one would probably be small. Stealing or hijacking a nuclear weapon from one of the present five nuclear-weapon powers, however, would be a very difficult task and hence one that terrorists might regard as least likely to succeed.

A different problem arises in the event that a number of new nuclear-weapon powers emerge in the next decade or two. As indicated above, many of them probably will not be able to apply as strict physical security measures and supervision as do the great nuclear powers. Nor are they likely to have the sophisticated locks and other control devices (PALs; see Chapter 4) that the more industrialized powers employ. Questions of command, control and communications, problems of inventory control, and the risk of the theft of a nuclear weapon, are still matters of serious concern even for the United States, the most sophisticated of all countries in these areas.[8] It therefore seems likely that the theft or seizure of some nuclear weapon will become a much less difficult task as more countries acquire their own nuclear weapon stockpiles. No matter how effective safeguards and physical security measures may be in the more advanced industrial states, if they are not equally effective in all other countries, the high technology countries may find themselves threatened by nuclear materials stolen in some other part of the world.

Much more is known about the dangers of diversion, theft, or seizure of fissionable material from civilian facilities or plants. Fissionable materials can be stolen either from a uranium enrichment plant, a fuel fabrication plant, a fuel reprocessing plant, or from facilities used for storing the growing stocks of plutonium. Fissionable material in transit between these various stages in the fuel cycle would be most vulnerable. Special security problems which affect material in transit either within a country or between countries have not been satisfactorily solved. While efforts are being made to improve the level of physical security and safeguards, the record is spotty and varies from country to country. In the last few years there have been a number of reports of thousands of pounds of enriched uranium and plutonium simply disappearing and remaining unaccounted for.[9] A General Accounting Office report released by the US House Sub-committee in August 1976 stated that more than 50 tons of fissionable material was unaccounted for in 34 facilities operated by the Energy Research and Development Administration and that the controls were so poor that recovery actions were precluded.[10] A later report on the 15 civilian facilities operating under licence by the Nuclear Regulatory Commission indicated some additional thousands of pounds were missing.

Once a well-organized terrorist group succeeded in obtaining the necessary fissionable material by theft or seizure or purchase on the black market, the actual designing and manufacturing of a 'home-made' bomb would not present a great obstacle.

While there is some disagreement about just how difficult it is to make an atomic bomb, many experts regard it as a comparatively simple matter. The technical information necessary to construct a bomb is all available in the open literature. The Encyclopedia Americana contains an outline in detail of how to make a fission bomb.[11] In 1966, the Atomic Energy Commission conducted a study at the Lawrence Livermore Laboratory in California to test the ability of persons without special expertise to design a nuclear weapon. Two young PhD physicists, using unclassified material, designed a bomb in six months which AEC experts said would come within 10 per cent of the predicted yield if exploded. Similar experiences have been reported with some frequency in recent years. The fact that young scientists and even bright undergraduates[12] can design a nuclear bomb does not mean that they would find it easy actually to build a practical device. It seems clear, however, that a team of scientists and engineers could do so. As indicated previously, a dedicated and well-financed terrorist organization could probably hire the necessary personnel from the tens of thousands already trained, or even arrange for the training of some of their own members. It therefore seems reasonable to conclude that a determined terrorist group would be able to manufacture, steal, or otherwise acquire nuclear weapons, if it chose to do so.

RADIOLOGICAL WEAPONS AND NUCLEAR SABOTAGE

The explosion or threat of explosion of a nuclear bomb undoubtedly poses the greatest conceivable danger from terrorism, but they are not the only forms of nuclear terrorism. Another danger, although a lesser one, is that plutonium or other radio-active nucleides could be used for the dispersal of radioactivity.

Plutonium is one of the most poisonous of all substances and small particles of powdered plutonium oxide, if inhaled, are exceedingly toxic and can cause death within a period of weeks or years depending on the level of the dosage. A plutonium dispersal device such as an aerosol canister would be an effective radiological weapon if introduced into the ventilating system of a large office building or factory, and could lead to the death of several thousands of people. It could also be released by attaching a leaking container to a taxicab, dropping it from the window of a tall building, or by the explosion of an ordinary time-bomb.[13] While the actual health effects might not be felt for some time, perhaps even years, the psychological effects could create immediate panic and necessitate the evacuation and decontamination of the downtown areas of a number of large cities. If one such terrorist attack with radiological weapons succeeded, subsequent similar threats would be encouraged and be more likely to achieve their aims.

Another danger of dispersal of radio-activity arises from the possibility of sabotaging a nuclear power station.[14] Radio-active materials contained in the core of a typical nuclear power reactor, if dispersed in the atmosphere upwind from a heavily populated area, could cause thousands of human casualties and long-term health effects, as well as land contamination. However, to sabotage a power station and to cause the core to melt so as to release a substantial portion of the radio-activity would require a highly organized effort for success. Even if it did succeed, the consequences of such an act of sabotage would be much less than that of a low-yield nuclear explosion in a highly populated area, or the effective dispersal of a kilogram of plutonium throughout a very large office building. While the threat of the use of radiological weapons by terrorists, or even the sabotaging of a power plant, is a distinct future possibility, it cannot be regarded as effective a means of creating terror as the threat of exploding a nuclear bomb. The latter is the supreme instrument of super-terrorism.

SCENARIOS FOR NUCLEAR TERRORISM

The type of terrorism that most concerns us is that undertaken by political groups such as revolutionaries, extreme nationalists, rebel military forces, and other such groups that aspire to change a government or take over control of a state. Such groups are likely to be not only the most highly motivated and dedicated, but also well organized and financed, and to include highly skilled and trained personnel among their members. Fortunately, until now, terrorists have concentrated their actions on conventional weapons. However, as both the opportunities for undertaking nuclear terrorism and the vulnerability of potential targets for such terrorism continue to increase as the nuclear age evolves, we can begin to envisage a wide range of possible scenarios.

The following brief outline of possible scenarios is not intended to be exhaustive, but is meant merely to provide examples of some of the more obvious ways in which nuclear terrorism might operate.[15]

The first and most simple way is for a revolutionary group publicly to threaten to use one or more nuclear weapons against the capital or governmental buildings (and their occupants) or against one or more large cities in the group's own country, unless their demands are met. Their demands might include dismantling of armed forces, transfer of governmental powers to a new body, release of political prisoners, redistribution of land, payment of enormous sums by way of ransom, etc. A small nuclear bomb might be exploded in an uninhabited area to provide the terrorist threat with greater credibility and coercion. Except for the attempted evacuation of the threatened cities, which might not be possible because public panic and a spontaneous mass exodus blocked all the highways and created chaos, the threatened authorities would have little or no alternative but to comply, or make the best deal possible.

In the case of a national liberation movement demanding independence or freedom from domination, the threat could be carried out either against the government of the dominating colonial or imperialist power in its country, or against the local administration or occupying forces in the case of a colony or dominated state. Since the terrorists would be unlikely to want to wreak disaster on their own people, they would probably proceed against the foreign territory.

A second set of scenarios can be developed in the case of a 'stable' country that is a nuclear-weapon power. If there is civil strife, rebellion, or civil war, some competing military group or faction might seize all or part of the country's nuclear stockpile. An official army command opposed to its government, or a cabal of fanatic colonels, might seize the nuclear weapons and undertake a coup d'état supported by a threat to use the weapons either in the home country or a foreign country in order to take over the government. For example, in 1967, during the Cultural Revolution in China, there were reports that the military commander of Sinkiang Province had threatened to seize the nuclear base there if the Maoists attempted to take over the provincial government.[16] A somewhat similar example relating to nuclear materials occurred in March 1973, when an armed terrorist group attacked and temporarily occupied the Atucha nuclear power plant in Argentina. It is easy to visualize circumstances in the case of a civil war, revolution, riot or guerilla activity where nuclear materials can be seized by one of the contending parties or by desperadoes for sabotage, dispersion of radio-activity, or fabricating a bomb for purposes of terrorism.

As nuclear weapons continue to proliferate over the next two decades, in particular to countries prone to instability because of domestic or foreign political crises, the possibilities for and likelihood of nuclear weapons falling into the hands of unauthorized groups will increase.

A third scenario concerns the use of nuclear terrorism for 'proxy' nuclear warfare, or what is sometimes called 'surrogate' warfare. In such a case, the actual use of the nuclear weapons becomes important, rather than the threat of its use. It therefore differs from the usual case of nuclear terrorism where the terrorists seek publicity, where success depends on the threat producing the desired result, and where the actual use of the weapon might become counter-productive. The surrogate act might be initiated by some 'crazy state' and be carried out by it clandestinely or through some non-governmental terrorist group.

An example of such use of nuclear weapons might be to upset peace negotiations between Israel and one or more Arab states, negotiations which might be regarded as inimical to Palestinian interests. Either the PLO or some other extremist Palestinian group might be used as a proxy or front by one of the 'rejectionist' Arab states. Another example of such terrorism might be for some truculent state or group wishing to undermine détente between the US and USSR, or to block political, military, or SALT negotiations between them that seemed likely to succeed. In such a case an alien third party or alienated military organization might even arrange for a terrorist group to 'steal' one of its nuclear weapons in order to appear to be itself innocent. Another possibility would be for some terrorist group to explode a nuclear bomb anonymously and without advance warning in order to destroy or damage the military power (selected armed forces and armaments, or war industries) or the economic power (selected industries, plants or natural resources such as oil fields) of a perceived hostile or enemy state.

ASSESSING THE LIKELIHOOD OF NUCLEAR TERRORISM

From all of the foregoing it would seem reasonable to conclude that both the scale and scope of violence and terrorism will increase in the years to come; so too will the vulnerability of society and the opportunities for engaging in all forms of terrorism.[17]

Terrorism today, particularly international terrorism, may still be in its infancy. So too are international efforts to curb it or cope with it. Indeed these efforts must be described as a failure up to the present time.[18] Terrorism is a human, psychological and political problem for which there is no technological 'fix'. It is a matter of surprise and concern that national governments have paid relatively little attention, and taken less action, in efforts to deal with terrorism on either a national or international scale.

In the highly complex society of today and tomorrow there is a web of relationships linking human activities. The food we eat and the goods we produce depend in very large part on power, on the supply of energy, on transportation, and on oil. If any link in the chain is broken the whole complex can be interrupted. As a result the targets for terrorism multiply, as also do the consequences.

Jenkins sums up the results of the research on terrorism at the Rand Corporation as follows:

'The increasing vulnerabilities in our society plus the increasing capacities for violence afforded by new developments in weaponry mean that smaller and smaller groups have a greater and greater capacity for disruption and destruction. Or, put another way, the small bands of extremists and irreconcilables that have always existed may become an increasingly potent force. This could have profound political consequences. Nations maintain their credentials in the last resort by maintaining their monopoly over the means of violence.

'As the balance of military (destructive) power shifts away from national armies toward smaller armed groups that do not necessarily represent or confine their activities to any particular nation, national governments may lose their monopoly over the means of large-scale violence and we may see the emergence of permanent subnational and transnational entities.

'The world that emerges is an unstable collection of nations, ministates, autonomous ethnic substates, governments in exile, national liberation fronts, guerrilla groups aspiring to international recognition and legitimacy via violence, and a collection of ephemeral but disruptive terrorist organizations, some of which are linked together in vague alliances, some perhaps the proteges of foreign states. ... It is a world of formal peace between nations – free of open warfare except, perhaps, for brief periods – but of a higher level of political violence.'[19]

There is no evidence that terrorists up to the present have made any serious attempts to acquire nuclear weapons or the material for making weapons, or for use as a radiological weapon. As to whether terrorists will go nuclear in the future, Jenkins has noted the attractions of nuclear weapons and concluded: 'It cannot be assumed that these possibilities have been ignored by existing or potential terrorists or that they will not be considered in the future.'[20]

As indicated previously, the continuing vertical and horizontal proliferation of nuclear weapons in the world, as well as the proliferation of nuclear reactors, will increase the likelihood of the occurrence of nuclear terrorism. The increasing acceptance of and familiarity with nuclear weapons and materials will tend to erode or breach the psychological barrier or taboo which separates nuclear from conventional weapons. Finally the increasing frustrations, resentments and, indeed, desperation of the poor nations of the world because of their economic and social conditions, and the growing development gap between them and the rich nations, may well turn them or non-state groups and organizations to the consideration of blackmail, violence, and terrorism as possible ways of solving their problems. Within a decade or two more than a score of these countries will have the technology and the nuclear materials that will give them a nuclear weapon capacity. The temptations to exploit this capability may become irresistable.[21]

The successful attacks by Israel at Entebbe, by West Germany at Mogadishu, and the more costly Egyptian attack at Larnaca, may indicate a trend for governments to take matters into their own hands and counter terrorist threats by military force. Such actions may be expected to increase in the future and may continue to be successful against conventional forms of terrorism (such as the hijacking of planes and the holding of hostages or the seizure of plants – nuclear or otherwise). It is much less certain that they would be successful against nuclear threats. There would be a risk that the military action might in fact precipitate the threatened explosion of the nuclear weapon with all its disastrous consequences. If the terrorist threat also involved the use of the weapon in a foreign state, military action against the terrorists would become much more complex and could itself create dangerous international tensions. Thus, if the use of military force is likely to be more effective against conventional rather than against nuclear terrorism, this may have the effect of hastening the advent of nuclear terrorism.

On the basis of the evidence available at present, and despite the hazards of attempting to predict the future, it seems reasonable to conclude that it is increasingly likely, indeed almost inevitable, that terrorist organizations will move into nuclear terrorism before the end of the century.

NUCLEAR TERRORISM AND NUCLEAR WAR

Even if nuclear terrorism becomes, as we have said, increasingly likely, indeed almost inevitable, the question remains as to whether it would tend to increase the likelihood or chances of a nuclear war.

The various scenarios for nuclear terrorism outlined above are 'worst-case' possibilities. They are none the less technically feasible and politically plausible. The chances of one or more of them leading to nuclear war cannot be ruled out. While most observers would regard the danger of their occurring at present or in the near future as posing a very low probability, and of their resulting in a nuclear war an even lower one, the consequences are appalling and the margin for error is very slim. It is not possible to predict or assess with any degree of accuracy how and to what extent the dangers will increase after the next five years or during the next two decades, but it seems reasonable to expect that increase they will.

Here again we can project various scenarios all of which could result in nuclear war or a real risk of such war.[22] So long as the threats or actual use of nuclear weapons are confined by the terrorist groups to actions within their own countries under the first and second scenarios, the risk of another country becoming involved and the dangers of a nuclear war occurring would be minimal. But if the revolutionary or liberationist group, or the military group wanting to engineer a coup d'état, wished to spare their own people and country by threatening a foreign country or a neo-colonial power, there would be an immediate possibility of strong military action by the threatened state. If the threatened state were itself a nuclear-weapon power, or were allied to one, there would always be some risk that nuclear weapons would be used or, at least, threatened to be used as a deterrent to the nuclear terrorism, or in retaliation for it. This could result in a game of 'nuclear chicken', where the odds might be on the side of desperate terrorists, with the possibility of the use of the weapons by both sides.

In the case of the second scenario – i.e., in a civil war or an attempted coup d'état – there would be a race by both the government forces and the rebels to seize the nuclear weapon stockpiles or to deny the other party access to them. If either or both warring factions managed to seize all or some of the nuclear weapons, the situation might become unstable and hazardous. Can one have much doubt that in such conflicts or civil strife as existed in Northern Ireland over the years, or in Lebanon during the height of the civil war there, if either or both factions had gained possession of nuclear weapons there would be a high probability that they would have been used?

Perhaps the greatest danger of nuclear war would arise in the case of the third scenario, where nuclear terrorism is used as a form of surrogate warfare in a proliferated world.

In any case of acute political confrontation or conflict between two states, whether it be North and South Korea, China-Taiwan, India-Pakistan, Israel-Egypt, Black Africa-South Africa, or other such confrontations where survival was in issue, if the parties were in possession of nuclear weapons, their use or threat of their use can be visualized not only by the governments concerned but also by non-governmental military or political groups, with or without governmental connivance. Such action might occur earlier as a result of some party wishing to launch a pre-emptive strike in order to win quickly or by a party facing imminent defeat in a conventional attack.

In such cases the reluctant involvement of the super-powers can easily be visualized either as guarantors or committed allies, or even as interested parties, on opposite sides of local nuclear confrontations. It can, of course, be assumed that the super-powers would do their utmost to keep from becoming too deeply involved and that they would attempt to undertake war-avoidance and damage-limiting efforts which might even amount to disengagement. Nevertheless, in certain circumstances, for example, if Mongolia were to become involved in a nuclear confrontation with China, or Warsaw Pact allies with some West German nuclear terrorists, it might not be easy for the Soviet Union to stand apart. Similarly, in a proliferated world, it would be difficult for the United States to avoid becoming involved in the event that South Korea, Israel, Saudi Arabia, West Germany, or Japan were the subjects of a surrogate nuclear attack by some nuclear terrorist group.

While the involvement of the super-powers or other great powers possessing nuclear weapons would not, of course, necessarily result in nuclear war, it could lead to nuclear confrontations that greatly increased the risks of such war by accident, by miscalculation, by human or mechanical breakdown, and by inadequate command, control, and communications procedures and measures.

CONCLUSION

Among the complex of problems in modern society that make possible the development of nuclear terrorism, the most important is widespread nuclear proliferation. Even on a local or regional level, the spread of nuclear weapons and technology could lead to nuclear terrorism and to the undermining of the stability of world order. The legitimacy and viability of governmental authority might come into question, as would the credibility of the existing alliance systems, and a situation verging on international or global anarchy could develop. In such a world tensions and crises would multiply and the actions of states, both great and small, would become impossible of accurate calculation. A highly unstable and dangerous world situation would develop. The concept of mutual nuclear deterrence could become meaningless, and might indeed be replaced by a situation of constant nuclear threat. In such a world the risk of nuclear war resulting from nuclear terrorism would certainly increase. It would be a rash or irrational man who did not take this risk seriously.

NOTES

1   Various authors have proposed definitions of terrorism and international terrorism, none of which are wholly satisfactory. See Brian M. Jenkins, 'International Terrorism: A New Mode of Conflict', in Carlton and Schaerf, eds., *International Terrorism and World Security* (London, 1975); and Mason Willrich and Theodore B. Taylor, *Nuclear Theft: Risks and Safeguards* (Cambridge, MA, 1974). For a discussion of the anatomy of terrorism and of non-governmental proliferation generally, see chap. 19, 'The

Danger of Proliferation to Terrorists and Criminals', in William Epstein, *The Last Chance: Nuclear Proliferation and Arms Control* (New York: The Free Press, 1976).

2   Personal letter to the author from Brian Jenkins, Director of Research on Terrorism at the Rand Corporation, Santa Monica, CA, 1978

3   Robert H. Kupperman, Chief Scientist, US Arms Control and Disarmament Agency, 'Facing Tomorrow's Terrorist Incident Today,' 1, 2, and 25

4   Jenkins, 'International Terrorism'

5   Projections of the proliferation of research and power reactors and of fissionable material in the world are contained in Willrich and Taylor, *Nuclear Theft*; Epstein, *The Last Chance*; and SIPRI, *The Nuclear Age* (Stockholm, 1975). The International Atomic Energy Agency (Vienna) and the US Energy Research and Development Administration (Washington) make annual surveys and forecasts.

6   'Nuclear Power and the Public Interest: A Watchdog's View', *Bulletin of the Atomic Scientists*, December 1976, 27

7   See Roberta Wohlstetter, 'Terror on a Grand Scale', *Survival*, 28, no. 2 (May-June 1976)

8   Lloyd Dumas, 'National Insecurity in the Nuclear Age', *Bulletin of the Atomic Scientists*, May 1976. Also Bruce G. Blair and Garry D. Brewer, 'The Terrorist Threat to World Nuclear Programs', *Journal of Conflict Resolution*, 21, no. 3, (Sept. 1977)

9   L. D. DeNike, 'Radioactive Malevolence', *Bulletin of the Atomic Scientists*, 30, no. 4 (April 1974), 16-20

10   *New York Times*, 6 August 1976

11   See the discussion in Willrich and Taylor, *Nuclear Theft*.

12   *New York Times*, 27 February 1975; *New York Magazine*, 18 July 1977; and *New York Times*, 26 March 1978

13   Willrich and Taylor, *Nuclear Theft*. See also the discussion of radiological weapons by David Krieger in 'What Happens If ...?' 'Terrorists, Revolutionaries and Nuclear Weapons', *Annals of the American Academy of Political and Social Science*, March 1977, 44-57

14   Michael Flood, 'Nuclear Sabotage', *Bulletin of the Atomic Scientists* (October 1974)

15   See the following sources for a discussion and analysis of a number of possible scenarios: Carleton and Shaerf, *International Terrorism*; Willrich and Taylor, *Nuclear Theft*; Blair and Brewer, 'The Terrorist Threat'; Krieger, 'What Happens If ...?'; Lewis A. Dunn, 'Nuclear Proliferation and World Politics', in *Annals of the American Academy of Political and Social Science*, March, 1977, 96-109; David M. Rosenbaum, 'Nuclear

Terror', in *International Security* (Winter 1977), 140-61; and Thomas C. Schelling, 'Who Will Have the Bomb?', ibid., 1, no. 1 (1976), 77-91. Schelling says, 'The organization most likely to engage in nuclear terrorism will be national governments' (84).

16 D. G. Brennan, 'The Risks of Spreading Weapons: A Historical Case', *Arms Control and Disarmament*, 1 (1968), 59-60, cites both these examples.
17 See Jenkins, 'International Terrorism'; Krieger, 'What Happens If ...?'
18 See Seymour Maxwell Finger, 'International Terrorism and the United Nations', in Yonah Alexander ed., *International Terrorism: National, Regional and Global* (New York, 1976); Fereydoun Hoveyda, 'The Problem of International Terrorism at the United Nations', in *Terrorism: An International Journal*, 1, no. 1 (1977).
19 Brian Jenkins, 'Rand's Research on Terrorism', in *Terrorism*, 1, no. 1 (1977), 94.
20 Brian Jenkins, 'The Potential for Nuclear Terrorism', P-5877 (The Rand Corporation, Santa Monica, May 1977)
21 See Epstein, *The Last Chance*.
22 See Dunn, 'Nuclear Proliferation', ref 17.

9

Local Wars and Their Escalation

SHALHEVETH FREIER

Forecasts often go wrong. This is true in particular of sombre forebodings. It is in the nature of things that misfortune can be more compellingly argued than propitious constellations.

In many countries, hatreds are nursed and military ascendancy and the successful use of force fire national ambitions. Such attitudes are common to many of the candidate countries for local wars, in Africa and the Middle East. But such wars by the end of the century cannot be discounted either in Southeast Asia or South America. These ambitions are, moreover, often fanned by the support the contestants enjoy from the big powers. If these attitudes, ambitions, and practices continue to prevail, then indeed a steady rate of up to five local wars a year may persist twenty years from now.

There may be crude nuclear weapons and means of delivery available in the areas mentioned above, with none of the refinements of the balance of terror which restrain the super-powers. Their employment in war will seem more tempting and less fateful, since their number and power, when pitted against the size and vulnerability of the victim, may not add up to a crippling blow. It is unlikely that by their nature such weapons will make a local war more contagious. Rather, local wars are likely to escalate through the growing involvement of the super-powers in local conflicts. If the super-powers realize their interests and responsibilities in time, it is just possible that the worst can be avoided.

FORECASTS GO WRONG, AS OFTEN AS NOT

Forecasts of the type attempted in this paper suffer from an important disability. They are made by extrapolating from present attitudes and situations and take no account of abrupt changes which intervene for better or for worse in the shaping of the future. Let me illustrate this point with a few examples.

Up to the Cuban crisis of 1962, the possibility of a war over divided Germany and Berlin loomed large on the European scene. The Cuban missile crisis added no new knowledge concerning the destructive potential of nuclear weapons, but brought the super-powers within the immediacy of a nuclear exchange. As the super-powers managed to pull back from the brink, tension in Europe subsided and has not again risen to the level of those times. The stark realization of nuclear annihilation as an alternative blunted the acerbity of the European confrontation. It was the experience of the Cuban crisis, and no new knowledge or thinking, which induced that sudden relaxation.

Just as circumstances – such as the Cuban crisis – could bring about an abrupt change of thinking, it is leaders at all times who have surprised and successfully defied conventional logic. Churchill defied the odds which were heavily weighted against his country's chances in the Second World War; de Gaulle conferred independence on Algeria in 1962, and the much vaunted rising of one million Frenchmen in Algeria against this decision never came to pass; Ben Gurion went ahead with the establishment of Israel in pursuance of the UN resolution in this sense, even though it appeared likely that the infant state would be crushed by the invading armies of the countries around.

Thus it is manifest that circumstances or people often sway the course of events in unpredictable fashion. But it is with an attempt at prediction that we are supposed to deal. This will be done with appropriate diffidence.

LOCAL WARS ARE LIKELY TO CONTINUE

Between now and the year 2000, changes for the worse are to be expected in a number of respects. World population may increase from four to six billion people, and the provision of food, energy, and other resources is likely to become less adequate through scarcity and inefficient distribution. It may be doubted that resolute and comprehensive action will be taken to forestall the impending aggravation, without intervening upheavals and disasters being required to convey the message to governments. There seems no way out but that the super-powers come around to the view that joint action for the benefit of the globe has precedence over the pursuit of their conflicting interests. If the pressures that lead to local wars persist, as I believe they will, the most likely areas for such wars in the coming two decades would presumably include Africa, the Middle East, and to a lesser extent Southeast Asia and South America. It is unlikely that there will be local wars in Europe at all, or, at any rate, wars of appreciable duration. As long as war between the super-powers remains a possibility, a local war in Europe could quickly degenerate into a general war or would otherwise be quelled quickly in order to avoid this calamitous contingency.

This statement may need elaboration. Peace in Europe is manifestly tied to the military balance between the NATO and Warsaw Pact alliances, for the time being. The outcome of war, say, between East and West Germany, would vitally affect the credibility of both alliances – in proportion to the fortunes of their champion – and it is hardly thinkable that the United States and their allies or the Soviet Union and its allies could remain passive by-standers in such an appeal to arms. Also, if Greece and Turkey, both within NATO, were to come to blows, it is likely that every effort would be expended by the NATO allies to bring such a war to an early end. A protracted war could seriously undermine that part of NATO and invite Soviet support for one of the contestants.

It could be argued that the super-powers would try to keep local conflicts local just because they are mindful of the dangers of a possible escalation. I doubt that this is feasible if there were a war in Europe or that it will be feasible eventually anywhere.

Why do local wars seem likely in the areas I have mentioned? It is, I believe, generally true (though there are exceptions) that there are differences of attitude between the established, industrialized countries and the developing countries. There are national ambitions and sources of pride in the established, industrialized countries which can be satisfied from within. These goals include social advancement, productivity, scientific attainment, realization of the human potential, and a greater awareness that what one lacks cannot be obtained by taking it or demanding it from someone else. What sins these industrialized nations have committed, they have committed in the past. Their present state of attainment is sensitive to war and there is greater emphasis on exertion in peaceful areas of endeavour. Such elements tend to mitigate what temptations for war there might exist.

These inhibitions, however, cannot weigh as strongly in the balance of considerations of the developing, or in particular, the new countries. They stand to lose less by war, and success in a warlike exchange – if it comes their way – is more manifest than the slow and tortuous advance which comes from sustained peaceful effort.

Countries ruled in dictatorial, arbitrary, and mercurial fashion in the extreme instance, and with one or two of these attributes in less extreme cases, are more likely to engage others in wars and seek fulfilment in enhancing their rule. Such tendencies are furthered by the more arguable concern with resources, outlets to the sea, the location of ill-defined borders, and the support the parties obtain from other countries or the super-powers.

It seems probable that many of these countries will more quickly absorb arms and learn the use of them than merely seek satisfaction (or be allowed by their neighbours to seek satisfaction) in improving the quality of life of their citizens. It is generally recognized that the developed countries lag behind in coping socially with the scientific and technological skills of which they dispose. This is truer still of the developing countries, many of which believe that technology transfer alone is the chief ingredient of advance.

In Africa, a situation such as I have described may obtain twenty years from now. In the Middle East and North Africa the fast-changing pattern of alliances made and disrupted (irrespective of Israel) between the countries stretching from the Persian Gulf to the Atlantic Ocean will, I believe, continue to harbour the seeds of local conflicts. Israel itself will continue to attract the animosity of all or some of those countries.

Southeast Asia has been rent by wars for decades, and they continue to occur. However, it may be hoped that the kind of stability which reigns in Europe will settle on that area by the end of the century. The vicinity of the Soviet Union and of China, and the danger of their involvement, may cause more restraint to be imposed on that area by the time this century runs out.

In South America, more so than in the other developing areas of the world, there are countries in which the sense of achievement by realizing their material and human potential, is fast gaining ground. What violent unrest there is upsets mainly the internal fabric of many countries, and it is just possible that this subcontinent will be spared the incidence of local wars by the end of this century – though a nuclear build-up could itself be the cause of tensions that lead to war.

ESCALATION OF LOCAL WARS – NUCLEAR WEAPONS

The Non-Proliferation Treaty has undoubtedly served as a brake on the indigenous development, production, and testing of nuclear weapons. However, it is agreed that a determined effort on the part of governments to subvert their commitment can succeed. Nuclear weapons-free zones are for the time being only convincing as far as the Antarctic and the Moon are concerned.

It seems, therefore, quite possible that within twenty years further nuclear capabilities will appear in areas in which local conflicts are likely, and that the development of nuclear weapons – manifest or surmised – by one party to a potential conflict is likely to be followed by a sense of need on the part of the other. If one contemplates the worst contingency, a good part of the indigenous technical or scientific infrastructure, generally associated with the ability to produce weapons, can be dispensed with. There will be enough expertise commercially available in the industrialized countries in order to enrich uranium with the aid of even non-economical enrichment processes, or to build small heavy water reactors and reprocessing plants in order to procure plutonium. Moreover, there is no absolute need for self-sufficiency. Indeed, countries may divide the labour between them, each contributing whatever their technical expertise and political circumstances permit, and then sharing the spoils.

Despite constraints, present practice in the nuclear market bears out that some of the supplier nations will trade knowledge and plants, with moderate scruples, for commercial benefit and long-term involvement in the recipient countries. This practice causes one to believe that, on balance, the mutual temptations which tie suppliers and customers will win out over the containment of nuclear capability.

If nothing changes, there might be a good number of countries in twenty years from now with a nuclear weapons potential in possible areas of conflict.

In Africa, at least, the uranium producers will legitimately wish to install enrichment services and thereby enhance their profits. If nuclear power successfully rides the storm of controversy, as I believe it will, the suppliers of enriched uranium may not only capitalize on their resources financially but also use nature's dispensation for political leverage, in the image of the oil-producing countries.

It is worth mentioning that there are at present six countries in Africa which have at least one element of the nuclear fuel cycle on their territory (Angola, Gabon, Mauritania, Niger, South Africa, Zaire). Of course, there is no comparison with respect to nuclear capability and political circumstance between South Africa, which produces enriched uranium and is highly industrialized, and Mauritania, which merely has plentiful uranium ore. Yet, if the political motive exists, there could be one or two countries below the Sahara, and in addition to South Africa, which might dispose of nuclear weapons by the end of the century.

In the Middle East, Israel is reported to be able to marshal adequate competence, if a decision to develop nuclear weapons were made. Egypt and Iran could presumably do likewise, and by the end of the century Iraq and Syria could well acquire the requisite knowledge and plant. In North Africa, Col. Qaddafi of Libya has been trying to shop for nuclear weapons for a long time. These attempts have been generally laughed off. But Libya has a firm industrial program for the expansion of its heavy industry (including at least a 10 per cent share in Fiat). If the quest for nuclear weapons continues, Libya may obtain them by the end of the century. Libya's neighbours in the Maghreb may in turn be induced to parry the mounting danger to themselves.

In South America, Argentina, Brazil, and Mexico are building nuclear industries and are certain, if they feel the need, to have a nuclear weapons potential by the year 2000. Of course, other countries in South America could do likewise.

In Southeast Asia, it seems evident that Pakistan would wish to have nuclear devices, now that India has set one off. And if one seeks further potential nuclear weapon countries, Vietnam and Indonesia could conceivably qualify.

These speculations, which will be moderated in what follows, suggest that ten or more countries in the conflict areas defined might have nuclear weapons by the end of the century. If they do have weapons, these will be few in number, crude, perhaps untested, and presumably fit for delivery from planes only. It would also seem that their employment in a local war would not extend beyond the local range and that the possible destruction wrought on the victim of a nuclear attack would not impair the viability of the country so struck. The small number of bombs at the disposal of the attacker, the large size of the victim, and the wide spread of its means of livelihood make it appear in most of the instances described above that a nuclear blow would not be altogether crippling, and consequently that the use of nuclear arms would not necessarily involve other countries in war.

This is a rather disturbing assessment of further proliferation of nuclear weapons in countries which might engage in local wars, even if an escalation of conflicts by reason of such weapons is not necessarily indicated. However, this prospect should be qualified.

The acquisition of nuclear weapons will probably continue to place a heavy political liability on the country that has chosen this course, and such liability should cause restraint. It is certain that countries suspected of wishing to acquire nuclear weapons will be closely watched and that the super-powers at least will attempt to forestall such an eventuality. Such attempts, and their likelihood of success will, of course, differ from one country to another. For example, no one would interfere with the Chinese nuclear program. India incurred temporary censure when she set off her nuclear device, but her international standing has not been impaired. South Africa, on the other hand, whose internal practices have been singled out for general disapproval, was recently warned by the US not to proceed with a nuclear test (if the newspaper reports are correct). It is anybody's guess what reaction there would be to a nuclear weapons enterprise by Brazil, for example, which looks to a future of political and economic strength and is treated with some deference in international councils. Thus, while restraint can be imposed by the super-powers on countries which contemplate a nuclear weapons program, such imposition is likely to be selective.

Further instances can be adduced which tend to temper the desire for the acquisition of nuclear weapons. Some of the candidate countries, for instance, have no democratic practices. Their rulers have trouble maintaining themselves in power and just as they cannot at all times be certain of the loyalty of their entire armed forces, they might hesitate to arm these forces with a very powerful device which might be turned against the government.

A sufficient supply of conventional weapons or the hope of other benefits could also curb the temptation to acquire nuclear weapons. On balance, however, I believe that in view of present circumstances there will be additional nuclear-weapon countries in the areas discussed, by the year 2000.

ESCALATION OF LOCAL WARS: INVOLVEMENT OF OTHER COUNTRIES

The question can be asked whether the possession of nuclear weapons by additional countries and their employment in war increases the chances of a local war developing into a world war. If this question is asked with respect to the year 2000, I believe the answer is no. It is not by reason of a tenuous nuclear weapons capability (in power, number, and range) of the warring parties themselves that a local war would escalate.

This answer does not, however, dispose of the question of escalation in general. As long as war between the two super-powers is not ruled out and their opposing forces are deployed across the earth, opposing involvement in local wars is bound to become more frequent and to make the threat of escalation more imminent.

This argument can be contradicted. It can be said that the wars in Korea, Vietnam, and East Africa demonstrate that the super-powers can tacitly agree to contain conflicts.

Things were different, however, during the Yom Kippur war of 1973, when the Soviet Union indicated that it might unilaterally place forces in Egypt, as a peace-keeping force; whereupon a precautionary alert of US forces was ordered. It has been said on good authority that such an alert is not uncommon, that it served merely as a token of serious displeasure, and that the US did not for a moment believe that its confrontation with the Soviet Union might lead to war. This is probably true. But I suggest there is more truth in the impression created at the time and such as lives on in memory than in the subtle sobriety of the policy-makers. The simple fact is that signalling by way of nuclear alerts is very dangerous (see Chapter 3).

The Middle Eastern pattern is, I believe, the more likely one, as additional areas gain the prominence of the Middle East in the super-power quest for strategic advantages. With this trend emerging, there will be rapid developments in future local conflicts. They will either be quelled fast, by mutual consent of the super-powers, or one of them could degenerate quickly into a general war. The likelihood of a protracted local war is, I believe, on the decrease.

The incidence of local wars, additional nuclear-weapon countries, and a growing involvement of the super-powers in local wars seem on balance a likely extrapolation for the year 2000. This prospect is sharpened by shortages of resources that are envisaged even at a stationary world population, let alone a population which will have gone up by one half of its present size.

THE CESSATION OF LOCAL WARS
DEPENDS VITALLY ON THE SUPER-POWERS

Seasonal attrition of the human population through wars and wants is not a prospect to be viewed with equanimity. Even disregarding moral strictures, the fortunes of the nations of the world are increasingly linked with one another, and in the long run it is doubtful that one country will be able to reap the benefit from the distress of another. If a major war is to be avoided, this can only come about through a gradual accommodation on

the part of the super-powers. Such an accommodation would certainly
tend to contain or even to stifle local wars, which at present solicit super-
power support and carry the seed of escalation. Such an accommodation
would also cause the super-powers to give pre-eminent attention to the
problems which face the globe. Moreover, a super-power accommodation
would reduce the bargaining power of the developing countries whose
standing, ambition, and weight in international councils have been so
largely abetted by super-power competition.

One may ask how such an accommodation could come about. I could
imagine the presidents of the United States and the Soviet Union conven-
ing for summit meetings on problems we are told will face the globe in
the decades ahead with respect to food, resources, energy, and environment. If these topics were elevated to the summit level, this would be an
entirely new development in international life. Even though such an
initiative would be fraught with great difficulties, I believe the attempt
is worth while since the crises just mentioned are inexorably moving
towards us. Such a move could lead to a more real assessment of the
hierarchy of our concerns and would show the arms race to be of little
pertinence against this background.

The suggesion for a joint super-power initiative invites two objections.
First, the importance conceded to joint action by these powers smacks of
imperialism. Second, there appears to be no good reason why the US and
the Soviet Union should do better in resolving global issues than in
nuclear arms reduction and control, in which they are not doing so well.

Taking the second objection first, I believe there is an inherent frustration in discussing arms reduction as detached from the motives and
causes which bring about the arms build-up. One cannot reasonably hope
that negotiations on arms alone will ever cause the super-powers to
renounce their ability to destroy each other several times over. The
vocabulary of the balance of terror, however discerning, just cannot come
up with anything but a balance of terror, at best. However useful these
negotiations are in ensuring contact on the issues and an agreed perception of the perils attendant upon them, they hold no promise beyond
buying time. And this is a frustrating exercise if the time so bought is not
used in order to remove the urge to prepare for war. It is for that reason
that I propose global concerns be raised to the level of prominence now
accorded to arms negotiations. These concerns are more real in the sense
that they are inescapable and can be spelt out in kind, scope, evolution,
and consequence. It is just possible that their recognition at the supreme

level, and the manifest urgency for anticipatory action, will create a sense of purpose and priorities, against which arms procurement and preparations for wars will pale in pertinence.

Now, the second objection bears on the preponderant role of the super-powers. I believe that without joint action by them and without a certain amount of bullying, there is little chance that global issues can be approached with any chance of a mature, comprehensive, and steady commitment. Even though this affirmation of power by the mighty states would be resented during an initial period, it is in the nature of the issues and the interdependence inherent in their resolution that the bullying would give way to an agreed set of rights and obligations in the management of the earth. Without such leadership, I see no way of arriving at a consensus among the nations of the world. They are just too heterogeneous. With such leadership, however, I imagine, many countries would right from the start wish to participate in such a forward-looking venture.

It is idle to speculate whether another world war or local disaster must precede a more reasonable arrangement on earth or whether the powers will forestall the worst before it happens. If accommodation between the big powers does occur before the end of the century, local wars may by then be a matter of the past.

10

Nuclear War between the Super-powers

GEORGE W. RATHJENS

In testifying two years ago on civil preparedness and limited nuclear war before the Joint Committee on Defense Production of the US Congress, Herman Kahn observed that fifteen years earlier when he was deeply involved with such issues he found that analysts concerned with nuclear war spent 90 per cent of their effort on scenarios that began with 'a surprise attack directed at cities' and the other 10 per cent on scenarios that began with 'a surprise attack out of the blue which hit military bases'.[1] They did this not because they judged such scenarios either very probable or important, but, according to Mr Kahn, because 'they simply were the easy things to study and talk about'. The proportions are a bit different now – the question of the vulnerability of ICBMs to a surprise disarming strike appears to be getting more than 10 per cent of the attention – but otherwise things haven't changed much: the scenarios that are most easily dealt with analytically still get disproportionate attention. Kahn is right in saying that 'comparing today's discussion to the sixties, there has been very little substantial improvement'. (Maybe he is even right in suggesting that there has been a retrogression. After all, no one has written anything in the 1970s quite like his *Thinking the Unthinkable* or *On Thermonuclear War*.)

But if there has not been an improvement in the quality of discourse, the same cannot be said of the weapons, particularly delivery systems. They have developed, seemingly inexorably, along with improvements in command and control capabilities, and there is little reason to believe the trend will moderate. Whether nuclear war might look different as a result merits comment. Many 'doves' argue that with increased numbers and greater sophistication of strategic weapons, nuclear war is more probable and, if it occurs, will likely be more damaging than it would have been in past decades. And many alarmists – I choose that term as more accurate and perhaps less pejorative than 'hawks' – will argue that the growth in strategic strength of the Soviet Union relative to that of the United States makes a substantial difference. Are they right? Let me try to deal with these and related questions from necessarily an American and subjective perspective.

DETERRENCE VERSUS 'WAR FIGHTING'

When I was initiated into the arcane world of war planning twenty-five years ago there were, as I recall it, three objectives to be served by nuclear weapons: the 'Bravo' – 'blunting' – mission, involving delivery of weapons against military targets in the Soviet Union to blunt its ability to launch nuclear strikes; the 'Delta' – 'destruction' – mission aimed at the destruction of Soviet war-making potential, the analogue of the strategic bombing efforts of the Second World War against Germany and Japan; and the 'Romeo' – 'retardation' – mission to interdict and delay an expected movement of Soviet forces into Western Europe. Underlying this structure were 1 / the belief that the major 'threat' of concern was a Soviet attempt to take over Western Europe; 2 / a hope that the knowledge of US strategic bombing capabilities would deter such an attack; and 3 / a resignation to the fact that if deterrence failed, the Soviet attack could not be immediately contained, but rather that the best that could be done would be to slow the advance in the hope that, with time and the destruction of Soviet war-making potential, a favourable outcome would result. As might have been expected, there was conflict over allocation of effort to the three missions: arguments about which allocation would have the most favourable effect on war outcome – significantly, not about whether allocating more resources to, say, the 'Delta' mission would enhance deterrence. It was a Second World War type of scenario and thinking carried over into the early 1950s, something not surprising considering the carry-over in personnel involved in war planning and the scepticism – voiced perhaps most persuasively by P.M.S. Blackett[2] – that atomic weapons would be immediately decisive in a Soviet-American conflict.

But such views eroded rapidly, beginning with the development of thermonuclear weapons which resolved all doubt about whether strategic bombing could have immediately decisive effects. Then, there developed an appreciation – particularly after a notable war game, Carte Blanche, in 1955 – that the use of nuclear weapons tactically would lead to very heavy damage to civilians and property in Europe. With this, and the growth in Soviet strategic weapons capabilities – development of both thermonuclear weapons and intercontinental delivery systems – interest in both Europe and the United States turned increasingly from 'war fighting' to deterrence of war.

The effects were most notable in political circles; less so among the military who went right on writing war plans and specifying weapons requirements pretty much as they had in the past. Thus, while Robert McNamara, Secretary of Defense, argued that ability to inflict unacceptable damage on Soviet population and industry should be the principal criterion to be used in measuring the adequacy of strategic forces, a substantial fraction of the weapons in the SIOP* were allocated to military targets and few, if any, explicitly to destroy population, if my memory is correct. In a way, it hardly mattered. There was little flexibility in the SIOP – at least in the first one – and if executed, virtually all of our strategic force would have been used. The targets the military had selected would have been demolished, but because of their collocation with, or proximity to, population centres, and because of the size and numbers of weapons in the force, most of the industry and virtually all of the urban population of the Soviet Union would have been destroyed as well.

'ASSURED DESTRUCTION' AS A CRITERION FOR FORCE DESIGN AND APPLICATION

McNamara never professed to know precisely how much damage-inflicting capability would suffice to deter, but he suggested destruction of 20 to 25 per cent of population and 50 per cent of industry was surely enough – an upper bound for what he called an 'assured destruction' capability. While these levels seemed large, they were easily achievable, even neglecting fall-out and the synergistic effects of the near-simultaneous delivery of large numbers of weapons. Thus, the 'assured destruction' criterion and policy could be, and were, used to resist service pressures for what McNamara regarded as undesirable increases in numbers of strategic weapons. Had the SIOP been executed at any time during the 1960s, or since, the assured destruction levels would surely have been exceeded, even had the Soviet Union struck first.

Three serious criticisms were levelled against a strategic weapons posture and policy based on such criteria. The policy was held to be immoral, inadequate, and not credible: immoral because it put at risk many who

---

* The Single Integrated Operation Plan for employing the nuclear weapons of both the Strategic Air Command and the submarine missile force.

would have had little or no role in the instigation of events that might bring about their destruction and because it posed the possibility of destruction grossly disproportionate to the triggering event; inadequate because deterrence might fail, and in that event efforts to limit damage at least, and perhaps to secure a 'favourable' outcome vis-à-vis one's adversary, ought to be taken; and not credible, at least with respect to many contingencies, because an adversary, the Soviet Union, would not believe that we would risk enormous destruction to defend less than vital interests.

With these objections, there were several attempts to get away from a policy of deterrence based on 'assured destruction': a brief flirtation in 1962 by McNamara with a proposed 'spare the cities' doctrine for the use of strategic weapons against the Soviet Union; a modest but unsuccessful effort to sell civil defence in the early 1960s; pressure to deploy an ABM defence of cities, resisted by the Kennedy and Johnson administrations until 1967; and the development of interest in, and capabilities for, flexible and limited use of *tactical* nuclear weapons.

All such moves were resisted in varying degrees by the 'orthodox' arms control community, most of whose members were, and remain, committed to the maintenance of a hostage relationship based on 'mutual assured destruction', MAD, to use Donald Brennan's acronym. Many go further, favouring an extreme variant, 'minimum deterrence', i.e., a policy based on a reduction of strategic forces to levels that would pose a substantial threat to an adversary population – hundreds of weapons capable of causing tens of millions of fatalities – but which would not be optimized for, or allocated to, attack against adversary military targets. Their objections to departures from 'assured destruction' type deterrence have been based on the beliefs that: such moves would be met by adversary counter-moves, the result being an arms race with no obvious end-point; such commitments would make arms control and disarmament efforts more difficult and less likely to be fruitful; and developments that hold out the possibility of nuclear weapons being used selectively and on a limited scale would make their use more likely.

FLEXIBLE OPTIONS:
THE LIMITED USE OF STRATEGIC WEAPONS

As far as I know, there was little serious attention paid in developing the American SIOP during the 1960s to the possibility that *strategic* weapons might be used very selectively either by the US or the USSR. Rather, analysis of 'central war' focused, as Kahn remarked, on massive attacks by the super-powers against each other.

For most of the 1960s such attacks could be, and generally were, heavily discounted as being extremely improbable, considering the likelihood of devastating retaliation that either side would have had to expect were it to initiate such an attack. The strategic balance proved to be very stable, at least from an American perspective, not 'delicate' as Albert Wohlstetter had suggested it might be in a celebrated article that had appeared in 1959.[3]

Yet the delicacy argument was destined to be revived, even as Blackett had foreseen in a 1961 critique of the Wohlstetter thesis when he warned that 'the arguments which have been used, in my view, falsely, to prove the balance unstable in recent years may be used in the future to prove it again unstable'.[4] This occurred in 1969 when, as a rationale for an ABM defence of American ICBMs, Secretary of Defense Laird was driven to resurrect the possibility of a massive Soviet disarming attack, at one point stating that Soviets were 'going for a first strike capability. There is no question about that.' There were a lot of questions about what Secretary Laird meant. Some of the time he seemed to have in mind a disarming attack by Soviet ballistic missiles against US ICBMs; at others, against US bombers as well; and at his most extreme, also against the US missile-launching submarines by means undisclosed – indeed, I believe, unimagined.

Few took the Laird scenario in its extreme form seriously, his successor, James Schlesinger, saying of it: 'There is just no possibility that a high confidence disarming first strike is attainable for either side, even against the ICBM components of the strategic forces on both sides and certainly not against both sets of forces, SLBMs and ICBMs.'

Recognizing this, and that the 'assured destruction' role for strategic forces was one of dubious and diminishing credibility because of the growth of Soviet capability to inflict damage on the United States in the event of its implementing an 'assured destruction' attack against the USSR, Schlesinger concluded that the Soviet Union might use its strategic forces in a selective and limited way. He went on to argue that the US should be prepared to do so too, either in response to such a Soviet use or to other Soviet attacks or provocations. The result was the promulgation of a doctrine of limited strategic options.

In fact, had US strategic nuclear forces been used during the Kennedy-Johnson years, they in all likelihood would have been employed in a very selective way under direct and detailed presidential control, the inflexibility of the SIOP notwithstanding. Certainly, that is the lesson of the Cuban missile crisis. What Schlesinger did was to make it clear that provisions would be made in advance that would facilitate their being so used, i.e., in ways more proportionate to the provocation than the old Dulles 'massive retaliation' concept of implementation of the total SIOP would suggest. The new doctrine was widely seen, as it was intended, as an attempt to make strategic forces usable for deterrence of lesser provocations and, if need be, for 'war fighting'.

ATTACKS AGAINST ICBMS AS *THE* LIMITED OPTION

The policy was criticized by some who believed it would make a nuclear holocaust more likely, especially inasmuch as they believed policy-makers might underestimate the magnitude of 'collateral' damage to population and hence the likelihood of escalation. These concerns were reinforced when the Defense Department released estimates of damage to US population, assuming Soviet attacks limited to US strategic force bases, that seemed unrealistically low.*

Notwithstanding Schlesinger's having argued that implementation of his flexible options policy was dependent mainly on re-targeting, not on changes in force posture, others were sceptical, seeing in it a rationale for the development and procurement of additional strategic weapons. These concerns were fuelled at the time with the implementation of missile-accuracy improvement programs. And since then a particular limited option – an attack against ICBMs, reminiscent of the less extreme version of the Laird scenario – has been much discussed, indeed, virtually to the exclusion of others involving the use of nuclear weapons against the Soviet Union and the United States.

This scenario has one side, usually the Soviet Union, attacking the other's ICBM sites, while retaining a capability to destroy population and industry as a deterrent to a counterattack. The events leading up to the attack on ICBMs are rarely specified. It is argued that by executing such an attack the Soviet Union would greatly improve its strategic posture vis-à-vis the US: it would have used a portion of its ICBM force to destroy the bulk of the American force, the result being an increase in the ratio of Soviet to American deliverable 'throw-weight', i.e., aggregate payload deliverable by the residual strategic forces. Even though the United States

---

* The Department of Defense originally estimated up to 800 000 fatalities for a Soviet attack of one 1MT warhead against each of the U.S. Minuteman silos. The figures were challenged by, among others, the Arms Control and Disarmament Agency which suggested that an attack involving two warheads per silo could be expected to produce 4.5 million fatalities and might produce as many as 13 million and perhaps even as many as 50 million, not counting those in rural areas. (The Department of Defense argued that the last figure – 50 million – was too high by a factor of seven.)[5]

would retain a retaliatory force in its SLBMs, its use would be deterred by residual Soviet capabilities, and the US would be seen as a much weakened guarantor of the security of its allies. The scenario has been used as an argument:

for the MX missile, which by virtue of its mobile launching mode would make an attack more difficult than against Minuteman ICBMs and, by virtue of large payload and high accuracy, would make US attacks against Soviet ICBMs more feasible;

for defending Minuteman missiles, the ABM treaty notwithstanding;

for making provision for launch of Minutemen on warning of attack; and

by some, who favour none of these alternatives, for phasing out ICBMs as a component of the strategic force.

ALTERNATIVE LIMITED USE OF STRATEGIC FORCES

It is all a bit bizarre. If one considers scenarios involving the limited use of force by the Soviet Union and the United States against each other, an attack that is massive but limited to adversary ICBM sites would seem implausible – certainly such a remote possibility that it ought to command little attention in defence planning.

It is highly probable that in any further confrontation between the United States and the Soviet Union involving nuclear weapons (we have had one – the Cuban missile crisis), the question of communication of resolve will be very prominent and very likely the immediately dominant issue. Now, if the objectives to be served by the first use of nuclear weapons are to send a clear signal *and* to avoid escalation, as is likely, the side first using them will presumably attach great weight to the predictability of the outcome. Moreover, it may have a special desire to *restrict* damage to military targets. These considerations argue persuasively against selecting ICBM silos – especially in large numbers – as targets for early attack.*

---

* Note in this connection, the estimates, given in the footnote above, of collateral damage to US population from a hypothesized Soviet attack against US ICBMs. The extremes in the range of fatality estimates, 145 000 to 50 000 000+, are *in part* a consequence of different assumptions about the details of the Soviet attack. Nevertheless, it would seem plausible that estimates of fatalities for a *given* attack would vary by a factor of five or ten. Moreover, because of uncertainties about missile reliability and accuracy, about the effect of the detonation of one nuclear warhead on others – the 'fratricide effect', – and about the vulnerability of missile silos to weapons effects, not to mention the possibility of missiles being launched based on warning that they were about to be destroyed, there would also be uncertainty about the effectiveness of an attack against ICBMs in destroying its intended targets.

It is much more likely that a demonstration of resolve would involve attack by nuclear weapons against immediately threatening forces in a tactical situation – say, Soviet ground or air forces in Europe in the event of a conflict there – or perhaps, even more likely, against an isolated target, or targets, that could be destroyed with high confidence and little collateral damage. Ships at sea, remote radar stations, and satellites are obvious examples of the latter.

While such a demonstration might lead to the resolution of the crisis in question, it is also possible that escalation would result. Were this to occur, and develop, whether it be over a period of hours or days, the constraints which are of such importance in the limited response scenario – indeed, they virtually define it – including trying to minimize collateral damage to population and civil structures in the vicinity of military targets – these constraints would almost certainly be increasingly subordinated (as has been common in conventional conflict in the past) to the objective of destroying the adversary's war-making capability.

In that event, or even if the objective in the first use of nuclear weapons were to inflict substantial damage on adversary nuclear capabilities rather than to demonstrate resolve, other targets – notably air bases and nuclear submarines at sea or in port, and in the case of the United States, aircraft carriers – would likely be attacked before large numbers of ICBMs. This is because the former are much more attractive targets if the measure is nuclear capability destroyed per weapon expended. While one warhead might destroy a single ICBM, at most, that same warhead or a smaller, less accurate one could destroy a submarine in port carrying 12 to 24 ballistic missiles, or even several such submarines; or it might destroy many aircraft, each carrying a number of bombs or missiles. Thus, if, in a nuclear war-fighting scenario, escalation were to go very far, it is likely that all submarines in port, and some at sea, and all aircraft carriers would have been destroyed before missile silos would have been brought under attack. All strategic air bases (and many others) would also have been attacked, probably repeatedly, and with substantial collateral damage. (If an exchange had not yet escalated to the point where such targets had been attacked, it is at least questionable whether a nation that still possessed vulnerable aircraft or sea-based delivery systems in port would wish to attack adversary's ICBMs, considering that such an attack could well result in their launch against those vulnerable targets.) Should an exchange develop to the point where the most lucrative remaining targets would be ICBMs, it is hardly credible that an attack against them would bear much resemblance to the disarming scenario that currently commands so much attention. Among other things, the 'attacker' could not have much hope that further escalation would not follow their attack.

I do not want to suggest that the scenarios I have outlined are either an exhaustive or even a very probable description of how nuclear war might begin and develop. I do suggest that such scenarios are more plausible than the one which so dominates debate about weapons acquisition and arms control and disarmament policy today, specifically, the massive disarming attack against ICBMs, delivered in the expectation of no retaliatory response. I also suggest that, however one may feel about it, there is likely to be continuing, and I believe probably increasing, interest in the use of strategic weapons in a 'flexible response' mode, i.e., for 'nuclear war fighting'.

The question of such use merits an additional remark. I have already noted that it has become a matter of orthodoxy in 'the arms control community' to argue that acceptance of, or movement toward, a 'nuclear warfighting' posture and policy is undesirable on the grounds that, with it, nuclear war will become more likely. This is, of course, an undecidable proposition. For while with such a policy and posture the use of nuclear weapons may be more probable, *given conflict*, the very *likelihood* of conflict may be reduced. Hence, the sign of the change in the compound probability is not obvious – nor, I believe, determinable. More generally, there can be no solid basis for asserting that the expected damage integral will increase, or decrease, with changing emphasis on 'nuclear war fighting'.

THE FUTURE

In conclusion, a few speculations about trends.

First, I would observe that the continued growth in Soviet strategic strength relative to that of the US, as measured by such indices as throwweight megatonnage, numbers of warheads, and hard target kill capability, is not likely to have much impact on the likelihood of central war involving US and Soviet forces, nor on the way it will develop in its early stages, should it occur. The numbers and hard target-kill capabilities of the two sides could make a difference, if we get to the point of ICBM duels, but that is likely to be the case, if at all, only late in the game. Notwithstanding this observation, it is likely that concern about a massive disarming attack against ICBMs will continue to influence US force posture and arms control policy unduly for two reasons: 1 / that adduced by Herman Kahn – because the scenario commands disproportionate emphasis by virtue of its susceptibility to analytical treatment; and 2 / because it provides a powerful rationale for weapons development and acquisition programs. Whether it will ever be such an issue as it was at the time of the missile gap seems doubtful, but considering the attention paid to 'first strikes' in the late 1960s and in the last couple of years, it is perhaps premature to dismiss Blackett's warning of the likely recurrence of alarms about strategic instability.

Second, to the degree that there is interest in being able to use nuclear weapons flexibly, in deterring an adversary's ability to so use them to one's disadvantage, and in holding open the hope of being able to terminate conflict in its early stages, superior command and control capabilities and the ability to destroy targets with little variance in the predictability of effects will be far more important than the indices mentioned in the paragraph above.

Third, we are likely to see a continuing trend of improving capability to use strategic weapons selectively, including quite possibly against targets which might previously have been assigned to tactical delivery systems. As a related point, it is likely that the distinction between tactical and strategic nuclear delivery systems will be increasingly blurred with the deployment of more 'grey area' systems, of which cruise missiles, the SS-20/16, and the Backfire bomber are examples.

Fourth, it is possible that civilian fatalities and other collateral damage to non-military targets might be held to lower levels than would have been likely had nuclear war occured in the recent past. This is mainly the result of improvements in missile accuracy. Lower aggregate megatonnage – at least in the US strategic force – could also contribute to this. While I am deeply sceptical about many of the recent claims about Soviet civil defence effectiveness, it too could contribute to a reduction in civil casualties. Moreover, as missile accuracy improves further, it may be that civil defence will have more potential for effectiveness in the future. These remarks might be read as suggesting that capabilities of destroying population and industry are likely to diminish. That would be a mistake: *capabilities* are not likely to diminish; they may well increase. What I am suggesting is that *if the attacker wishes to do so* it will be increasingly possible to destroy many military and industrial targets with nuclear weapons while limiting damage to civilians and other industry to lower levels than would have been possible heretofore.

Fifth, the chances of terminating conflict after a few nuclear weapons have been used are probably somewhat better than they were some years ago and will improve further. This follows because of improvements in command, control, communications, and damage assessment capability, as well as because of the likelihood of less collateral damage having been inflicted with the first weapons that might have been used. Recognizing these possibilities, the restraint in using nuclear weapons shown by us, and our adversary, may diminish.

Sixth, while one cannot logically argue that the impact of these trends on policy will be desirable or undesirable if the measures are the likelihood and consequence of war, the hands of those who favour a flexible options policy seem destined to be strengthened as a consequence of technological developments at the expense of those committed to 'mutual assured destruction'. This may augur poorly for the control of nuclear arms. Commitment to 'assured destruction', and even more so to 'minimum deterrence', as a basis of policy implies acceptance of a belief in rapidly diminishing returns from both increased numbers of weapons and great sophistication in technology, and hence a basis for both unilateral and mutual restraint in weapons development and acquisition. In such a context arms control is conceptually at least *relatively* easy, although perhaps not very important from a narrow military perspective. As flexible options command increased attention, there may be a greater military pay-off in arms control, but it will be more difficult. Marginal differences and particularly qualitative advantage will be seen to be important, and hence hard to forgo. Thus commitment to 'flexible options' is likely to contribute to a continuing arms race. God forbid that we be caught in an 'options gap'!

All this will doubtless be read by some as suggesting diminishing prospects for nuclear arms control and/or disarmament and an increasing acceptability of the use of nuclear weapons as instruments of policy. Technological developments, including particularly the extension of the capabilities of conventional and nuclear systems to attack point targets with great precision, and also the blurring of the distinction between tactical and strategic nuclear capabilities, do indeed point in that direction, in my view.

However, that is only part of the story. Whether nuclear weapons will be used or whether there will, at long last, be some substantial progress in arms control and disarmament efforts will depend far more on political than on technical developments. These questions are, however, subjects for another paper: not one on scenarios of nuclear war but rather on scenarios for its avoidance. That is a harder paper to write and one that will be more contentious; for difficult as it is to imagine just how nuclear weapons might be used in conflict involving the super-powers, it is more difficult in the light of the record of the last third of a century to argue with any persuasiveness that there can be a resolution of political and philosophical differences so that conflict between them will be less likely.

Clearly, there is now a consensus that the survival of existing political systems and the welfare of those who live under them are less jeopardized by a continuing confrontation, of which nuclear weapons are a part, than they would be by political changes that would be required, including intrusions on sovereignty, so that differences could be substantially reduced and better mechanisms established for the peaceful resolution of those that remain. Whether the consensus is correct must be doubted, especially inasmuch as it is based in part on two premises that are, if not patently false, at least questionable: that nuclear weapons can be used in a controlled and limited way, for which there is no evidence; and/or that there can be truly meaningful nuclear arms control and disarmament in the absence of radical political change, for which there is much contrary evidence. While it is easier to believe in one or both of these premises than to face up to the necessity of choice between political change and the probability of an eventual holocaust, it is the problem of a paper on scenarios for the *avoidance* of nuclear war, and the ultimate challenge to political leadership, to do just that, recognizing, and exposing, the risk in the first premise and the limited utility, if not sterility, of the second.

NOTES

1 'Civil Preparedness and Limited Nuclear War', *Hearings* before the Joint Committee on Defense Production, Ninety-Fourth Congress, US Government Printing Office (Washington DC, 1976), 9

2 P.M.S. Blackett, 'The Military Consequences of Atomic Energy (1948)', in *Studies of War* (New York, 1962)

3 'The Delicate Balance of Terror', *Foreign Affairs*, January, 1959

4 P.M.S. Blackett, 'Critique of Some Contemporary Defense Thinking (1961)', *Studies of War*

5 'Briefing on Counterforce Attacks', *Hearings* before the Subcommittee on Arms Control, International Law and Organization, Committee on Foreign Relations, United States Senate, Ninety-Third Congress, US Government Printing Office (Washington DC, 1975), 13, 31, 30, 33

Retrospect and Prospect

11

Forum: Remarks Made at a Special Session with the Prime Minister of Canada

1 Georgi A. Arbatov

We are attempting to assess the dangers of nuclear war by the year 2000. While I am not in a position to summarize the various points of view expressed here, it would be fair to say that all of us share feelings of concern and some see cause for serious anxiety. In discussing the dangers of war, and ways to avert it, we must pay great attention to the arms race itself, seeking ways to curb it and begin a process of disarmament. There are few who do not acknowledge that bad political relations and an atmosphere charged with mistrust encourage arms race activity. Today, in addition, we know that such behaviour can flourish under different circumstances. The arms race, as we have recently learned, can go on even in a time of remarkable political improvement and can eventually undermine good relations by fomenting mistrust and suspicion. The conditions are then set for a deterioration in the political atmosphere and in relations between countries.

The arms race, in the opinion of many people – and I share this opinion – has become a major source of danger of nuclear war. Today, the world finds itself on the threshold of a new round of the arms race which is fraught with grave dangers. These dangers are not simply in the possibility of development of some particular weapons but in the pace of development of weapons technology under present political conditions, a trend which can be detrimental to stability and peace.

The continuing military rivalry between major world powers cannot but increase the danger of proliferation of nuclear weapons. Recognition of this truth should not be an excuse for those leaders and governments that may in the years to come opt for nuclear armaments. Under any circumstances such an option will be a bad and dangerous one. It can only greatly impair the security of any country choosing this road and jeopardize international security as a whole. All nuclear powers will continue to bear a special responsibility; if they fail to curb the arms race, the risk of proliferation of nuclear weapons may increase and even become inevitable in certain political situations.

However serious the problem of proliferation of nuclear weapons may be, it is not the only danger in the continuing arms race. The number of stockpiled weapons of mass destruction, the emergence of new systems, and the new strategic concepts that appear as a result of these, increase the danger of nuclear war. The development of MIRVs, despite all the justifications given by the United States at the time, resulted in a growth in the number of nuclear warheads that far surpassed the needs of 'deterrence'. Military planners immediately began to seek a rationale for the 'redundant' warheads or, in other words, to look for new targets for them. In this way, the idea of 'counterforce' use of strategic weapons was revived at a new and more dangerous level. This led in turn to the development of new programs designed, among other things, to improve accuracy, terminal guidance, flexibility in retargeting, and miniaturization of warheads.

It is clear that, cumulatively, all of these developments can have far-reaching consequences. In particular, the achievements of military technology have given a fresh impetus to the idea that nuclear war is a possible instrument of foreign policy. In this context the restatement by the United States in 1975 of its policy of possible first use of nuclear weapons seemed particularly alarming. All the more so since it came in the context of new attempts to convince the public that increased accuracy and development of small-yield weapons or neutron weapons would reduce losses in a possible nuclear war to 'acceptable' dimensions. It was argued that these would be used 'only' against military targets and the hostilities would thus not escalate into an all-out nuclear war. All this doubtless contained a good measure of blackmail levelled against political adversaries of the United States. However, it is rightly pointed out both in the Soviet Union and other countries that a by-product of this campaign was to scale down public opposition to nuclear war, to make the idea of such a war a 'thinkable' alternative in the eyes of the public.

Set against the background of possible future breakthroughs in the sphere of anti-submarine warfare, the revival of the 'counterforce' concept and the relevant armament programs gives a new impulse to fears of a 'first-strike' capability. I do not believe that qualified experts, let alone responsible statesmen, would consider a first strike truly feasible. There would, for example, always remain the possibility of countering this threat by developing mobile launching installations or, as a last resort, relying upon a 'launch on warning' strategy, however dangerous this may be.

One cannot fail to see, however, that these trends of the arms race will destabilize the strategic situation and increase the risk of a dramatic, fatal mistake under conditions of acute international crisis. Moreover, another menace may be discerned: the arms race could take a course (and to a certain extent is beginning to do so) which would make new agreements on limiting and reducing armaments far more difficult, if not altogether impossible, due to the insurmountable obstacles entailed in verification of some new weapons. This is, for instance, one of the negative consequences of the development of the strategic cruise missile or the MX mobile missile.

It must be stressed that the continuing arms race is highly unlikely to produce any immediate, let alone long-term, advantages for either side. But it does create grave threats for both parties as well as for world peace and security. This is so because the arms race increases the danger of nuclear war even though no government may want such a war or plans deliberately to unleash one. In this sense, the decades ahead may differ sharply from the sixties and seventies. These developments are already under way. We must act and act quickly to avoid the dangers. One has to agree with ambassador George Kennan who recently warned that time is running out for all of us.

I believe that there is increasing need to understand that the Soviet Union and the United States, East and West, face in their relations and their negotiations – including arms control negotiations – an impersonal adversary that overrides any specific threat one side may see in the other. This adversary is the looming danger of nuclear war, whatever may be its concrete scenario. With all our differences and contradictions we have an overwhelming mutual interest in seeking to avert the threat of war. This interest compels us to be persistent in our efforts to promote détente and to secure arms control and disarmament.

Another mutual interest, one which transcends the borders of each state and which also demands détente and disarmament, is the increasing complexity and urgency of global problems. It seems to me that actions which impede détente not only hinder the strengthening of peace and world security but also ignore the fundamental requirements of social progress all over our planet. I have in mind the emergence of such problems as limited energy resources and shortages of other raw materials, difficulties in providing food for the world's growing population, pollution of the environment, and so forth. It is good that in recent years active discussion of these problems has begun. But it is a pity that they are so rarely posed in the context of their interconnection with and dependence on the world situation. Yet such a relationship exists and it is a direct one.

Scientists estimate that by the year 2000 the Earth's population will increase by the number of people our planet had at the beginning of this century. A colossal amount of building will be required since in less than a quarter of a century the world will have to build as much as was constructed in several previous centuries. If present trends continue, about 900 million people on the Earth will need jobs by the beginning of the next century. Development of the Third World will pose tasks of unprecedented dimensions. Energy and food problems will become increasingly acute.

These are only some of the global challenges we will face in the year 2000. Even allowing for error on the part of scientists, it must be admitted that they are very grave. Yet they can and must be solved.

If problems of this magnitude are on the agenda one may legitimately ask whether the people of the world, especially those in countries with the most advanced economies, science, and technology, can afford to continue to spend an enormous portion of their brain and labour power, of their means and resources, on the arms race and the needs of war. Can these countries afford not to make maximum efforts to concentrate their resources on tackling the global problems mentioned above, on developing the closest and broadest possible co-operation to this end and on establishing an international political atmosphere that is conducive to such co-operation? It is true that détente will not solve all the world's problems by itself. But without it mankind will hardly be able to start coping with them in any sort of fundamental way.

We have, then, tremendously important mutual interests which make détente not only desirable but the only reasonable policy for the future. At the same time we have to be aware of the fact that states, like people, have not always acted in keeping with their own best interests – otherwise history would have spared us a great many wars and conflicts. Efforts to curb the arms race lag far behind the pace of military technology. This could lead once more to an unwanted major conflict. Special efforts must be made to avoid this development. Quick and effective measures in the field of arms control are imperative.

The Soviet Union considers arms control and disarmament to be the dominant objective in all its efforts in international policy. As Leonid Brezhnev recently affirmed (*Pravda*, 26 April 1978), 'there is no type of weapon, above all, weapons of mass destruction, that the Soviet Union would not be ready to limit, to ban on the basis of mutual agreement with other states, and then to exclude from the arsenals.' We stand for the speediest conclusion of the SALT II negotiations on the basis of equality and equal security. We stand for effective verification measures which are no less important to us than to the West. We are actively pursuing the goal of banning underground nuclear tests. We are strongly committed to the task of arms reduction in Central Europe. To quote again the recent statement by Leonid Brezhnev reported in *Pravda*: 'In contrast to the NATO countries, we have long refrained from increasing our armed forces in Central Europe and do not intend – let me emphasize it with all strength – still do not intend to increase them by a single soldier or a single tank.'

The Soviet Union keeps coming up with fresh proposals aimed at curbing and ending the arms race. On 25 April 1978 in an address to the 18th Congress of the Young Communist League, President Brezhnev appealed to the West to consider a concrete program designed to end further quantitative and qualitative growth of the arms and armed forces of states having large military potential. This program included ending the production of all nuclear weapons, banning all the other weapons of mass destruction, stopping the development of new conventional arms of great destructive force, a refusal to increase the armies and conventional armaments of the permanent Security Council members, as well as their military allies. The Soviet Union also announced its decision to join the international ban on nuclear weapons in Latin America.

In concluding, I must stress that we are hopeful for the future of détente. As President Brezhnev said to the heads of diplomatic missions in Moscow in July 1977: 'We trust, we firmly trust, that political realism and the will for détente and progress will ultimately overcome, and mankind will be able to step into the 21st century in a peace as secure as never before. We will do all we can to make it happen.'

2 P.R. Chari

The dangers of nuclear war arise at one level from increases in the number and sophistication of nuclear weapons available. They arise also from the likely increase in the number of international actors possessing these weapons. The trend towards vertical and horizontal proliferation of nuclear weapons and their danger to international stability must, however, be properly evaluated before initiatives to reduce these threats can be discussed.

In a sense the nuclear Non-Proliferation Treaty represented a contract. It was entered into by over one hundred countries of whom three were nuclear-weapon powers. The contract was that the non-nuclear-weapon powers party to the Treaty agreed to abridge their national autonomy by abjuring the nuclear option: in return nuclear-weapon powers signing the Treaty undertook to take meaningful steps towards cessation of the arms race prior to achieving nuclear disarmament. France and China did not join the Treaty. Neither did those non-nuclear-weapon states who had acquired significant nuclear technological capabilities. But these dissident nations might have perceived incentives to join the Treaty if any reasonable hope could be entertained that nuclear disarmament was likely in a reasonable interval of time.

But what has been the record? Actions by the nuclear-weapon powers, especially the super-powers, are quite naturally more significant than declarations of intent. It is clear that the total number of nuclear weapons has increased over the last decade. It is equally obvious that the nuclear arms race proceeds as part of an unending action-reaction phenomenon. The very great destructiveness of nuclear weapons and additions to the size of nuclear arsenals add to tensions and instability. It is argued that nuclear weapons serve the ends of deterrence. Can constantly increasing levels of nuclear weaponry be justified to secure these ends? Is it not rational to assume that unacceptable damage can occur at lower (but significant) levels of destruction? Assuming the rationality of leaderships should it not be expected that nuclear deterrence and stability might be sought at lower rather than progressively increasing levels of nuclear capability?

But quantitative increases in nuclear arsenals do not represent the major danger to international stability. This comes from three other directions. First, qualitative increases in nuclear weaponry are potentially destabilizing. Developments like multiple warhead missiles, for instance, add qualitatively and quantitatively to the capacity of nuclear arsenals. At another level, the development of weapons like cruise missiles and land-mobile missiles like the SS-20 and MX add, not merely to the qualitative capabilities of nuclear arsenals but consequently to difficulties in verification of their numbers and, therefore, to difficulties for future arms control negotiations.

Second, the deployment of newer types of tactical nuclear weapons, which are essentially battlefield support weapons, adds to the credibility of the nuclear war scenarios. The danger from enhanced radiation weapons, munitions using depleted uranium and future developments in this genre of nuclear weaponry arises because they blur the distinction and hence diminish the fire-break between nuclear and conventional weapons. Any effort to 'conventionalize' nuclear weapons is very destabilizing. More importantly, deployment of such weapons is likely to create the reprehensible psychological belief that nuclear weapons are indeed usable. Since no nuclear war has, fortunately, yet been fought it is unclear whether the defending nuclear power would rightly perceive a nuclear conflict as being intended to be limited and would refrain from escalating the exchange to general war levels. Further, the deployment of particle beams as anti-satellite weapons threatens the technical means recognized as necessary to verify existing arms control agreements.

Third, it is dubious whether existing consultative and other confidence-building measures reassure us that a congruity exists between strategic perceptions among super-power leaders regarding the utilization of nuclear weapons. The history of past nuclear crises, such as the Cuban missile crisis, give the impression that nuclear crises are really a game of chicken. Believing in the righteousness of their cause, convinced that the adversary would ultimately back down, unwilling to compromise till the last possible moment, a nuclear confrontation is *per se* highly dangerous. That it would not lead to a nuclear conflagration assumes that national leaderships continue to remain rational under conditions of extreme stress. Can this be depended upon?

Vertical proliferation represents only one source of danger from nuclear weapons. Indubitably, another source of danger arises from the horizontal proliferation of nuclear weapons to new powers. Whatever be the confidence reposed in existing command and control arrangements – and there is little reason that such measures would not be equally tight in newer nuclear-weapon powers – a statistical probability must be accepted that nuclear war by inadvertence might occur. A nuclear exchange by accident or misunderstanding is recognized as possible. This statistical probabililty can only increase with an increase in the number of independent nuclear actors. Furthermore, the existing pattern of nuclear deterrence, essentially bipolar in character, would have to be converted into a chandelier balance of increasing complexity. In these circumstances the chances of nuclear instability and nuclear war can only increase.

How can the danger of nuclear conflict be reduced?

Is it possible for the nuclear arms race to be reversed?

No solutions are feasible without national sacrifice and this must commence with the nuclear-weapon powers, especially the super-powers. These sacrifices go to the heart of the politico-economic structures in the United States and the Soviet Union. The strength of their military-industrial and military-bureaucratic complexes must be appreciated. (A military-academic complex must also be recognized which provides the intellectual sustenance for prevailing strategic theories and nuclear arms racing.) Unless national governments, therefore, are willing to ignore or curb these powerful domestic interests it is unlikely that military research or testing, production and deployment of nuclear weapons, which propel the nuclear arms race upwards, would be reversed. The problem lies *within* the nuclear-weapon powers – adversary relationships provide only a plausible reason for the relentless drive towards quantitative and qualitative improvements in nuclear arsenals.

An indirect effect of the continuing arms race must be noted. Nuclear weapons have come to be imbued with almost mystic qualities. They provide both prestige and perceived security. More importantly they permit a challenge to the existing international power structure. These false values are strengthened by theses justifying the development of nuclear weapons to provide deterrence, stability, prestige, and the capability to exert influence abroad. Unless the mystique attached to nuclear weapons is reduced by stressing their non-usability – most credibly, by a meaningful reduction of nuclear arsenals with a hope of their ultimate elimination – more non-nuclear-weapons powers will be tempted to obtain them by any means.

A technological solution to the problem of horizontal proliferation, by seeking to bring transferred nuclear material, technology, and equipment under international supervision, is a short-term solution. This would be resisted as discriminatory by non-nuclear-weapon powers, since it is not the intention to place the military nuclear facilities in nuclear-weapon states (which are the more dangerous) under similar safeguards. In any case technological fixes can at best postpone horizontal proliferation; they cannot prevent it.

3 Richard L. Garwin

The problem which I address here is not novel, but it is still important. It is that of the strategic offensive forces of the United States and the Soviet Union. I have long had contact with this problem, both in US government activities dealing with national security and arms control, and also in academic and international circles. The prime question pertaining to the future of strategic forces and their relationship to nuclear war is how best to maintain this bulwark against nuclear war while minimizing the extent to which strategic forces may *cause* such a war.

Experience shows, however, that:

Forces are built against worst-case anticipations. For instance, multiple independently targeted re-entry vehicles (MIRVs) were largely justified as a means of assured penetration of ABM systems expected to be built by the other side. Similarly, the possibility of destruction before launch (i.e., pre-launch vulnerability) has led to substantially larger forces than would otherwise have been built. Predictably, the worst-case does not materialize, and we have forces which are excessive both qualitatively and quantitatively.

The continued existence of these excessive forces are then justified by clever arguments rather than by need. Design groups, development engineers, and manufacturers – whether in the US, the Soviet Union, or another nation – find themselves idle, and don't like it. The large numbers of warheads, built against the worst case (which has not materialized) are *not* idle; they are assigned to targets of questionable value for deterrence, simply because warheads exist.

Weapon *characteristics* are thus driven by technological challenge, rather than by an agreed need.

The result is that the forces are always perceived as being *marginal* in capability to perform the assigned task of deterrence, since the assigned task is continually revised upward to encompass current destructive power. A prime example of this took place in the 1969 debate over deployment of the Safeguard ABM system in the United States. Defence circles maintained that a very modest number of Soviet missiles, the SS-9 Model 4 (with three re-entry vehicles per missile), could destroy some fraction of Minuteman force and so compromise US deterrence (interpreted as the ability to cause unacceptable damage in the Soviet Union). What the Defense Department did not volunteer was that fewer than 10 per cent of the US strategic warheads were assigned to targets relevant to deterrence; the rest, being normally surplus to that task, were assigned to military targets of lesser deterrent value. Thus, a vast resource was available to the US strategic planners at that time, who could, simply by the stroke of a pen, transfer warheads from targets of lesser importance to those on the deterrent list, to counter what was viewed then as an alarming Soviet development.

The process which I have sketched continues. The solution is to go back to fundamentals. No matter how few ICBMs, SLBMs, or airfield-based payloads are available, the easiest, most valuable, and most effective targets for a deterrent force are the opponent's cities and productive capacity. Even those arguing for ICBMs capable of destroying the other side's silos (not his missiles, since they can be launched before they can be destroyed) close their scenarios with 'and after having destroyed the U.S. Minuteman force, and Soviet Union presents the U.S. President with an ultimatum to concede or surrender – or else see the destruction of U.S. cities'.

So cities are the deterrent targets, and no government has any goals (except survival of the nation) worth the destruction of its cities. But 'counterforce' is where the action is, because one can have an interesting technological arms race towards this end, which, very unfortunately, may imperil the stability of deterrence based on the ability to destroy population and industry of the other side. Fortunately, it is largely within the capability of the US or the Soviet Union to control its strategic forces, which have a physical aspect, a doctrinal aspect, and a declaratory aspect. These matters are discussed more fully in my chapter in the Council on Foreign Relations book, *Nuclear Weapons and World Politics* (New York, 1977).

In general, since neither the US nor the USSR is going to give up nuclear weapons to the extent that it will not have a city-destruction capability, the least likelihood of nuclear war and the least destruction if war should come would be obtained if the strategic nuclear capacity were *limited* (either by agreement or unilaterally) to an assured, robust capability to this end. Measures which should be taken toward this goal are:

A strategic reserve. Rather than to assign targets for every existing warhead, strategic weapons which have been built against some future enemy threat and which are surplus against the present enemy threat should not have targets assigned, but should be disabled in such a way that it would take some weeks to restore them to active service. This might be done with land-based ICBMs by burying them under 10 or 20 meters of earth, which would have to be bulldozed away. In this fashion, there would not be recurrent arguments that existing forces are 'fully committed' (to an artificially inflated task) and any growth on the opposite side thus leads to inadequate deterrent capability.

Launch under attack or launch on reliable detection. A land-based ICBM force is not threatened by a few warheads launched out of the blue; it would require a force of many hundreds of missiles, with thousands of warheads, to threaten the survival of the Minuteman force. Nothing in existing agreements or international law compels a nation to watch its strategic forces being destroyed. When nuclear weapons begin to burst in the Minuteman fields, after a half-hour of strategic warning from infra-red satellites and other sensors, the ICBM force can be launched against its strategic targets rather than await destruction. Of course, the very capability and commitment to launch the strategic force will prevent attack upon it. There are easier ways for the Soviet Union to destroy its own cities (or *vice versa*) than to provoke the enemy ICBM force to do so.

Minuteman defence. Strategic attack on ICBM silos can be prevented if it is made clear that such an attack will fail in its goal. Previous means for defence of hardened silos used radar and interceptors very similar to those which had been developed in the hope of defending cities. The large size and extreme vulnerability of cities (and of the radars themselves) rendered this primary task infeasible. However, until the last few years, little attention has been paid to defences of silos which actually capitalize on the extreme hardness of the silo, capable of withstanding pressures and environments which would destroy the incoming re-entry vehicle. One such defence would consist of a buried nuclear explosive about 2km north of each silo to be defended, triggered (*after* the system has been switched on by the national command authority) by a very small radar a few kilometers farther north. This radar has nothing in common with air defence or ABM radars, but looks like a highway speed-control radar (except for being mounted in a concrete block). These buried explosives, since they can be large and heavy, can be made both cheap and clean – having perhaps 1 per cent as much fission products and radioactive material produced as the incoming enemy warheads. The detonation of such an explosive would throw into the air near the silo hundreds of thousands of tons of soil and debris, preventing effective attack by the re-entry vehicle about to explode. Furthermore, as this material rose to higher altitude, it would prevent further re-entry vehicles from attacking for an hour or more. Of course, the availability of such a defence means that there would be *no* attack of the silos, since it would serve no end. A somewhat more expensive and less effective version of such a defence would use ordinary explosive and hundreds of tons of steel chunks.

Flight test restrictions. Finally, it would be useful to have flight test restrictions on ICBMs, to reduce the rate at which progress can be made in accuracy and reliability, and to deny firm knowledge of reliability which is essential particularly for attack against enemy strategic forces. Thus, a total of 6 or 12 ballistic missile launches per year could be allowed each side, and no testing of manoeuvring re-entry vehicles (MaRVs) would be allowed.

The problem posed would, in my opinion, be properly solved by the suggested measures. Strategic nuclear forces would be assigned the mission which they have the inherent capability to perform. There would be no more arguing about the adequacy of the strategic forces for missions for which they are only marginally suitable (namely the destruction of an opponent's ICBM force – termed 'counterforce').

Substantially smaller strategic forces on the two sides would be acceptable, and they could stay in service longer. They would no longer be challenged by possible destruction before launch and they would not require ever-increasing numbers and accuracy in order to carry out their marginal tasks of counterforce.

In order for this view to prevail, those who are concerned with national security in the broad sense will have to become more deeply involved with national security as it is embodied in the various aspects of the strategic nuclear force – physical, doctrinal, and declaratory.

4 George Ignatieff

While we are particularly concerned in Canada at this time with the question of national survival, President Brezhnev is reported as having told the German Chancellor only recently that the world may be engulfed in thermonuclear war unless the east-west armaments race is halted. Relations between the People's Republic of China and the Soviet Union, two nuclear powers, are also strained and could spark a world war. Our Symposium has tried to look at this danger from the perspective of the next twenty-five years or so. We do not regard ourselves as prophets but as people attempting to analyse risks and what might best be done about them.

First of all, there is always the danger of confrontation between nuclear powers of the kind that arose over the Cuban missile crisis. We are assured that this risk is reduced as a consequence of the very strict command and civilian control procedure applied by the United States and, no doubt, by the Soviet Union. However, the process of 'vertical' proliferation of nuclear weapons goes on almost automatically, powered by the on-going momentum of research, weapons testing and weapons development. Decisions on weapons systems seem to be made less on the need for any new weapons system but rather on the basis of technology, economic considerations, and political pressures. Considerations of prestige also enter the picture; 'what they can do, we can do better.'

Another danger arises from the possibility of conventional wars escalating into nuclear war. Any forces engaged in hostility and determined to win are apt to use the weapons necessary to prevent defeat. If such forces have access to nuclear weapons in any form, such as the neutron bomb and other tactical nuclear weapons, they are likely to use them. This threat of escalation arises from the trend to make tactical nuclear weapons into a natural, though more powerful, extension of conventional weapons, in order to offset the advantages in manpower of the adversary or for alleged reasons of economy. Moreover, there are hostilities going on in different parts of the world, in the context of the north-south dialogue, in which countries supported by powers equipped with nuclear weapons, are directly or indirectly involved – especially in the Middle East and parts of Africa – this too poses the threat of escalation.

There is, in addition, the increased risk of further countries acquiring nuclear weapons without the structure of political-military restraints which have been accepted over the years by the super-powers.

What can be done to reduce the danger? First of all, if there is to be nuclear disarmament, we have to start by continuing to stem or stifle nuclear proliferation at source, primarily by 'psychological denuclearization' – that is to say, a diminished reliance on nuclear weaponry – as well as actual arms control measures. We have to assume that the knowledge and means to build nuclear weapons will continue to spread. It is the terror of the consequences of the use of nuclear weapons, in terms of mass destruction, that will continue to be the main sanction against dangerous nuclear policies. But anyone who suggests that nuclear weapons can do anything but deter or prevent nuclear war would be doing a great disservice to the cause of peace between now and the end of this century.

Only if the nuclear powers succeed in stopping the nuclear arms race, which goes on apace, do we have any real hope of preventing the spread of nuclear weapons to additional countries, i.e., succeed in stopping horizontal proliferation which is tied, but not indissolubly tied, to such legitimate motivations as the need for additional sources of energy, including nuclear energy.

If the psychology of fear is to work as a deterrent against nuclear war, more must be known about this nuclear threat and what can be done about it. The present Pugwash Symposium is a contribution to this end. It must be realized that once a nuclear weapon is used in a conflict between nuclear powers there is no clear way to prevent escalation, until the war ends in mutual annihilation. There is no way in which you can fight a nuclear war which will only strike against the armaments of your adversary without risking the destruction of population, cities, and industries – and indeed civilization as we know it.

In addition to reducing the secrecy surrounding nuclear war and its dangers, each of the super-powers should declare that it is prepared to renounce the idea of a pre-emptive or first strike war. Such an undertaking would at least halt the search for ever more elaborate and costly systems to get the upper hand, which only raise the fear that the other side is preparing for a possible first strike.

Also, we must press for an end to the development and deployment of new nuclear weapons systems, and in particular those that would blur the threshold between nuclear and conventional warfare. Nuclear weapons should be recognized exactly for what they are – weapons of mass destruction to be used for deterrence only.

But even nuclear deterrence may not work forever, particularly in a world of many nuclear powers. The kind of arms control measures that could give credence to such a declaration against first-strike or pre-emptive warfare would include the prohibition of all nuclear testing as well as the testing of delivery vehicles. Any arms control measures, to be effective, must be based on the realization that security does not rest ultimately on the development of weapons which in some way are going to make warfare less likely in the year 2000, or less destructive than it was when this century began. Security depends upon the strengthening of international organizations, amelioration of economic and political disputes, and the promotion of co-operation between countries willing to support international peace-keeping forces. Such measures would reduce dependence on national armaments and armed forces. So long as a state of anarchy prevails in our interdependent world community, the risk of world war will be with us.

5 Lord Zuckerman

During the past days we have been discussing the possibility that war in which nuclear weapons are used might occur within the next twenty years. We have not been talking about war in general, nor about a major war that opened with an all-out nuclear exchange, but of the possibility that, given an armed conflict, nuclear weapons might be used. Our concern has therefore been with what is essentially a process of transition, and with the circumstances in which such a process might occur, and how it could be averted.

We all accept that the devastation which would be caused in a nuclear war would be vast and terrible. But I believe that the greatest danger of nuclear weapons being used is that people do not realize, that they are unable to visualize, what this would mean.

Even at this meeting, we began with too depersonalized, too clinical, an account of what would be the result of the explosion of nuclear weapons. We speak of them as though they imply single isolated disasters. We have not tried to visualize the picture of the virtually total destruction, not of one, but of several related cities or, given an 'all-out' nuclear exchange, not just of several cities, but in effect of the effacement of the major cities of Western Europe, of the USSR, and of the US, beyond all possibility of reconstruction in any realistic period of time.

Writers in the United States, a country which did not suffer damage in any of the wars of this century, talk about 'levels of acceptable damage', of 'assured destruction', of '100 million U.S. citizens being killed in a nuclear exchange'. Words like these carry no meaning. To understand our subject we should have had at our table a survivor of Hiroshima, or of Hamburg or Dresden, or someone who had been on the spot when some vast area of London was flattened. Drawing concentric circles on a map showing the areas where radiation would be lethal, where fire would spread, and where blast would have its effects provides no glimmering of what would be the consequence of the explosion of a single megaton or of a seven megaton bomb on a city of, say, a million inhabitants. If a single megaton bomb were ever to burst over an English city like Birmingham, about a third of its population would be immediately killed or crushed under debris. The remaining two-thirds would be extricating themselves from radio-active rubble as they sought help and shelter. There would be floods and fire. There would be nowhere to turn, no possibility of help if at the same time neighbouring cities had been struck. In modern society one major focus of destruction interacts with another; there is a multiplying effect.

When the Russians carried out their last series of atmospheric tests, Mr Khrushchev, when referring to a 57 megaton burst, said that it could have been made bigger, but the danger then was that all the windows of Moscow, hundreds of miles away, might have been broken. This was a gruesome joke; but I believe he understood what he was saying! My first point is that one real danger of the possibility of nuclear war is that we have ceased to understand what we are talking about. How can one imagine the reality: the possible elimination, not only of say half the population of the Northern hemisphere, but also the elimination of the better part of the cultural history of our globe? We need education in these matters. Each new sequence of generals, of admirals, of air marshals who come to positions of power, needs to be educated afresh about these things. So too do politicians and prime ministers. They come and go but, as someone said earlier at this Symposium, they come as freshmen to a university. One generation of freshmen as it moves on to its second year does not inoculate the one which follows with its wisdom. And the wisdom becomes thinner as the years pass.

If we go on talking about the use of nuclear weapons as though this was a real option in world politics, then they will be used. That is a danger I see worsening in the years ahead.

The second and related danger which I see has been already referred to this afternoon by Dr Arbatov and Dr Chari, and by one or two other speakers earlier on. It is a technological trend which aims at obliterating the critical difference between nuclear weapons on the one hand and so-called conventional weapons on the other. We persuade ourselves that nuclear weapons can be made small and precise, and not as harmful as an equally precise conventional weapon with more destructive power. In my view this trend undoubtedly lowers the nuclear threshold, at least partly because it encourages people to believe that nuclear weapons (for example, so-called neutron bombs used ostensibly to hold up a massive tank incursion) can be real weapons of choice.

This leads into the third danger I see – the growing belief that nuclear weapons could be used in what is now fashionably called a 'theatre war'. I do not believe that any scenario exists which suggests that nuclear weapons could be used in field warfare between two nuclear states without escalation resulting. I know of several such exercises. They all lead to the opposite conclusion. There is no Marquess of Queensberry who would be holding the ring in a nuclear conflict. I cannot see teams of physicists attached to military staffs who would run to the scene of a nuclear explosion and then back to tell their local commanders that the radiation intensity of a nuclear strike by the other side was such and such, and that therefore the riposte should be only a weapon of equivalent yield. If the zone of lethal or wounding neutron radiation of a so-called neutron bomb would have, say, a radius of half a kilometer, the reply might well be a 'dirty' bomb with the same zone of radiation, but with a much wider area of devastation due to blast and fire.

To the best of my knowledge, no one has yet suggested a mutually agreed mechanism for controlling escalation on a battlefield. Until we are assured that there could be one, we have to see any degree of nuclear destruction as part of a continuous spectrum of devastation. Having some knowledge of the way generals and air marshals discharge their responsibilities in war – having understood why they do as they do – I have no faith that they would behave differently in any future war. What Admiral Miller has told us about the chain of command in the control of the use of nuclear weapons makes it inevitable that if the concept of tactical nuclear warfare were to have any meaning at all, there would have to be the authority for 'prior-release' as soon as hostilities begin. Another speaker, in his explanation of the concept, has told us that if a division or a brigade feared that it was going to be overwhelmed then, according to NATO doctrine, it would have to resort to the use of nuclear weapons. Were this indeed to happen, we would be talking not of nuclear tactical warfare, but about kamikaze warfare leading to mutual annihilation. Wars are fought on the ground, and by men, and not in accordance with some pre-ordained scenario, and not by moving little flags around on maps on a wall in Moscow or Washington or Paris or London. Wars may start as central planners predict; but history shows that they rarely, if ever, proceed, or indeed end, as predicted.

The next, and again related, danger which I see as possibly leading to nuclear warfare is, of course, the proliferation of nuclear-weapon states. Some countries which might 'go nuclear' are undoubtedly encouraged by the belief that nuclear weapons – weapons which we cannot wish away – have a tactical or battlefield value. This promotes a belief in their utility. There is also a false belief that the possession of nuclear weapons implies political power. But the greater the number of nuclear-weapons states, the more difficult the maintenance of the present situation of deterrence between the few existing nuclear powers.

People forget that when nuclear weapons were first developed in the US, in the UK, and then in the USSR, it was believed that in effect they were just super-bombs capable of providing, in a phrase now happily forgotten, 'more bang for a buck'. It was only when the risks associated with their possible use became appreciated that the concept of mutual nuclear deterrence emerged. The idea of deterrence then moved inexorably to the idea of equivalence of nuclear power, and then to questions of control. But today, even though knowledgeable men, for example Kissinger, ask what meaning can be attached to the concept of 'nuclear superiority', even when wise men have long known that 'enough is enough', the nuclear arms race continues unabated.

There is, of course, a danger of the control system that maintains the state of deterrence inadvertently breaking down. We have heard at this meeting that, during the Cuba crisis of 1962, some American warships were not fully under command from the top. In times of war, control systems do become precarious. When asked what he thought of the political control of nuclear weapons in Europe, Field Marshal Montgomery said publicly that he would seek permission to fire only after he had fired. The present system could also break down because national sovereignty implies that the much smaller nuclear arsenals of the United Kingdom and France could independently trigger nuclear war. If a British ship in, say, the Indian Ocean, were to launch nuclear missiles at Russian targets, how would the Russians know under which flag they had been fired?

I keep asking myself whether it was wrong to treat Szilard's solution – to have built under Moscow a nuclear fortress manned by American personnel in communication with Washington, with a corresponding fortress manned by Russians under Washington – as a joke.

The next danger which might trigger nuclear war derives from the momentum of the technological arms race itself. We in the West are fearful of the build-up of Warsaw Pact conventional forces in the same way as the Russians are fearful of the possible introduction of cruise missiles and other new types of delivery systems. As we have been told by Admiral Miller, who knows more about strategic targeting than most of us, new nuclear warheads have to be assigned targets as they are produced, whether or not there is a requirement for additional destructive capability. Political fears and reciprocal suspicions have inevitable reactions. The technological arms race cannot but be politically destabilizing.

Finally, I see as another danger which might trigger nuclear war, the continuing competition in the sale of arms – conventional arms, it is true – but none the less a transfer of destructive power which might generate situations in which nuclear weapons could be used.

These are the dangers I see. What then would be my priorities in their reduction? Here I agree completely with Dr Arbatov that the first thing to do is to slow down the arms race, and if possible to reverse it. I am not a dreamer. I do not visualize disarmament as a practical goal; I would be content with arms control.

The first measure which I regard as important is the reduction in the race of proliferation of nuclear weapons. The United Kingdom is committed to the Non-Proliferation Treaty and to such other treaties as have been agreed in order to reduce the dangers which face us. I see as critical to the Non-Proliferation Treaty an unqualified complete test ban. When states began to negotiate for a non-proliferation treaty, they were concerned with the spread of nuclear weapons to non-nuclear countries. Then we started hearing about the 'horizontal proliferation' which the nuclear powers wanted to prevent, and the concept of 'vertical proliferation' which non-nuclear countries, for example India, saw as continuing between the nuclear powers. I believe it to be essential that a Comprehensive Test Ban (CTB) is agreed in such a way that potential nuclear powers will not be able to build up their own arsenals, and the nuclear powers will be unable to elaborate what they already have. That, in all logic, comes first.

Next, I believe it is essential for the world that the SALT talks achieve some measure of success, and that they succeed in full public view. There should be no hitches here. It is a fact of history that with every delay in reaching an agreement in the control of nuclear arms – due to a failure to agree to this or that at any given moment – nuclear stocks build up at such a rate that the best that could be achieved later is worse than the worst that might have been concluded a year or two before. With every delay, our mutual peril becomes greater.

I have said that I see a Comprehensive Test Ban as a *sine qua non* for the achievement of non-proliferation. As my colleague Lord Trend knows, I was personally involved in the negotiations that led up to the Partial Test Ban Treaty of 1963. I soon became acutely conscious of the fact that heads of state are accountable to different constituencies. Whatever the President of the United States may agree, he has to carry the Senate with him. Like him, the Senators are under pressure from their own constituents and in part from the views of the military chiefs. While the military chiefs may have to defer to the views of their commander-in-chief, the President, they also have their own public to deal with.

I do not know what the position is in the USSR and what influence the military have on the Secretary of the Party and on the Central Committee. But I do know that from the moment he began his crusade for a test ban, Harold Macmillan was personally committed as a statesman to the achievement, first of a complete test ban, and then, when he was driven to appreciate the difficulties with which President Kennedy was wrestling, of a Partial Test Ban. And I also know that in stating his position publicly, he did not feel it necessary to consult either his Chiefs of Staff or the heads of our weapons laboratory.

However difficult a CTB, it would be far easier to monitor than any other kind of treaty. Let us therefore start with it. Another measure which might avert some of the dangers was touched on during the course of our meeting; namely, sanctions against any non-nuclear state which decides to 'go nuclear', or which undertakes a nuclear test.

I come back, inevitably, to my first point. However difficult the task, let us find a way to educate people properly about the dangers.

We realize that by the year 2000 there will be problems before the world even more serious than the dangers of a nuclear war in the intervening years. The global population will by then greatly exceed that of today. Poverty will still be with us. We shall still have our energy problems. The Third World will be struggling to catch up. All these matters will have to be settled internationally. As was said earlier on at our meeting, the arms race is a luxury which not even the super-powers can afford any longer.

Stopping the arms race is a matter for political determination. It is not an issue which should or can be decided on the basis of bickering arguments either between so-called military analysts or weapons specialists. If war is too serious a matter to be left to the generals, peace certainly is. The nuclear arms race can be halted only by those statesmen, on both and on all sides, who refuse to allow their view of the world to be blinkered by illusory experts.

12

A Forecast

FRANKLYN GRIFFITHS

What are the dangers of nuclear war to the year 2000? A danger is of course a peril or harmful consequence to which one is more or less liable. Neither the consequences nor the possibilities of nuclear war can be estimated with assurance. Yet we do need an idea of how the nuclear threat to humanity might develop in future if we are to take appropriate action now.

Uncertainty in the face of the many nuclear wars that could in principle occur before the end of the century may be reduced, albeit arbitrarily, by considering those combinations of actors, capabilities, and contexts that initially seem most likely to engender war, and that have evoked most concern. Uncertainty may further be reduced if assumptions are made about the political and military setting in which decisions about nuclear war and peace will be made. The rudimentary forecast that follows will accordingly consider the dangers of general and limited nuclear war and of nuclear terrorism in a changing poltical-military environment. What dangers do these various forms of nuclear war present to humanity, and are they likely to increase, diminish, or remain unchanged over the next twenty years?

GENERAL WAR

General war entails exchanges of nuclear blows between states possessing advanced long-range systems in number and kind sufficient not only to devastate one another but to visit destruction upon the population, civilization, and physical environment of the planet as a whole. Only the Soviet Union, the United States, and possibly China seem likely to have an authentic capacity to wage general war by 2000. To attain this questionable status, other states would have to produce not only sufficiently large numbers of nuclear warheads to pose a threat to the global population and environment, but also the means to deliver them effectively against the economically and technologically most powerful of societies. Others (for example, France, West Germany, or Japan) might succeed in doing just this. But here it is assumed the impediments will be too great. The danger of general war is likely to be associated primarily with the behaviour of the present two super-powers and increasingly with the conduct of China.

The present-day consequences of an unlimited strategic exchange between the Soviet Union and the United States are examined in stark and detached fashion by Carson Mark in his contribution to this volume. Presented with a vision of devastation that is already virtually beyond comprehension, it is appropriate to ask whether the outcome of general war could become significantly more adverse.

Although science may reveal to us new and even more catastrophic effects from the detonation of very large numbers of nuclear weapons, any further increases in the destructiveness of general war must surely be of marginal significance only. Humanity has already entered the twenty-first century in so far as the capacity of some to shorten the lives and destroy the habitat and civilization of all is concerned. Nor is the destructiveness of general war likely to diminish markedly over the next two decades without the erection of international institutions that effectively provide new sources of safety. For in the absence of such institutions, a substantial reduction in the destructiveness of nuclear war would serve to weaken the deterrence that is born of terror in the face of its consequences.

If the peril posed by general war is at present staggeringly great and may be expected to stay that way to the end of the century, what of the likelihood of an unlimited nuclear exchange between super-powers?

The observations of McGeorge Bundy, Admiral Miller, and George Rathjens indicate that currently the likelihood of general war as the result of an intentional or inadvertent massive surprise attack is small. So also is the risk of an unlimited exchange following upon the accidental or unauthorized release of a limited number of nuclear weapons in a non-crisis setting. This situation seems likely to persist, granted one assumption: that a radical discontinuity does not occur in the political leadership of a super-power to place in authority a group of adventurers or lunatics ready to accept formidable risks in the use of nuclear weapons. For the latter to occur, politics within as well as between major nations would have to approach anarchy in the next twenty years – a possibility but not one that is here assumed to be great.

In effect, acute super-power crisis is now and will doubtless remain a precondition for the occurrence of general war. To inquire into the likelihood of general war is therefore to consider the likelihood and character of super-power crises – the potential they present for miscalculation, for inadequate control of national strategic forces, and for mutual loss of control over escalation of the crisis itself. John Steinbruner's account of the vagrant strategic anti-submarine warfare operations of the US Navy during the Cuban missile crisis of 1962 shows just how things might begin to go wrong. And this was at a time when political leaders sought to exercise intense political control over military forces far less complex and elaborate than exist today.

During the next twenty years the occurrence of general war as a consequence of super-power nuclear crisis would seem on balance to be increasingly likely. A vast assortment of cross-cutting processes and influences will be at work, only a few of which can be considered here.

To begin with, international relationships appear destined to become less stable and orderly as we witness a redistribution of power and influence, well-being, and status among the members of the international community. The order-producing activity of states may succeed in averting some of the most severe consequences of redistribution. But it will probably not keep pace with the growing disarray in world affairs. Indeed, while bilateral and multilateral co-operation should add structure to the process of international change, it is also likely to create new agendas upon which to divide – as is already indicated by the American-Soviet strategic arms limitation talks (SALT), the Helsinki and Belgrade meetings on European security, the United Nations Conference on the Law of the Sea, and so on.

Whether it be energy shortages, uneven rates of technological innovation and transfer, unbalanced economic development within as well as between nations, explosive population growth, widespread poverty and starvation, or transformations in the sense of purpose and identity of entire societies, powerful forces are altering the capabilities, ambitions, and prospects of states. The astonishing rise of OPEC, the recognition of new limits to American power, the new foreign activity of China and the ensuing deterioration of the Soviet outlook, the growing menace of nuclear proliferation, the alarming potential for a division of the globe along north-south lines – these developments may be viewed as harbingers of substantially changed international relations by 2000. The rapidity and scope of redistribution among the members of the international system are, of course, highly contingent. But there can be little doubt that the occasions for international violence will become more frequent as the relatively settled world order of recent times gives way to a setting of systemic change.

All of this is to suggest that the underlying circumstances of world politics to the end of the century will serve to sharpen rather than attenuate conflict between China, the Soviet Union, and the United States. The leading powers will be presented with more frequent opportunities and doubtless the perceived necessity, as voiced by articulate internal constituencies, to intervene in local conflicts and otherwise to seek a favourable disposition of an increasingly complex and mobile balance of global advantage. Continued awareness of the threat of nuclear war may at the same time be expected to keep the risks of confrontation high in comparison with the benefits of indirect intervention and limited aid to client or 'proxy' states.

Where the past two decades have seen only two super-power nuclear crises, one of which was severe, the greater international disorder of the next twenty years could yield at least the same number and possibly more if the next one or two were not acute. Furthermore, the implications of success or failure in crisis for a major power's sense of purpose and standing in world affairs could come to be regarded as more momentous than is the case today. A more active manipulation of nuclear weapons to back bargaining positions in crisis might accordingly be seen as more necessary than at present. In such a setting, the possibilities of disaster through miscalculation and escalation, emphasized most strongly by John Polanyi and Lord Zuckerman in this volume, could be expected to increase.

In sum, the underlying process of change in international relations may broaden the crisis path to general war in the years ahead, unless effective countervailing action is taken on behalf of arms control and other forms of collaboration among the super-powers. They must lead the way.

As George Ignatieff states in this account of the arms control effort to date, the super-powers have been more interested in crisis management than in the limitation and reduction of strategic forces. Both the Soviet Union and the United States will presumably continue to rely upon strategic nuclear weapons for security and presumed political advantage. Moreover, as China moves toward the essential equivalence that neither of today's super-powers will allow another to exceed, each of the three may in the long term have to retain sufficient forces to counter the other two, despite the selective rapprochements and détentes of the moment.

As several of the contributors to this book imply, the strategic arms race appears to be here to stay in greater or diminished form to the end of the century.

In this context, the SALT negotiations, eventually widened to include China, will be of especial importance in affirming the existence of barriers to general war as a consequence of nuclear crisis. This could be accomplished primarily through the elaboration of a sense of mutual restraint and the expectation of accommodation, as observed by Steinbruner in his account of the resolution of the Middle East crisis of 1973. In addition, the participants in SALT or its successor negotiation may come to agree increasingly upon the need to structure and control their strategic forces with an eye to greater military stability in crisis. Though it is greatly to be hoped that SALT will also increase physical security by the reduction of super-power strategic forces, the prospects in this regard are not encouraging, and may better be realized through unilateral restraint in defence management, as suggested by Richard Garwin. The significance of SALT may therefore remain essentially political in fostering a shared awareness of the common interest in survival – an awareness that could gradually moderate the future crisis behaviour of the super-powers.

The extent to which the likelihood of general war as a result of crisis in an increasingly disorderly world is held in check or reduced by co-operation and restraint among the leading powers is impossible to predict. A formidable array of influences will again be at work, most of which will act in spontaneous fashion and only some of which can be considered here.

On the one hand, widespread apprehension about nuclear war may be expected to grow, and to bring with it a greater tendency to restraint, if not co-operation. Similar but more pronounced effects could be produced by an acute nuclear crisis that stopped short of war and did not result in a major political defeat for one side. Unfortunately, it must also be recognized that the cautionary political lessons of a generalized perception of greater danger or a close brush with nuclear war would pale before the consequences of the first use of nuclear weapons after Nagasaki. Should the first use occur in a local war between smaller nuclear-weapon states or in a terrorist attack, an unusual opportunity for super-power collaboration on behalf of arms control and moderated competition could arise.

In addition, as Shalheveth Freier and Walter Schütze point out, further nuclear proliferation could oblige the super-powers to act with greater prudence in intervening in local conflict areas that might otherwise provide a greater occasion for crisis. Indeed, Schütze goes on to suggest that additional proliferation might eventually reduce the super-powers' capacity to influence developments in the southern portion of an international system fragmented along north-south lines, so much so that they would virtually be excluded from competition in the area.

Further, there is the possibility, discussed by George Rathjens, of the Soviet Union and the United States taking advantage of innovation in military technology to develop the capacity to wage limited strategic war as an alternative to the choice between suicidal massive exchanges or political defeat in crisis. In Rathjens' opinion, a commitment to limited nuclear options could make the use of nuclear weapons more probable in an acute super-power crisis; but once nuclear weapons had been brought into use, the likelihood of escalation to general war might be somewhat reduced.

Most of this sounds like making the world safer by making it more dangerous. And so it would: direct experience of greater danger would help to create the political will required for more extensive collaboration among adversaries. But this is by no means the whole story.

Mounting apprehension at the growing danger of nuclear war could equally well lead the Soviet Union, the United States, or China to rely still more heavily upon policies of strength and opposition. An acute nuclear crisis could result in a striking setback for one rival, an extremely unsettling outcome if the victim then resolved to seek compensation and otherwise to avoid subsequent losses. As to the first use of nuclear weapons after Nagasaki, if it took the form of a limited exchange between major nuclear powers, the devastation could be so great and the circumstances so complex as indefinitely to prevent postwar co-operation among the belligerents. Similarly, while nuclear proliferation could cause the super-powers to exercise greater caution in Third World conflict situations, it would also give smaller nuclear-weapon states powerful instruments with which to provoke super-power intervention in local wars and hence to invoke general war.

Finally, it would be extremely risky to believe that the limited use of strategic nuclear weapons in a super-power conflict would stop at that and not prove to be but a way-station between nuclear alert and general war. Wars do not run according to plan. As Bundy notes in speaking of Europe, no one really knows what would happen once nuclear weapons had been brought into use. Moreover, to develop the capacity to strike selectively at the opponent's strategic forces would be to raise the threat of a pre-emptive first strike, and thus to further a climate of suspicion that would surely reduce the propensity to collaborate.

To sum up, we are faced with extraordinary uncertainty in attempting to estimate the course of relations among the super-powers, whether it will on balance favour co-operation or the sharpening of conflict. Each of the major variables in the situation is capable of working in widely divergent ways. There is, however, reason to believe that underlying processes of systemic change in international relations will enlarge the potential for super-power conflict and increase the need for super-power co-operation in the years ahead. The incidence and severity of super-power crisis, and hence the likelihood of general war, will probably grow. Indeed, they could grow substantially if we are not brought to recognize the dangers far more clearly and to insist on moderation in foreign and military policy.

LIMITED NUCLEAR WAR

Where the routes leading to general war seem few and comparatively well marked, the picture for limited nuclear war resembles a city map studded with large and small intersections. Many potential belligerents are involved. These range from the Soviet Union and the United States, who could conceivably engage in limited nuclear war as matters stand, to nuclear war near the end of the century between a minor North African state and a nearby power equipped with conventional weapons only. In between there is the possibility of limited nuclear war in Europe, between China and the USSR, in the Persian Gulf area or the Middle East, in outer space or at sea, between Argentina and Brazil, and so on.

To simplify matters, let us briefly consider the future dangers as they concern first the major nuclear-weapon states of today, and second the lesser nuclear powers that could come into being as a result of further proliferation.

Where Britain, China, France, the Soviet Union, and the United States are concerned, the danger of limited nuclear war may be expected to increase in response to processes of systemic change and in the degree that awareness of the growing threat does not impose greater restraint in foreign and defence policy. The outlook here is broadly the same as for general war, and for broadly the same reasons. This much said, some distinctions are in order.

In the first place, the future likelihood of limited nuclear war among the major powers would seem to be somewhat greater than is the case for general war.

Aside from the fact that currently there are two more major powers capable of waging limited as opposed to general war, limited nuclear war is at least temporally a precondition for general war. It cannot be assumed that every nuclear exchange among major powers, whatever its beginnings, would proceed to develop into general war. Nor should it be assumed that general war would be initiated with a massive attack. If strategic war occurred among major powers, it would more likely commence after the panoply of conventional and tactical nuclear weapons had been brought to bear in comparatively 'restrained' attacks. As long as the ensuing exchanges continued to be subject to calculated control, the possibility of a decision to terminate the use of nuclear weapons would remain, as would the possibility of loss of control. In these circumstances every effort would be made to avert mutual annihilation in general war.

This is by no means to suggest that nuclear war is controllable, or that it would be desirable to act as though it were. Rather the point is that of the range of possible outcomes of nuclear conflict among major powers, for example in Europe, ascending degrees of limited war are considerably more numerous, separated in time, and open to cessation than is the case for the variations in unrestrained strategic attacks. In principle, though this could not be relied upon in practice, limited nuclear war would seem the more likely outcome once nuclear weapons had been brought into use.

Secondly, the interaction of politics and the evolution of military technology is encouraging the belief, as Zuckerman puts it, that nuclear weapons are real weapons of choice. The development of enhanced radiation or neutron weapons and very low-yield fission weapons deliverable with great accuracy are instances in point. They further the view that nuclear war, if it occurred, could be held to low levels of destruction with greater assurance than when more powerful weapons were used. Similar processes are at work on the strategic plane, where the development of weapons systems with lower explosive yields, greater accuracy and reliability, and ultra-secure, surgically exact command and control is regarded as permitting controllable limited strategic exchanges as opposed to the choice between general war and political defeat.

Should the United States and its allies, followed as technology permits by the Soviet Union and China, set themselves up to fight limited nuclear war, they would probably increase the likelihood of its occurence. The opposing view has it that with an alternative to political defeat or annihilation, nuclear crises that might otherwise lead to general war could be averted. This might be. But once an acute crisis had led to war with conventional arms, the likelihood of nuclear weapons being used would rise substantially over present levels. If the view that nuclear weapons are weapons of choice is permitted to stand, the prospect of their being chosen will surely grow, as will the intention to wage limited nuclear war if necessary.

Third, whereas limited nuclear war among major powers would appear to be somewhat more probable than general war, and could become still more likely owing to technological trends, the consequences of limited nuclear war for humanity would be less adverse and conceivably much less adverse. At the one extreme, the battlefield use of tactical nuclear weapons or a limited nuclear war at sea could be held to a comparatively small exchange in a war otherwise fought with conventional weapons. At the other, the cataclysmic consequences of a limited strategic exchange involving American-Soviet counterforce attacks and a hard-fought 'limited' nuclear war in Europe, would in many respects be indistinguishable from those brought on by general war. Nevertheless, when the extremes are set aside, limited nuclear war could be expected to yield death and destruction on a scale that defied the imagination, but not devastation of a magnitude that directly threatened human civilization and the planetary environment.

Where limited nuclear war among new nuclear-weapon states is concerned, the adverse consequences for humanity would be still less. Aside from the likelihood that only India, Israel, and South Africa could currently deploy a small number of nuclear weapons on short notice, the limited explosive yield and range of these weapons would confine their effects to limited areas in comparison to those engaged in nuclear war among major powers. This would be of absolutely no consolation to those Third World societies and cities that could be subject to risks of devastation greater than the global norm. But when viewed from a planetary perspective, the adverse consequences of limited nuclear war among new nuclear-weapon states do pose a diminished danger.

As both Freier and Schütze suggest, at least some further increase in the number of nuclear-weapon states is to be anticipated in the next twenty years. Just how large the increase will be should depend upon success or failure in strengthening the non-proliferation regime, particularly the degree to which the Soviet Union and the United States set an example of reduced reliance on nuclear weapons by honouring their commitment, made in the Non-Proliferation Treaty, to reduce their strategic forces. Among those more likely to acquire nuclear weapons Schütze lists Algeria, Argentina, Brazil, Chile, Egypt, Indonesia, Iran, Iraq, Libya,

Nigeria, Pakistan, Phillipines, Saudi Arabia, South Korea, Syria, Taiwan, and Zaire.

The nth powers that actually proceed to acquire nuclear weapons will do so in a context that favours their use to a greater extent than would be the case for major nuclear-weapon states. Aside from processes of systemic change in international relations that will entail regional as well as global realignments of power and position, and hence continued Third World regional conflicts, attitudes toward nuclear weapons and war may also be rather different in this quarter. Freier points out that notions of mutual deterrence and assured destruction could prove to be quite foreign to the leaders of less developed states. Whether or not they are prone to behave in dictatorial, arbitrary, and mercurial fashion, they may, as Freier suggests, be acting in a setting where national antagonisms are strong and where success in foreign ventures could seem an attractive means of strengthening national self-esteem.

In addition, the military-strategic setting in the developing areas could make war rather than deterrence the order of the day. As is pointed out by Schütze, the assurance provided to most of the major nuclear powers by their alliance systems would not be at hand to mute the insecurity of newer nuclear-weapon states. Moreover, the weapons themselves would be more vulnerable to surprise attack and pre-emptive use. Lacking the protection of great distance from the opponent, and without extensive warning systems or hardened basing facilities, the new nuclear-weapon state, as Garwin reminds us, will be more likely to employ its forces in a crisis.

Indeed, of the various combinations of actors, capabilities, and settings that have been considered thus far, limited nuclear war between new nuclear-weapon states would appear to be most likely to occur between now and 2000. Further, should one or more lesser powers not only resolve to produce nuclear weapons but then succeed in using them for blackmail or self-defence, a major stimulus would be given to further proliferation, and hence to a still greater likelihood of limited nuclear war among smaller states. Where the first use of nuclear weapons after Nagasaki might serve to bring the developed countries together on behalf of greater co-operation in international security affairs, it could equally well drive the less developed countries apart.

In sum, limited nuclear war among major powers appears to be somewhat more likely than general war, and the likelihood itself will increase over the next twenty years for broadly the same reasons that apply in the case of general war unless the will is found to moderate the risks through greater co-operation among the potential belligerents. Where new nuclear states are concerned, the risks of limited war to the year 2000 will probably grow at a greater rate if governments fail to lend stability to a changing world through further development of the nuclear non-proliferation regime and super-power arms reduction in particular. At the same time, the adverse consequences of limited nuclear war for humanity would by definition be less destructive than those encountered in general war, and considerably less so where war between new nuclear-weapon states was concerned.

NUCLEAR TERRORISM

There is also a possibility of warfare at still lower levels of nuclear violence. Here we are concerned with non-state organizations and groups that regard themselves as being in a state of war with governments and social systems, and whose actions may lead to the detonation of nuclear explosives or the release of radio-active material into the environment.

Nuclear terrorism is the least destructive of the hazards we face and perhaps the most likely to occur before 2000.

As is the case with other forms of nuclear war, the destructive consequences of nuclear terrorism could be quite varied. A portion of a large city could be annihilated with great loss of life if a bomb were detonated. Or conceivably an attack could result in only the relatively ineffectual use of a radiological weapon or the partial destruction of a nuclear generating station.

At this level of nuclear warfare, adverse political consequences would also loom large in relation to population loss and environmental destruction. Here again the range of possible effects of one or more acts of nuclear terrorism might be quite large. An authoritarian protective reaction destructive of civil rights could sweep the liberal democracies. Other terrorist organizations could be encouraged to follow the first. Or, as William Epstein notes, inter-state war could result if one government believed that the attack had surreptitiously been sponsored by another. More generally, the capacity of nuclear terrorism to heighten insecurity and to further a climate of opinion in which nuclear war seemed imminent, should not be underestimated. If the first act of nuclear terrorism did not lead to a more vigorous effort to strengthen international security through arms control and the building of new institutions to lend order to an uncertain world, subsequent terrorist attacks could have quite disastrous effects on national foreign and military policies.

As to the likelihood of nuclear terrorism, Epstein suggests that although the current probability is very low, it is almost certain to increase to the point of inevitability by 2000. This alarming prediction is based upon a variety of considerations including the potential for nuclear proliferation and hence nuclear weapons theft from a new nuclear power, the increasing availability of fissionable material with which to construct explosive devices, and the wider access to technical experts and expertise necessary for manufacturing nuclear weapons.

Although the ease or simplicity of constructing a workable nuclear weapon is debatable, as is the degree to which terrorists regarding themselves as the vanguard of a mass movement would resort to the use of such weapons, it remains that only a very few individuals dedicated to social revolution, national autonomy, or a transfer of wealth would have to make the decision to proceed. Where domestic and international impediments to the use of nuclear weapons by states are likely to be substantial even in the case of new nuclear powers, the political constraints experienced by the individuals forming a terrorist organization would be comparatively slight. Moreover, the social setting within the developed countries and in the poverty-stricken areas of the southern hemisphere will presumably continue to give rise to individuals capable of truly desperate acts of terrorism, and possibly in greater numbers should frustration and despair continue to increase.

International co-operation may again serve to reduce the future risks, but the prospects for joint counter-terrorist action do not currently appear to be great. Unless this pattern changes, the more likely outlook is one of growth in the threat of nuclear terrorism from its present low level to pose a prominent if not a major threat to humanity in the years ahead.

CONCLUSIONS

Each of the dangers of nuclear war considered here will increase unless countered by imaginative and determined action. They will not go away or look after themselves. They are sufficiently complex and deeply rooted in domestic and international society to require extraordinary creativity and political will if they are to be resolved. Their resolution ultimately requires the improvisation of new forms of governance adapted more to global than to national needs of order and well-being. This, however, is a task that promises to occupy us for generations to come. For the remainder of this century our primary need is to avert the worst and to secure the time to grope toward a new world order.

Of the nuclear dangers that must be faced, general war is unquestionably the gravest in view of the virtually unimaginable consequences it would visit upon us. Limited nuclear war, while it would appear to be somewhat more likely than general war where major powers are concerned, and considerably more likely for any new nuclear-weapon states that appear, presents in comparison a diminished threat owing to the lesser destruction that would follow. As to nuclear terrorism, it offers the smallest of the hazards of nuclear war, despite its still greater likelihood. There is obviously a pattern here, one that suggests the greater the nuclear calamity, the less likely it is to occur. This should not, however, cause us to focus our attention in future upon what seem to be the more probable forms of nuclear war as presenting the most urgent threats. The destructiveness of general war and, to a lesser extent, of limited nuclear war among major powers, is such as to offset the diminished possibilities and to produce dangers of unparalleled magnitude.

It should also be noted that we have been considering various hazards of nuclear war in isolation, and with certain assumptions about the development of international relations to the year 2000. A combined assessment of the possibilities suggests a still larger risk that nuclear weapons will be brought into use during the next twenty years. And if we relax the assumption made at the outset that Japan and Western Germany will continue to abstain from the acquisition of independent nuclear forces, the prospects of human survival become considerably more perilous. Similarly, if we set aside the further assumption that greater turbulence and disorder in world affairs will not at some point threaten anarchy as a consequence of acute energy shortages, the cessation of economic growth, or unexpectedly adverse climatic change, the outlook for the avoidance of nuclear war could decline very sharply indeed.

A worst case estimate of the dangers of nuclear war is not at this point any more appropriate than most worst case arguments in favour of acquiring new weapons systems. The menace that faces us is not overwhelming. There is time to summon the imagination and the will to avert nuclear war.

13

The Dangers of Nuclear War

JOHN C. POLANYI

Looking back over the papers presented here, which reflect – as one would wish – the varied backgrounds of their authors, and recalling the days of discussion at the Symposium, one is struck by the fact that something approaching a consensus should have emerged. The Statement at the outset of this volume gives concise expression to that consensus. The objective in this closing chapter is to present a more personal view of the discussion, which, at the same time, reflects its dominant themes.

One of the contributors remarked that: 'It is in the nature of things that misfortune can be more compellingly argued than propitious constellations.' If 'compellingly' denotes 'arrestingly', then the point is well taken. If, however, 'compellingly' is to mean 'convincingly', one must demur. Human imagination is too feeble to encompass the level of misfortune implied by the gloomier prognostications for the year 2000. Even the relatively modest scale of disaster that unfolded in 1914 and once again in 1939 went far beyond the most fearful expectations – their magnitude was in fact only grasped in retrospect.

It is quite true, of course, that prophets of doom are a more common spectacle than prophets of joy, or even prophets of muddling through. 'The End is Near' has a more arresting ring than 'More-of-the-Same Is Near'. None the less – and this is the point that needs to be made – it is the latter that we choose to believe, as our daily actions amply testify. Indeed it is not only our daily actions (which matter less) but our actions at the fateful junctures of history that give evidence of the human tendency to turn away from what is awful to contemplate. Thus Barbara Tuchman in *The Guns of August* remarks: 'One constant among the elements of 1914 – as of any era – was the disposition of everyone on all sides not to prepare for the harder alternative, not to act on what they suspected to be true.'[1]

George Rathjens says something akin to this when he stresses that the scenarios for nuclear war which attract the keenest attention and most voluminous analysis are those which are the simplest to grasp. We must guard against the supposition that they are the most likely to occur. Lord Zuckerman expressed the thought most clearly in his remarks addressed to the Prime Minister when he gave prime place to the following proposition: 'My first point is that one real danger of the possibility of nuclear war is that we have ceased to understand what we are talking about. How can one imagine the reality: the possible elimination, not only of say half the population of the Northern hemisphere, but also the elimination of the better part of the cultural history of our globe?'

The consequences of a major nuclear exchange between the Soviet Union and the United States are set out in the opening chapter of this volume. Many scores of millions in the two countries would die promptly, to be followed by more millions of deaths among those exposed to radioactive fall-out, those enfeebled by a multitude of injuries, and those who were in other than robust health at the time of the cataclysm and must contend with harsh circumstances of life. Carson Mark's dispassionate account steers clear of the elements in the picture that are hardest to quantify; for example, the fact that many millions who die in the aftermath of a massive nuclear exchange will die most horribly in a society that can no longer offer the comforts of warmth, shelter, food, uncontaminated water, and medication. The millions of injured who survive in a condition of reduced health (blinded, burnt, maimed, or weakened by the effects of radiation) will provide a fertile ground for plagues of contagious disease. Those fortunate enough to escape the war and its aftermath without visible scars will live in fear that their long-term health may have been impaired, their environment poisoned, and their future progeny imperilled for generations to come. The sense of demoralization, and its consequences for the orderly process of reconstruction, defy imagination. No parallels can be drawn (though sometimes they are) with the deaths and carnage of previous wars. The compression into a matter of hours of events more terrible than those that took place in other times over a period of years will shred the fabric of society rather than – as previously – severely strain it.

The consequences of a limited nuclear blow in which intercontinental ballistic missiles (ICBMs) are used to reduce an opponent's ability to retaliate do not differ as vastly from the foregoing picture as was once supposed – both Mark and Rathjens comment on this important point. (It is a measure of the inevitable crudity of such calculations that neither author

184 John C. Polanyi

remarks on the fact that a by-product of such a 'surgical' nuclear strike if it were aimed at the US would be the death of roughly one million Canadians.[2])

Given the appalling consequences of nuclear war, it is almost tautological to point out that the major danger of a war that unleashed ICBMs armed with hydrogen-bomb warheads stems from inadvertence. It is evident from the foregoing chapters that the two most feared forms of inadvertence are miscalculation and escalation.

MISCALCULATION

The majority of participants in this Symposium conceded one central role for nuclear weapons, namely as a threat sufficient to prevent the employment by an opponent of his nuclear weapons. They warned, however, (in the Statement at the start of this volume) that: 'We have not mastered the paradox that the avoidance of nuclear war requires both stable general deterrence and deep restraint in reliance on nuclear weaponry of any sort.' The legitimate objective was seen, by most, to be the exploitation of nuclear weapons to avoid nuclear war. The danger sprang from reliance on nuclear weapons for purposes that might (rightly or wrongly) be construed as going beyond this. The latter would be the traditional purposes for which nations have employed armed might – as a threat, or in actuality, to compel others to yield on contentious issues.

If one were asked to say in a single sentence what, in the view of the participants, constituted the gravest source of danger of nuclear war in the coming decades, the answer would surely have been that the danger stemmed from the transfer of traditional notions of the functions of military power into the context of nuclear force. Accordingly, the remainder of these few retrospective comments will be devoted to this topic.

Deterrence has its dangers, and they are sobering. There is no guarantee, for example, that a fanatic can be deterred. This century has had more than its share of irrational acts by national leaders. A world in which the employment of nuclear weapons is held in check by the threat of horrible punishment will still be a dangerous place. It will, however, be incomparably safer than a world in which nuclear weapons are used by opposing parties as a means of demonstrating (through threats) or asserting (through acts) the extent of their national will.

Strategies which are genuinely designed to assure a sufficient and sane level of mutual deterrence offer the least possibility for miscalculation of an opponent's capabilities and intentions. At a Pugwash conference eighteen years ago Leo Szilard suggested that major nuclear powers agree to the emplacement of nuclear weapons, controlled from each other's command centres, beneath their major cities. The proposal was regarded at the time as a sort of macabre joke. In fact it represents the apotheosis of the trend toward institutionalized vulnerability exemplified, for example, in the SALT agreements which deny the signatory nations defence by anti-ballistic missile (ABM) systems or security from continual surveillance by satellites.[3]

By contrast, the exploitation of nuclear weapons for 'compellence' rather than 'deterrence' provides fertile ground for dangerous miscalculations of capabilities and intentions. Nuclear compellence implies nuclear competition aimed at ascendancy rather than rough parity. Though exaggerated claims of the requirements of deterrence have played their part in fuelling the arms race, the requirements for compellence – namely precision, flexibility, versatility, and modernity – provide an open-ended rationale for arms racing. The spectacle of the arms race, and the shifting panoply of nuclear capabilities that it produces, is itself a source of misunderstanding and hence misjudgment of intentions. Worse yet, the requirements of more effective compellence argue for policies which keep potential opponents guessing. This ambivalence is built into military doctrine which recognizes two distinct categories of policy, namely 'declaratory policy' mentioned by Lord Zuckerman, and 'action policy'; the former constitutes overt threats and actions, the latter embodies covert intentions and reservations. The whole could add up to a species of schizophrenia that presents grave dangers of confusion, not only between competing nations but within them.

During the Cuban missile crisis these dangers were clearly recognized and every effort was made to keep declaratory and action policy at one. Both sides, as Steinbruner points out in his carefully measured account, were extremely alert to the danger that they might become the victims of events that they had set into motion but could no longer fully control. However, notwithstanding precautions which could hardly be bettered on a future occasion (the crisis took place, after all, just off the coast of a nation with the most sophisticated command and control capabilities) 'the American military response to the crisis developed farther in the direction of global strategic operations than the President or the Executive Committee either intended or imagined in advance.' Steinbruner puts forth evidence that, expressing the matter starkly, in the Cuban missile crisis 'efforts to bring American policy under central direction must be said to have failed'.

This failure of central control can be seen to be virtually inescapable, even when, as in this instance, all pains were taken to establish and to retain the closest possible supervision on the part of the top executive level. Steinbruner expresses the matter succinctly: 'In order for the complex organizational system to work at all a great deal of authority to make preparations necessarily resides at low levels of the command structure. This very basic fact unfortunately provides ample means for the events of a crisis to exceed the control of central political authorities and the decisions they make.'

Admiral Miller's paper is highly pertinent to this question. He gives a remarkable overview of the network of channels that link the military command to the nuclear forces, and is led to ask whether the danger may not reside in a control so tight that the weapons appear unusable. He is surely not alone in this perception. It is for just this reason that the leash tethering nuclear weapons is visibly slackened at times of crisis. There seems to be no escaping the fact that it will be precisely at what are politically the most dangerous moments in world history that the decentralization of command will be implemented. Experience in operating the enormously elaborate military machine under crisis conditions is inevitably lacking. From one standpoint we may hope it will continue to be lacking; from another we have reason to fear the consequences of that lack.

These comments deal only with the simplest aspect of control, namely the relationship between levels of command within a nation. Additionally, at times of grave danger, there may be conflicting voices of authority within a threatened nation at the highest level (as appeared to be the case on the Soviet side in the Cuban crisis). Above all, we can expect misunderstanding between the contending parties as to intention and determination; here too the Cuban missile crisis is replete with fearsome examples.

It should be remarked that since the date of the Cuban crisis a 'hot-line' has been instituted linking the Kremlin to the White House. This is a heartening development. It falls far short, however, of allaying the fears that this sort of confrontation engenders. In a test of nuclear resolve nations communicate less by words than by actions. It is the ambiguity of these actions such as, in the Cuban crisis, the shooting down of a US reconnaissance plane, the tailing of Soviet strategic submarines, an incursion into Soviet airspace – all of which events occurred within a brief span of time – that will continue to provide the grounds for misunderstanding, miscalculation, and their attendant disasters.

The likelihood of miscalculation is at least as great in confrontations between small nuclear powers. There exists a possibility for quick action and reaction between belligerents, due to the small distances and exposed targets. In addition, there is likely to be a strong incentive for the speedy employment of such nuclear weapons as are available, before they are disabled by enemy action. One need only re-read Steinbruner's account of the days of the Cuban crisis, and the extraordinary efforts that were made to keep events under control and channels of communication open, in order to recognize how appallingly difficult it would be for a pair (or group) of small countries to control the outcome of a nose-to-nose confrontation in which their national existence was at stake.

There is one important regard in which these comments have failed to take a full measure of the danger of nuclear confrontations as a means to settling national differences – assuming that they are to be settled by negotiation or capitulation rather than by annihilation.

Even a rational, well-balanced leadership requires a longer time in order to take a longer view. It is a commonplace that men have killed themselves for grief over events that would have seemed tolerable enough after the lapse of time. National leaderships, one fears, might do the same. It is enough to mention Korea, Algeria, Suez, Cuba, Vietnam, Taiwan, in order to recall that the dictates of pride, honour, and public sentiment can shackle a nation to a position from which it can free itself only with the passage of some time. Neither the threat nor the actuality of nuclear war give time for such accommodation. Steinbruner points out that to the principals involved in the confrontation over the Soviet emplacement of missiles in Cuba nuclear war undoubtedly seemed close. There is, Steinbruner goes on, 'sober warning in the fact that men who believed it [nuclear war] was near were not thereby deterred from military actions'.

ESCALATION

It is well to recognize that there are two types of escalation that can lead to an increasing scale of nuclear conflict. 'Controlled escalation' forms a part of virtually every scenario for the deliberate use of nuclear force. 'Uncontrolled escalation', which is the topic under discussion, represents a category of miscalculation of such importance as to merit a separate section.

All-out nuclear war has a meaning which, on paper at least, is clear enough. Limited nuclear war is any act of nuclear war that falls short of this. We heard three types of limited nuclear war discussed in the course of this Symposium; a limited nuclear strike involving ICBMs, a limited ('theatre') war involving the use of tactical nuclear weapons, and a war limited to the lesser nuclear powers. In each case the danger of escalation appeared to be severe.

The notion of a war for limited objectives being fought out by the US and USSR as a duel between ICBMs is difficult to accept. George Rathjens put it this way: 'It is all a bit bizarre. If one considers scenarios involving the limited use of force by the Soviet Union and the United States against each other, an attack that is massive but limited to adversary ICBM sites would seem implausible – certainly such a remote possibility that it ought to command little attention in defence planning.'

And yet this scenario has held a central place in the planning of the US Department of Defense for years past. At a number of levels this would appear to be a frightening example of 'miscalculation' – miscalculation in time of peace by an organization that is in a far more favourable position to compute, to consider, and to respond to outside advice than any comparable military organization in the world.

At first the Pentagon underestimated the incidental casualties from such an attack by a factor of about ten. That error was corrected some time ago. The current thinking is that in such an exchange some ten million American plus ten million Soviet citizens would die (the numbers could be much higher). The reduction in either side's ability to launch a massive second strike (using residual ICBMs, the full complement of submarine-launched ballistic missiles, and aerial bombardment with hydrogen bombs) would be slight. The mood of horror, confusion, and hatred that would prevail defies comprehension.

To represent this as a viable option – a possible means of demonstrating resolve – would suggest a willingness to risk miscalculation on an epic scale. Perhaps this constitutes a case in which 'declaratory policy' and 'action policy' are believed by planners to be usefully separable. In practice such distinctions are likely to be lost on the rest of the world. What remains is the willingness on the part of a responsible great power to tempt fate in a fashion which has grave implications for the prospects of avoiding a nuclear conflagration – for assuredly the United States has no monopoly on folly.

The conclusions to be drawn from the next category of limited nuclear war – a great power conflict involving the use of tactical nuclear weapons in a limited theatre of war – are less obvious. Steinbruner's point that weapons, if they are to appear usable, must be transferred to a lower level of command applies with particular force in the context of a 'theatre' war, in which the targets are shifting on a time scale of days or hours. Zuckerman takes up this point and argues forcefully that a limited nuclear war would rapidly get out of hand.

Escalation would seem to be inevitable unless one supposes that the opponent for some reason might fail to respond in kind – a highly improbable supposition. A more plausible train of events would begin with one side finding itself at a severe military disadvantage in some forward area, and thereupon firing a nuclear 'shot across the bows' at its opponent, as evidence of its determination to escalate the conflict to a higher level if need be. The initiator of nuclear warfare would warn with all possible solemnity of the grave danger of escalation in the event that the opposing forces failed to withdraw. The victim of the nuclear attack, after alerting world opinion to the fact that he was indeed the victim and not the aggressor and that he had been struck a grievous blow, would in all likelihood respond not long afterwards with an attempt to achieve a genuine military advantage through the employment of tactical nuclear weapons in concert with armoured troops. It would then be the turn of the first party, who would have taken the precaution of putting his forces into a position of evident nuclear alert, to decide whether to take the actions implied by his threatening stance or whether to retreat. However prudent this latter course might be, it would involve him in a denial of his own solemn warnings, as well as in a virtually instant abandonment of his allies whose heartland was by then imperilled.[2]

A *volte face* of this sort on the part of the leaders of a major alliance would presuppose that they are prepared (organizationally, psychologically, and politically) to change direction by 180 degrees in the space of days, or even hours. Once again, this is highly improbable. It appears more likely that the initiator of the nuclear exchange, now gambling for far greater stakes, would seek to show his resolve in an unmistakable fashion by a more substantial flexing of his nuclear muscle. This could take the form, as Rathjens suggests, of an ICBM attack on targets chosen because they are more or less isolated geographically – ships at sea, power stations, or communications centres (satellites or radar facilities). The danger, as Rathjens makes clear, is that the damage may appear a great deal graver to the victim than to the attacker. It may appear more severe than was intended, due to failure of the attacker's chain of command to follow instructions to the letter, inexperience in the actual wartime use of ICBMs, an underestimate of the significance of the target in the military or civil context of the opposing side, changeable weather conditions that carry radio-active fall-out over populated areas, or a misreading of the scale and nature of the attack by observers on the opposing territory.

Since it is a great deal more painful to be struck than it is to strike, the path to escalation is an easy one. In his anxiety to act decisively, and thereby terminate hostilities, the attacker is likely to act forcefully. The victim of the attack will then ask himself whether the provocation that he offered could reasonably justify a blow of the force that he has sustained. If, as seems likely, the answer is in the negative, he is likely to be swept on a wave of national indignation in the direction of a further sharp escalation of hostilities – a minor escalation, as we have noted, would not serve his purpose which would be to put the opponent on notice that both sides now stand at the brink of disaster, and both must desist before it is too late.

The alternative to a further attempt to effect a final decisive escalation would be to accept the devastation that has already occurred, to accept the terms being offered, and to forgo the use of any further part of the vast arsenal of nuclear weaponry that has been amassed for just such an occasion as this and that waits only the command to fire. To fail to give any such command under these strained circumstances would require a leadership which was sufficiently far-sighted to make the decision to commit political suicide rather than risk national suicide (since the leadership would surely not retain power in the aftermath of surrender), and yet a leadership sufficiently in control to hold contenders for the position of command at bay.

If all these requirements were fulfilled then that particular nuclear war would have been fought and won. However, one is bound to raise the question whether, in the long run, this constitutes a promising way of settling the differences that divide us today, and the many more that will divide us in the future.

It would be repetitious to trace the steps by which a nuclear conflict between lesser nuclear powers could escalate into a major conflict. Where the United Kingdom and France are concerned, a prime incentive for obtaining nuclear weapons capability was to make the US nuclear guarantee more credible. The US might hesitate to take the first step which could lead to Armageddon on behalf of a European ally; the 'solution' was for the ally to place itself in a position where it could itself take the first fateful step under circumstances in which its survival was called into question. Neither the United Kingdom nor France could themselves threaten the survival of the USSR, but either could set in motion events that involved the United States to such an extent that the full armoury of deterrence would come into play.

It is harder to forecast the incendiary effects, on a global scale, of a one-sided or bilateral nuclear conflict involving China, the Middle East, Africa, India, South America, and so on. It seems improbable, however, that in the year 1990 or 2000 of our shrinking planet the nuclear middle powers and nuclear giants would adopt an isolationist stance while events of such enduring importance ran their course. It would be far more in keeping with current trends if they were to move with all possible speed into the arena with a view to damping down the conflict and also in order to make good on commitments that they had undertaken in advance of the outbreak of hostilities in the hope of averting them. Here again the time scale for intervention is likely to be measured in hours, and the problem of arriving at an accommodation between the intervening parties will be correspondingly severe.

The role of nuclear-armed terrorists, from within a country or from some neighbouring region, in precipitating a nuclear conflict by detonating a nuclear explosion, cannot be discounted. Epstein makes a convincing case for the potential importance of nuclear terrorism as an element in the politics of the year 2000. However, there is no argument about the fact that the most fearful dangers for the immediate future lie elsewhere.

CONCLUSION

We embarked upon this project with the knowledge that few things would be said that had not been said previously. We were concerned, however, with the totality of the picture that our discussion would bring to light. It may be that the contributions to this volume are open to very different interpretation. In these retrospective comments one participant registers his reaction. The Statement at the beginning of this book gives an indication of the response that these three and a half days of discussion engendered in the participants as a whole. Their feeling of concern, and its sources, are unmistakable. The danger that nuclear weapons will come to be used, in a world where such weapons form an integral part of the armouries of an ever increasing number of nations, is great. The likelihood that a limited use of such weapons will precipitate an avalanche of action and reaction is alarmingly high.

Despite all this, the prospects for reaching the year 2000, and beyond, without a nuclear conflagration are indeterminate. We are not the victims of immutable fate. To the extent that we are able to perceive our predicament, we shall be impelled to respond to it. The need to educate the world to the altered circumstances of the nuclear age has been with us for a quarter of a century. Some progress has been made. However, the greatest effort of education lies ahead.

The message that stands out most clearly in the foregoing pages, to this observer, is that we must abandon the idea of 'winning' nuclear wars. Though individually these weapons may in a few cases be less destructive than conventional weapons could be made to be, the nuclear armoury must be regarded collectively and not individually; the danger of nuclear escalation is too great to be countenanced.

If nuclear weapons cannot be used as the ultimate arbiter of national differences then, given the fact that nations are increasingly incorporating nuclear weapons in their military planning, it follows that they are increasingly debarred from settling their differences by force of arms. What Steinbruner called mildly 'the habit of negotiation' (albeit negotiation under political and economic duress) becomes, in an increasing range of contexts, the *only* option this side of insanity.

In the preceding paragraphs it was urged that the nuclear powers tailor their forces so that they are seen to have no more sinister purpose than deterring a potential opponent from using his nuclear weapons. If this were done, it could represent a dramatic and desirable reversal of present trends. However, when, as in this volume, we are thinking in terms of a time span of decades we should acknowledge that so long as a vast and readily accessible deterrent capability is in existence there will be pressure to use it to 'deter' an opponent from a wider range of activities than merely to counter an act of nuclear folly: there will be a temptation to rattle the deterrent in its scabbard at times of international crisis. We should plan to bury the deterrent ever more deeply so that ultimately it exerts its influence simply through its potential, rather than through the fact that it is continually poised for flight.

So long as the arms race continues, this is an idle dream. Today's weaponry is in a constant process of being refurbished and modernized. (One of the significant benefits of the SALT negotiations has been to keep the world mindful of the current deployment of nuclear weapons, as well as further weapons systems in the offing.) Some modernization can be justified within the context of deterrence on the grounds that the proposed new weapons could be less prone to 'crisis instability'. Unfortunately there is a circular process at work here. Much the same developments in science and engineering that brought these new weapons systems within reach gave rise to the *need* for them by rendering earlier systems vulnerable. Thus technological developments in the field of weaponry both create a need and fill it. The process is unending. By allowing it to proceed we are opting to run in order to stay still, and we are constantly raising the spectre on the other side that we are running in order to get ahead.

There is much to be said for Garwin's plea to his own government to abandon the attempt to maintain a lead in military innovation, and be content instead to respond to others' innovations. If others were to take this same enlightened view there would be an end to a senseless, wasteful, and dangerous competition.

The greatest danger of nuclear war has not, I believe, so far been mentioned in this discussion. It stems from the fatalism of those who believe that the actions required to avert disaster can only be taken after the meaning of a nuclear cataclysm has been made fully apparent – forged in the fire of the holocaust. This view denies the very elements in a civilization – such as human compassion and creativity – that make it worth saving.

NOTES

1   B. Tuchman, *The Guns of August* (New York, 1962) 39
2   Hearings on *Effects of Limited Nuclear Warfare* held before the Subcommittee on Arms Control, International Organizations and Security Agreements, of the US Senate Committee on Foreign Relations, September 18, 1975.
3   General Arthur S. Collins Jr., US Army (Ret.), Former Deputy Commander-in-Chief, US Army in Europe, Address to the First Nuclear War Conference, Washington, DC, 7 December 1978

Glossary

ABM   anti-ballistic missile

A-bomb   a thermonuclear fission weapon (the 'atom bomb')

^{28}Al   a radio-active form of aluminum; half life $\tau = 2.3$ minutes

ALCM   air-launched cruise missile

ASAT   anti-satellite devices

ASRO   anti-submarine rocket

ASW   anti-submarine warfare

AWAC   air-borne warning and control

β-radiation   high-energy electrons emitted in the course of radio-active decay of an atomic nucleus

CJCS   Chairman Joint Chiefs of Staff, USA

Cruise missile   most commonly, an air-breathing, low-flying, pilotless jet-plane, carrying a conventional high-explosive or hydrogen bomb warhead

CTB   comprehensive test ban

Enhanced radiation weapon   *see* Neutron bomb

Fission   decomposition of an atomic nucleus, with the release of a large amount of energy (due to the transformation of some of the mass into energy)

Fusion   combination of smaller atomic nuclei to form a larger nucleus, with the release of a large amount of energy (due to the transformation of some of the mass into energy)

γ-radiation   high-energy X-rays emitted in the course of radio-active decay of an atomic nucleus

Half-life (τ) time required for a radio-active substance to decay to one half of its initial activity (often symbolised $T_{\frac{1}{2}}$)

H-bomb   a fusion weapon

ICBM   intercontinental ballistic missile

km   1 kilometer = 0.6 miles
KT   1 kiloton; an explosive power equivalent to one thousand tons of
TNT (trinitrotoluene)

MaRV   Manoeuvrable re-entry vehicle
MIRV   Multiple independently targeted re-entry vehicle
^{56}Mn   a radio-active form of manganese: half-life τ = 2.6 hours
MT   1 megaton; an explosive power adjudged to be equivalent to one
million tons of TNT

^{24}Na   a radio-active form of sodium; half-life τ = 1.5 hours
Neutron bomb   or 'enhanced radiation weapon'. A fusion device, akin to
a small hydrogen bomb (H-bomb) but designed to emit a large number
of fast neutrons
Neutrons   uncharged highly penetrating particles, emitted in the course
of nuclear fission and fusion
NPT   Non-Proliferation Treaty

PAL   permissive action link; a coded lock preventing the release of
nuclear weapons, except following 'permissive action'
Prompt radiation   radiation that accompanies a nuclear explosion – in
contrast to secondary or delayed radiation stemming from material that
has been made radio-active as a consequence of a nuclear explosion.
Pu239   fissionable form of plutonium used in A-bombs. A by-product of
uranium consumption in civilian nuclear reactors

r   a unit of radiation termed a Roentgen. Lethality involves an accumu-
lation of approximately 600r over a period of a few days
Radio-activity   Emission from disintegrating atomic nuclei (such as β
and γ radiation; q.v.)
rem   a unit of radiation ('Roentgen Equivalent Mammal'), used to measure its effect on human tissue; approximately equal to a Roentgen

SACEUR   NATO Supreme Allied Commander, Europe
SAM   surface-to-air missile
SecDef   Secretary for Defense, USA
SIOP   Single Integrated Operations Plan for a massive nuclear strike at
the Soviet Union

SLBM   submarine-launched ballistic missile

^{90}Sr   a radio-active form of strontium; half-life $\tau = 28$ years

SSBN   nuclear-powered ballistic missile firing submarine

SSN   nuclear-powered attack submarine for use against the opponent's SSBNs and other military and shipping targets

Strategic use of nuclear weapons   use against the homeland of the opponent or his strategic weapons

Tactical nuclear weapon   at the time of writing this refers to a fission bomb of 'low' yield, i.e. 1-20 KT, intended for use by troops in field. The bomb that destroyed Hiroshima was a fission bomb of approximately 14 KT yield (SIPRI *Yearbook 1969/70*). In the future neutron bombs (*q.v.*) may be included in the arsenal of tactical nuclear weapons.

Tactical use of nuclear weapons   use in a battlefield or 'theatre' of operations

TERCOM   'terrain comparison' guidance for computer-controlled 'cruise missiles' (*q.v.*)

Thermonuclear explosion   a fusion explosion of the type characteristic of an H-bomb

USCINCEUR   US Commander-in-Chief, Europe